GENDER IN

Series editor
Lynn Abrams, Cordelia Beattie, Pam Sharpe and Penny Summerfield

━┼╼━╾┼━

The expansion of research into the history of women and gender since the 1970s has changed the face of history. Using the insights of feminist theory and of historians of women, gender historians have explored the configuration in the past of gender identities and relations between the sexes. They have also investigated the history of sexuality and family relations, and analysed ideas and ideals of masculinity and femininity. Yet gender history has not abandoned the original, inspirational project of women's history: to recover and reveal the lived experience of women in the past and the present.

The series Gender in History provides a forum for these developments. Its historical coverage extends from the medieval to the modern periods, and its geographical scope encompasses not only Europe and North America but all corners of the globe. The series aims to investigate the social and cultural constructions of gender in historical sources, as well as the gendering of historical discourse itself. It embraces both detailed case studies of specific regions or periods, and broader treatments of major themes. Gender in History titles are designed to meet the needs of both scholars and students working in this dynamic area of historical research.

Women of letters

Manchester University Press

OTHER RECENT BOOKS
IN THE SERIES

+⊨══⊨+

Love, intimacy and power: marriage and patriarchy in Scotland, 1650–1850 Katie Barclay
(Winner of the 2012 Women's History Network Book Prize)

Modern women on trial: sexual transgression in the age of the flapper Lucy Bland

The Women's Liberation Movement in Scotland Sarah Browne

Modern motherhood: women and family in England, c. 1945–2000 Angela Davis

Gender, rhetoric and regulation: women's work in the civil service and the London County Council, 1900–55 Helen Glew

Jewish women in Europe in the Middle Ages: a quiet revolution Simha Goldin

The shadow of marriage: singleness in England, 1914–60 Katherine Holden

Women, dowries and agency: marriage in fifteenth-century Valencia Dana Wessell Lightfoot

Women, travel and identity: journeys by rail and sea, 1870–1940 Emma Robinson-Tomsett

Imagining Caribbean womanhood: race, nation and beauty contests, 1929–70 Rochelle Rowe

Infidel feminism: secularism, religion and women's emancipation, England 1830–1914 Laura Schwartz

Women, credit and debt in early modern Scotland Cathryn Spence

Being boys: working-class masculinities and leisure Melanie Tebbutt

Queen and country: same sex desire in the British Armed Forces, 1939–45 Emma Vickers

The 'perpetual fair': gender, disorder and urban amusement in eighteenth-century London Anne Wohlcke

WOMEN OF LETTERS

GENDER, WRITING AND THE LIFE OF THE MIND IN EARLY MODERN ENGLAND

Leonie Hannan

Manchester University Press

Published by Manchester University Press
Altrincham Street, Manchester M1 7JA, UK
www.manchesteruniversitypress.co.uk

British Library Cataloguing-in-Publication Data is available

ISBN 978 0 7190 9942 7 hardback

ISBN 978 1 5261 2719 8 paperback

First published by Manchester University Press in hardback 2016

This edition first published 2018

The publisher has no responsibility for the persistence or accuracy of URLs for any external or third-party internet websites referred to in this book, and does not guarantee that any content on such websites is, or will remain, accurate or appropriate.

Typeset by Out of House Publishing

Printed in Great Britain by TJ International Ltd, Padstow

Contents

LIST OF FIGURES   *page* vi
LIST OF TABLES   vii
ACKNOWLEDGEMENTS   viii
LIST OF ABBREVIATIONS   x

Introduction   1

Part I: Women and learning   **33**

1   Getting started   35

2   Becoming an 'intellectual'   64

Part II: Putting pen to paper   **95**

3   Writing and thinking   97

4   Spaces for writing   123

Part III: Hearts and minds   **151**

5   Connecting reason and emotion   153

6   A seedbed for change   178

APPENDIX   185
BIBLIOGRAPHY   188
INDEX   201

Figures

1   A letter written by Mary Clarke and addressed to her husband, Edward Clarke, on 28 April 1690   *page* 55

2   A letter written by Mary Evelyn and addressed to her friend, Ralph Bohun, on 3 February 1668   68

3   George Ballard's letter book containing 140 original letters from female contacts, including Elizabeth Elstob   71

4   A letter written by Elizabeth Elstob and addressed to her friend, George Ballard, on 2 October 1735   75

5   A letter written by Elizabeth Elstob and addressed to Margaret Cavendish Bentinck, Duchess of Portland   78

6   A letter written by Cordelia Collier to her mother, Mary Collier, on 1 June 1735   100

7   A letter written by Jane Johnson to her son, Robert Johnson, on 15 November 1753   103

8   A letter written by Eliza Worsley and addressed to her sister, Frances Robinson, on 24 February 1749   126

9   A letter written by Mary Evelyn addressed to her brother-in-law, William Glanville, on 9 October 1671, copied into her letter book for future reference   162

10 An example of a letter written by Anne Dormer addressed to her sister, Elizabeth Trumbull, on 28 August *c.* 1686   170

Tables

1   Content analysis: selected letters of Mary Grey, 1740–41   *page* 185

2   Content analysis: selected letters of Elizabeth Elstob, 1736–37   186

3   Content analysis: selected letters of Mary Evelyn, 1667–68   187

Acknowledgements

The ideas that frame this book can be traced back to my earliest days of postgraduate research at Royal Holloway, University of London. Since that time, I have been incredibly fortunate in meeting with friends, advisors and supportive institutions who have made this work not only possible but also enjoyable. But there is one person who has had a defining influence on my development as a researcher, Professor Penelope Corfield, and this project owes an immeasurable debt to her intellectual generosity and firm guidance. I have also benefited hugely from the support and inspiration provided by Professor Margot Finn, Dr Susan Whyman, Professor Michèle Cohen, Dr Simon Werrett, Professor Lisa Jardine and Professor Amanda Vickery.

Various institutions have been critical to the completion of this research, in practical, financial, social and intellectual terms and they include Royal Holloway, University of London, University College London, the Institute of Historical Research, the British Federation of Women Graduates and, more recently, Queen's University, Belfast. I am also indebted to the conversations made possible by the mighty British History in the Long Eighteenth Century Seminar at the Institute of Historical Research in London, which have nurtured and developed my thinking over many years.

This book is the product of archival research and I am grateful to the very many archivists who have helped me and the archives that gave their permission for manuscripts to be quoted. They include: the Bodleian Library, the British Library, the Bedfordshire and Luton Archive Service, the Derbyshire Record Office, the Keep Archives at the East Sussex Record Office, Hertfordshire Archives and Local Studies, the Library of the Society of Friends, Northamptonshire Record Office, Somerset Archive and Record Office, the University of Nottingham Manuscripts and Special Collections and West Yorkshire Archive Service.

Throughout the research and writing of this book I have continued to work in other professional settings outside the very particular world of academic history. This book has, therefore, been shaped by the cultural influences and collegial support of a host of organisations, most importantly, Museums & Collections at University College London, Lifespan Research Group (formerly of Royal Holloway, University of London), Kensington and Chelsea College, Birkbeck College, University of London, the Highgate Literary and Scientific Institution, the Geffrye Museum, the Old Operating Theatre Museum and Herb Garret, the Hunterian Museum at the Royal College of Surgeons (London) and Milton Manor House. All of these environments and encounters have helped me think through my subject and have removed the possibility of holding a narrow perspective on the practice of history.

I am very grateful to the team at Manchester University Press for shepherding this book to completion and also to the anonymous readers for their rigorous scrutiny of the manuscript and helpful suggestions. I also want to thank Professor John Thompson for giving me a long-term future in academic research and the opportunity to write my next book.

For their personal and intellectual friendship I would like to thank Joey O'Gorman, Julie Mathias, Ananay Aguilar, Jane Hamlett, Polly Bull, Helen Chatterjee, Kate Smith, Eleanor Hannan, John Steward, Melanie Griffiths, Tabitha Tuckett and all of the 100 Hours Collective. A scholarly existence only gets you so far and time spent with all my friends has been crucial at every step. Finally, I owe a deep gratitude to Sheila and Patrick Hannan for imparting such a varied and vibrant childhood education that I could only presume it possible to pursue a life of the mind, and to Joey O'Gorman for sharing it with me.

Leonie Hannan
Belfast, June 2015

Abbreviations

BL	British Library
Add. MS	Additional Manuscripts
AP	Althorp Papers
BC	Birch Collection
CP	Conway Papers
EP	Evelyn Papers
HP	Harley Papers
PP	Portland Papers
PtP	Petty Papers
TP	Trumbull Papers
BLA, LP	Bedfordshire and Luton Archive, Lucas Papers
Bodl.	Bodleian Library
ColP	Coleridge Papers
MP	Madan Papers
DRO	Derbyshire Record Office
ESRO, SP	East Sussex Record Office, Sayer Papers
HALS, CP	Hertfordshire Archives and Local Studies, Cowper Papers
LSF, FP	Library of the Society of Friends, Follows Papers
NRO, IP	Northamptonshire Record Office, Isham Papers
ODNB	Oxford Dictionary of National Biography (Oxford: Oxford University Press, 2004); online at www.oxforddnb.com
SARO, SEP	Somerset Archive and Record Office, Sanford Estate Papers
UNMSC, PP	University of Nottingham Manuscripts and Special Collections, Portland Papers
WYAS, NH	West Yorkshire Archive Service, Newby Hall Papers

Introduction

Letters denote exchange, even the unsent letter locked in a bureau drawer speaks of the urge to converse if not the conviction to seal and send. For literate women in the seventeenth and eighteenth centuries, the letter was a powerful tool – one that privileged discourse, demanded reciprocity and drew letter-writers into a defining cultural practice of their era. The letters discussed here represent far more than the historical information they contain. As letter-writers put pen to paper they engaged in a very particular writing practice, one which saw its reflection in a wide range of print culture, from newspapers to novels. In this way, the practice of writing letters connected individuals with other texts and processes of textual production. However, these lines of ink on folded page are also remnants of an everyday habit which gifted the individual space for reflection and discussion. On a personal level, letters helped letter-writers negotiate relationships with their world but, collectively, epistolary practice fed cultures of friendship, kinship and business. Correspondence informed the literary, intellectual and creative cultures of its day and, in many cases, the familial overlapped with the literary; distant cousins became intellectual companions, neighbours became fellow readers. Networks of correspondents also connected groups of peoples separated by class, nationality, gender and location and in doing so linked 'men of letters' with provincial housewives, university scholars with amateur collectors, provincial poets with metropolitan coteries. Although the letter-writing public still reflected the striations of a society riven by social distinction, letters also spoke of the opportunities presented by epistolary aptitude to transcend such boundaries.

The study of letters entails encounters with both the typical and the eccentric and clues to the intricacies of early modern housewifery sit squarely alongside tracts of moral philosophy. This tendency to the diverse makes letters extremely difficult to categorise along lines of modern scholarly enquiry. Here, the focus will be on the 'familiar letter', which Susan Fitzmaurice has described as 'a pragmatic act that is embodied in a text that responds to a previous text, whether spoken or written, and at the same time anticipates new texts'.[1] This dynamic of exchange is integral to the character of the familiar letter, but the term also denotes the fact that such letters did not primarily communicate matters of business or affairs of the state (although these topics might be discussed) – they were instead rooted in personal relationships. This book makes no attempt to carve up the messy multiplicity of this encompassing category of correspondence and, instead, uses the familiar letter to explore the interconnected nature of women's domestic, familial, intellectual and social lives. Whilst the quiet solitude of a corner with table and book might have proved welcome to the serious reader, the table and corner were part of a greater household in which the reader also acted as housewife, child bearer, carer and teacher, wife, kitchen garden cultivator, provider of poor relief and host to neighbouring friends. These roles and responsibilities informed the rhythm of every day and also the ways in which women engaged with the life of the mind. Interior worlds were marked by exterior environments and the home proved to be the library and lecture theatre for many literate and self-motivated women of seventeenth- and eighteenth-century England.

By considering women's lives through reading their surviving letters, it can be shown that many more women than have previously been documented or studied engaged with a reflective life of the mind in this period. Literate women across England, who had the benefit of some spare time, access to books and a private space in which to study, could actively develop their inner lives – the evidence of this can be found in their letters, which survive in their many thousands in national collections and local record offices. The aim of this book is to establish the critical role of letter-writing in the process of women's engagement with the life of the mind and, through doing so, reveal the early modern letter as an analytical tool for historical scholarship.

Letter-writing has been the subject of much recent research and scholars have considered its connections to the literary world,[2] its role as a social and cultural force in national and global communications[3] and its status as a genre of life writing.[4] Here, the focus is on how women made use of letter-writing to further their own self-educational or intellectual pursuits. It is the process of engagement with reading, writing and ideas, rather than the product of those efforts, that provides the point of departure. Through this analysis of engagement with intellectual life, the varied contexts of childhood experience, personal relationships, family life and domestic space will come to the fore. Nonetheless, the primary concern of this book is with examples of intellectual motivation fostered by letter-writing and the implications these women's experiences have for our understanding of cultural life in this period.

Literacy, education and the life of the mind

In examining letter-writing as a conduit for intellectual engagement, levels of literacy and access to education for women correspondents naturally have a strong bearing. Literacy, the essential prerequisite for educational achievement, is measurable on a sliding scale, from the ability to sign a name to owning the versatility and finesse to write for reasons of communication, literary creativity or personal advocacy. Most women, like many working men, simply lacked the skills of reading and writing necessary to participate in intellectual life. David Cressy's important study of literacy found that women in the sixteenth and seventeenth centuries were much less likely to be able to sign their names than were their male counterparts.[5] Although literacy improved in the period 1650–1750,[6] it was only in London that female literacy breached 50 per cent; elsewhere in the country as a whole only about a quarter of women were classed as literate.[7] However, female literacy amongst the middling and upper sorts in seventeenth- and eighteenth-century England was high and literacy rates of 100 per cent have been claimed for society's elites.[8] Recently, Jacqueline Eales has shown that female literacy was compulsory within clerical families of the seventeenth century, most of whom firmly occupied the ranks of the middling sort.[9] Access to education inside or outside the home for young people in this period varied widely; the content, duration and results of that educational experience were correspondingly diverse.[10] It is also worth noting, that many women were taught to read without being taught to write, so for some women engagement with text began and ended with the read or spoken word.

Where erratic spelling in some women's letters of this period betrayed a deficient education, verbal fluency was often evident on the page, and from this starting point skills could be honed through activities such as letter-writing.[11] Susan Whyman has valuably highlighted the concept of 'epistolary literacy', seeing letter-writing as 'a training ground for composing other types of literature'.[12] Whyman advises that instead of looking 'for women's education in makeshift methods and informal places' historians need 'to recognize the importance of domestic literacy'.[13] More recently, Whyman has demonstrated widespread epistolary literacy across the social scale.[14] These discoveries are crucial to our understanding of female intellectual life in this period. Illiteracy and inadequate educational provision have been blamed consistently for women's silence on matters of academic note. Letters housed in archives and record offices point to a different story: one of widespread written literacy. But, more than this, correspondence collections highlight the adventurous use women made of the epistolary form. Letters were the home of ideas, perhaps erratically spelled, but nonetheless evident on the page.

Of course, well-to-do girls in the seventeenth and eighteenth centuries were expected to have an education of some degree during childhood. A small minority might even be sent away to school, and teaching provided adult women with a possible vocation and source of income. Mothers were key educators in the home, especially of very young children of both sexes, as most boys of middling or gentry families would not be sent away to school until they were seven or eight years old.[15] Mothers were usually responsible for their girls' educations throughout their formative years. Evelyn Arizpe and Morag Styles have explored the dynamic evidence of the Jane Johnson archive, which shows how Buckinghamshire clergyman's wife Johnson drew on her own reading and creative talents to develop effective materials for teaching her children at home in the 1740s.[16] Likewise, Michèle Cohen has argued persuasively that a domestic education was not necessarily an inferior education.[17]

Where childhood education had been sufficiently thorough, adult women could become readers. Indeed, the figure of the woman reader was a popular subject of literary and artistic representation but female reading could be both extolled as a rational pursuit and deplored as dangerously corrupting of women's characters.[18] Of course, a long tradition of morally sanctioned female religious reading existed and reading the Bible had a strong influence on early modern women's own writings.[19] However, there was a perceived difference between religious and informative kinds of reading and literature that engaged the imagination.[20] During the eighteenth century, concerns about the particularly damaging effects of novel reading on women abounded in popular culture and perpetuated a deeply polarised view on the 'proper' relationship between women and books.[21]

Despite a social context fraught with fears about both the morally corrupting qualities of reading and the capacity of this pursuit to take women away from their household and familial duties, women did read all of the genres (prohibited or otherwise) and discussed their reading in letters to friends. These epistolary conversations contributed to a broad culture of textual analysis, which has been linked to historical developments as significant as the changing status of the middle class or the emergence of the Enlightenment.[22] Indeed, detailed studies of reading practice are revealing about the ways in which early modern readers diverged from prescribed genres and availed themselves of impressively diverse reading matter. Using the records of Midland booksellers for the second half of the eighteenth century, Jan Fergus provides demographic information on who bought and borrowed fiction, concluding that – contrary to the fears of moralists – 'The raw numbers for women readers of novels and plays confirm that provincial women do not constitute a particularly large or broad market for fiction' in this period.[23] Other scholars have focused on individual readers so as to cut across genre and represent the experience of reading for early modern people.[24] A particularly illuminating example of this approach is Naomi Tadmor's exploration of two reading households, where she finds the practice of reading 'connected not to idleness, listlessness or frivolity but to a routine of work and religious discipline'.[25] This study shows that for a tradesman and his wife, reading was part of the household routine and books were picked up intermittently, between other domestic and business responsibilities, and also that reading moved between genres on a daily basis.[26] Other studies have confirmed that individuals of modest social standing might engage with a wide variety of literature, accessed not only through buying books but also through the use of subscription and circulating libraries.[27] Both the study of the distribution of books and the reading practices of individuals in this period show that the literate negotiated a range of strategies for getting hold of reading material and integrated time for reading into their often busy lives. Once literacy and access to reading material had been established, opportunities might present themselves for more in-depth intellectual exploration.

Women's intellectual lives in an era of Enlightenment

The eighteenth century is an era synonymous with the notion of rapid growth in rational and scientific thought. For many scholars this period is still directly referred to as 'the Enlightenment' and in its epistemological waters are traced the origins of subsequent scientific discovery.[28] Although men dominated institutions of political and intellectual note, women participated in the developments of their time.[29] However, in terms of women, it is the second half of the century that has drawn most scholarly attention as the era of Bluestockings and Wollstonecraft feminism. History titles that focus on the period after 1750 abound, but the late seventeenth and early eighteenth centuries fall between early modern scholarship and research which looks forward to the modern period.[30] Moreover, late seventeenth- and early eighteenth-century England deserves the attention of readers interested in women's mental worlds. After all, it was in 1696 that Mary Astell famously made *A Serious Proposal to Ladies* concerning their education. Formal institutions of the age, such as the Royal Society (founded in 1660), may have excluded women members, but a vibrant correspondence culture was commandeered by female thinkers who wished to contribute to the debates of their time.

Recent scholarship has shown the importance of letter-writing networks to cultures of knowledge in the seventeenth and eighteenth centuries. Increasingly, historians have been able to make use of the data provided by digital collections of correspondence to map these networks across Europe and North America and gain insights into the geographies of intellectual life.[31] Whilst many of the letters that have provided the focus for these studies have been those of the most well-known literary and scientific men,[32] studies have also begun to capture the women who were active in these networks.[33] These valuable works demonstrate that by the seventeenth century, correspondence was a well-established route for women's participation in scholarship.[34] Moreover, recent efforts to digitise these archival collections has emphasised the operation of networks over the works of individuals and helped scholars to see intellectual production as a collaborative venture which encompassed broader communities of individuals.[35] But women did not just participate in cultures of intellectual exchange, they also lent their social and financial support to knowledge production. In this way, correspondence networks connected distant individuals, promoted patronage and provided a space for discourse. Letters performed these functions for pairs or groups of women who wished to be in contact, but – likewise – for men and women who had intellectual interests in common. Together they formed a diffuse and diverse 'Republic of Letters'.

This book employs an interpretation of intellectual life that can more accurately be described as the 'life of the mind'.[36] The phrase, used most famously by Hannah Arendt in her exploration of the 'activity of thinking', is used here to emphasise the experience of thinking life as well as the tangible textual outcomes of thought.[37] In Arendt's discussion of the life of the mind, she identifies as a defining feature 'the habit of examining whatever happens to come to pass or to attract attention, regardless of results and specific content'.[38] This inclusive approach to human thought is helpful when considering women's epistolary writing in this period because it took such diverse forms and fulfilled multiple functions. Moreover, Arendt's conceptualisation of the life of the mind as being composed of three main mental activities: 'thinking, willing, and judging' bypasses traditional divisions between reason and intellect, contemplation and knowledge production.

The focus here on women as overlooked intellectual participants begins the important work of integrating gender and intellectual histories. However, many of the same arguments could be made for other marginalised intellectuals, such as amateur male scholars, collectors and readers who, whilst distant from institutions of intellectual note, remained fully engaged in research and writing. The examples explored in this book include female circles of intellectual acquaintance as well as cases of cross-gender exchange. Some made letters the primary forum for their considered thoughts and thereby perfected a mode of expression that both conformed to and competed with established ideals for feminine conduct. Others used their letters as spaces for rehearsal, their correspondents acting as critical friends. What is clear is that women used strategies to engage with the debates of their times which were achievable within their personal and social contexts.

Recent scholarship has highlighted the relatively limited number of early modern women writers typically discussed by scholars of literature and history. As Jeremy Gregory states 'the familiar names of Mary Astell, Anna Barbauld, Elizabeth Carter, Susanna Centilivre, Ann Finch, Eliza Haywood, Mary Leapor, Lady Mary Wortley Montagu, Hannah More, Ann Radcliffe, Elizabeth Rowe, Sarah Scott, Anna Seward, Mary Wollstonecraft, and Ann Yearsley recur time and again'.[39] Histories of philosophy could add, amongst others, Margaret Cavendish, Anne Conway and Catherine Trotter Cockburn to the list.[40] This reliance on a discrete canon of female creative talent tends to underline the broader presumption that very few women wrote anything of interest at this time. One answer to the question of why such a small pool of names is drawn upon to illuminate women's thinking lives is the over-reliance on biography in the evaluation of intellectual impact. There is a strong tendency in the recording of intellectual lives to make it just that, a 'Life and Works'. This need for an individual to have created work systematically over their lifetime disenfranchises many female participants from intellectual history altogether. Most women read and wrote when and where they could. Intellectual letter-writing could be interrupted, for years at a time, by the rigours of child-bearing and rearing; perhaps never to be returned to. This patchy and sometimes abruptly aborted activity does not lend itself well to an analysis of a lifetime of intellectual practice. Moreover, where poorly provenanced manuscript writings do appear in the archive, the lack of a definitive author, with a well-documented life story, makes the task all the more difficult. As a result, the evidence of women's contributions in this arena, where it does exist, is often overlooked. By making good use of the fragmentary manuscript evidence, as opposed to relying on published texts, it is possible to uncover the depth and diversity of female intellectual work in this period.[41]

When women have been considered by historians specifically as intellectuals, they are frequently subjected to a denial of their works' 'originality' amongst other techniques to depreciate the value of their contribution to the world of ideas.[42] It is now commonly agreed that women lent a hand in the collective task of generating new knowledge, but they are rarely described as the initiators, discoverers or founders of that knowledge. Women's critical reading and commenting on published literature is a good example of intellectual output that deserves greater attention. As Jaqueline Pearson has emphasised, women could read 'rebelliously and resistingly rather than compliantly'.[43] Nevertheless, women have often been characterised as passive readers, dutifully reading for self-betterment, rather than as informed consumers of texts who developed incisive critiques through writing to friends. This is the same kind of thinking that has led to women happily being designated as helpmeets to 'real', male thinkers, instead of innovators in their own right. Instead of acknowledging that women have often found their contributions systematically undervalued by their contemporaries, and then subsequently so by historical scholarship, this process of marginalisation is dressed up as the product of limited educational opportunity for women in their given period, be that the seventeenth, eighteenth, nineteenth or twentieth century. Women are not initiators, discoverers or founders because they could not compete with their better educated and resourced brothers. This explanation for women's non-achievement in the world of knowledge production simply does not hold true for the women letter-writers who are the subject of this book.

Historians of gender have sought out hidden women's histories, but there are still calls for more and better scholarship on women intellectuals.[44] Recent studies on the Bluestocking circle have certainly identified a wider culture of sociability that birthed and promulgated Enlightenment ideas but they retain a focus on the most prominent examples of that culture.[45] It is the ideas and writings of a broader cross-section of women of this period that are the primary concern of this book. This study is rooted in social history and it is therefore concerned with the practices that informed and gave access to intellectual study and the relationships participants had with the life of the mind. This is not a history that primarily concerns itself with women's interpretations of specific texts, or their development of particular ideas, although that will form part of the discussion. This book is concerned instead with women's engagement with, and experience of, intellectual life in all its manifestations. For some women that would be critical engagement with current affairs, for others it would be reading and responding to classical literature, for still others it would be tracts written on perfect friendship, drawing on a range of literary and cultural influences. Through this approach, new evidence will be presented in support of a social history of female intellectual achievement in an era well before women gained access to higher education.

Letters and letter-writing

This book uses manuscript rather than print letters as its source material and whilst it has long been understood that letters found in archives cannot be treated as 'unmediated historical artefacts',[46] there still exists a clear difference between letters that were written with the intention of being sent to, and read by, a specified person (or group of people) and letters that were written with a wider audience in mind. Nevertheless, however narrow or wide the intended readership, it is worth remembering that letter-writing did not represent an uncomplicated narration of life events or expression of self.[47] The publication of an individual's letters was only one way that correspondence might meet with many eyes; the circulation of manuscript letters beyond their original addressee was much more likely. In fact, this potential for a letter to attract multiple future readers provides a helpful way of thinking about the unpredictable afterlives of correspondence.[48] The permeable boundaries between the letter in manuscript and print form has been described by Clare Brant in terms of the letter as 'a junction or crossroad' between manuscript and print culture.[49] Nonetheless, manuscript letters betray a sense of the author's intention about the way in which they expected or hoped their letter would be read. The first few lines of a letter often refer directly to the practicalities of sending and receipt and the anxieties felt about regularity of contact and privacy of content. So whilst every letter sat within a complex web of relationships (with people, other letters, the letter-form in print and so on) there was often also an explicit intent for its status as a personal message or a more public statement.[50] Even those letters that were written in company and sent with the expectation that they might be read aloud to an assembled group were not, as a result, 'public' documents. An exchange of letters might represent a conversation between more than two people, but the intention of the letter-writer was still to communicate with a specified group with whom she had an established relationship. Of course, letters that were not initially intended for either circulation or publication might later find their way into other people's hands or into print.[51] Likewise, the habit of preserving sections of a family member's correspondence for the enjoyment and instruction of sons, daughters and grandchildren was also common. Whilst it is certainly true that letter-writers did not exert complete control over the end use of their missives, the reality was that most letters penned would not even survive in manuscript form let alone be transmitted onto the printed page. So, whilst letter-writers commonly expressed anxiety about the possibility of their letters being read by unintended eyes, they could – in most circumstances – still be confident of their letters reaching the addressee intact and being read only by them, especially once that recipient had tossed the letter into the fire. Here, familiar letters are the focus and the vast majority of these were intended to be read by just one other person or by very few people. Post Habermas, 'public' and 'private' are freighted terms, but – in respect of letter-writing – it is still useful to use the term 'private' both for the meanings it had in this period and also to describe the act of writing a message to be read by a particular person.[52]

The significance of the letter in early modern society and culture is difficult to overestimate. The establishment of the Post Office opened up new channels for communication for a growing proportion of the population.[53] Social spaces were created and imagined through letter-writing and increasing numbers of people were drawn into this powerful communicative practice. In larger and larger numbers, British men and women 'were able to seek to accomplish a variety of ends, solely though the persuasiveness of their writing'.[54] There have been many arguments made about the specific benefits brought to women by letter-writing and, through corresponding, women certainly did exercise agency for a truly diverse range of purposes.[55] But the force of letter-writing was perhaps most discernible in its ultimate permeation (in form and function) of social, cultural, economic and political life. Konstantin Dierks has described this process as the 'mediating force of letter writing' and the 'prescriptive force of letter writing', showing that letters were both an all-pervasive motif in text and also the method by which individual letter-writers acted, made meaning, communicated and formed identity.[56] In its inherent capacity for meaning-making, exchange and the formation of identity, letter-writing proved the perfect vehicle for intellectual exploration. More than this, correspondence provided a particularly important space for women. Whereas female authors were seen to be relatively quiet in published form as compared with men; women letter-writers were voluble.[57] Moreover, the act of letter-writing became integral to the process of identity formation for women who wished to discuss their reading and exchange ideas through correspondence.[58]

This book uses letters written by women to understand their experiences of intellectual life. However, for historians and critics interested in the frameworks within which women wrote, contemporary

advice literature has also been an important source.[59] Advice literature flourished in this period and epistolary practice did not escape
the printer's eye as countless volumes were produced advising the
reader on how to make the best use of this form of communication.
Considering the potentially complex deliberations involved in putting pen to paper, it is perhaps unsurprising that books were printed
and reprinted with guidelines to the keen but untutored letter-writer.
No doubt, nervous correspondents sometimes turned to the pages of
Polite Epistolary Correspondence[60] or *The Accomplished Letter-Writer*[61]
to help them perform, but it remains difficult to say with any certainty
how strongly the prescriptions of these popular books influenced the
practice of individual letter-writers.[62] For one, letter-writers rarely
acknowledged the use of a manual or guide. Moreover, knowing that
such books sat on the shelves of family libraries does not ensure that
they were read or that their rules were applied.

On reading and comparing advice books of this period, the immediate impression is one of repetition. The same themes, topics, stylistic
conventions and examples grace the pages of books published many decades apart.[63] So whilst claims were commonly made for the novelty of
the material contained, many manuals were simply recycling a previous
generation's prescriptions. However, this literature has been read as evidence of social regulation. The stark rules provided for proper behaviour
make for compelling reading and the genre – predictably – made women
readers a key target of its prescriptions. For example, Abbé d'Ancourt's
1743 publication, *The Lady's Preceptor* suggested that:

> THERE is not a more improving, as well as a more agreeable
> Entertainment, Madam, than that of Writing Letters. They are
> Emanations of our selves, by which we do, as it were, talk and act in
> several Places at a time. Besides, they are of the utmost Advantage in
> our Intercourse with the World.[64]

However, with these significant advantages in mind, it was warned:

> There are as great a Variety of Rules for Writing well, as for Talking
> well; the Ignorance of most of your Sex, therefore, in this Science, who
> generally are guilty of as many Faults as they pen Words, arises from
> their not caring to be at the pains required to excel in it.[65]

Moreover, d'Ancourt's promotion of the letter as a means to broaden and
maintain a woman's network of influence was strongly mitigated by his
final condition:

never, unless upon some singular Emergency which may warrant it, to write to any one but of your own Sex, nor to any but of such a Quality and Reputation as not to lose any of your own by it, nor to any one whomsoever, without the Permission of those under whose Jurisdiction you may be.[66]

This comment did not reflect the social reality of 1743. At this time, many women were active participants in social, political and commercial activities and interacted with broad networks of people, male and female. But the rule-providing remit of advice literature precluded such a diversified view of gender roles.[67] To most, this advice would have seemed terribly outmoded, but this is the point. These books were unlikely to have been read straightforwardly as rules to abide by. As Vivien Jones has argued, this literature was read for pleasure as well as instruction and she warns against a reading that sees the texts as simply 'truth-bearing'.[68] Advice literature was entertainment as well as instruction.

Whilst letter-writing manuals might have been read just as much for fun as for education, correspondents were subject to a host of other influences when they put pen to paper. Conversations, other letter-writers, newspapers, periodicals, plays, novels, songs, sermons and the Bible all played a part. Correspondents thus negotiated their own approach in the context of a wide range of influences, using, adapting and dispensing with convention as they saw fit. Moreover, the key process by which personal habits were formed was the act of letter-writing itself.[69] A letter-writer such as seventeenth-century gentlewoman Dorothy Osborne, whose letters to her future husband William Temple have been printed, was deeply influenced by her readings of French romances.[70] Similarly, for the more literary-minded, the printed letters of Madame de Sévigné and Madame de Maintenon could provide inspiration.[71] In May 1668, the cultivated letter-writer Mary Evelyn responded to being addressed by a fellow correspondent as 'Madam Balzac'. First she objected to the title because she did not value the French author, Jean-Louis Guez de Balzac's written style and suggested instead that 'Voiture seems to excel both in quicknesse of fancy easinesse of expression, and in a facile way of insinuating that he was not Ignorant of letters; an advantage the Court Ayre gives persons who converse with the world as well as books'.[72] In her lifetime, Mary Evelyn gave considerable thought to the letter as a space for critical and creative writing. However, this comment also reveals that she had engaged closely with the examples of published letters that were available at the time and had considered their influence on culture and society.

Engagement with literature in letter-writing sometimes took the form of critical discussion but it could also appear as passages in the style of a particular published letter-writer or author. Brant has referred to this as 'an aesthetic of imitation' and notes that it was particularly prevalent in the first of half of the eighteenth century, before concerns about copyright came to the fore.[73] In the case of the diarist Sarah Cowper (1644–1720), as Anne Kugler has shown, passages from published works mingled – unattributed – with Cowper's own life writing, a process by which Cowper reshaped the texts she had read and asserted her own identity.[74] This example shows that resistant reading could also lead to rebellious writing.

The letters researched for this book show that childhood education, family traditions, marital relationships and personal dispositions played a more important role in the character of women's letter-writing than the wisdom offered by published guides.[75] By far the most fruitful primary source for understanding gender roles, writing and the reasoning mind in this period are letters written by participants in that society – from these documents the strictures of conventional style, format and address can be detected amongst the great diversity and eccentricity of personal practice.

Sites and communities

The focus of this book is on the home as a site of female learning and on the communities of intellectual exchange that could be fostered through letter-writing. However, the more discrete spaces of epistolary activity discussed here can be usefully contextualised by the wealth of scholarship that has been undertaken on early modern sites, networks and communities of intellectual life. For a start, the period in question is central to historical accounts of the 'Republic of Letters' and anticipates studies focused on later eighteenth-century Enlightenment culture. As Anne Goldgar has described it, the Republic of Letters 'existed only in the minds of its members'; unlike a university or a literary society its 'regulations and even its membership were nebulous at best'.[76] However, Goldgar reveals that the Republic functioned via contact – in the form of correspondence, social visits and discussions in scholarly journals. In other words, networks of epistolary exchange provided support for their members and, collectively, these activities represented an incredible clamour of communication across traditional boundaries of nation, religion, gender and class.[77] Women were present in these communities of scholars, and recent research has elucidated how female intellectual communities operated and interacted with men of letters and wider networks of scholarly exchange. For Carol Pal, these intellectual networks were permeable and overlapping, focused around particular scholarly projects and generating new connections where shared concerns were realised.[78]

This characterisation of the way the Republic of Letters operated in late seventeenth- and early eighteenth-century society is a helpful one, and can be augmented by studies that consider the operation of patronage in this era. As Melanie Bigold has described, 'Well-placed, intellectually minded women also supported other scholarly women' and this was particularly true of wealthy aristocrats who could provide financial support for literary publication or the costs of living for struggling writers.[79] Letters fuelled this process, both by forming an important component of literary practice and by maintaining lines of communication which could facilitate the production and dissemination of literary works.[80]

However, for some of the women discussed in this book, the networks and communities of scholarship encompassed by the Republic of Letters would have felt a distant arena. Instead, communities of a more local kind served to generate intellectual friendship and exchange. Women of the landed gentry often lived for many months of the year in country homes, which were relatively distant from both metropolitan centres and the homes of other families of their class. However, in this context, neighbourhood sociability between families of similar social standing was important and this community was forged through reciprocity enacted by social visits and gift exchange.[81] Moreover, for the early modern landed elite, London also played an important satellite role in their geography of well-to-do sociability.[82] For many of the women discussed here, these neighbourhood contacts would have played an important role in their social world. But this society was not bounded and whilst relationships within the neighbourhood might be consolidated through thoughtful correspondence, its parameters could also be breached by the same means.

An interesting example of a community that embraced both the intellectual and the local, was antiquarianism.[83] With its interest in the sites and artefacts of ancient Britain, antiquarianism offered much scope for regional studies which drew on the evidence of local parish records, early churches and what would become known as archaeological heritage. For many gentry families, this study of local histories offered opportunities to trace illustrious family heritage back many centuries. The possibility of working in sites removed from the universities or metropolitan societies also made antiquarian research accessible to individuals outside main-stream scholarship.[84]

The home as a site of learning and intellectual exchange was not a boundaried space. Instead, the household represented a place of circulation (of goods, people and ideas) and a location that was embedded in a network of other households and sites of social interaction. However, each household shared many domestic practices in common. As Karen Harvey has discussed in relation to men and masculinity, 'Through oeconomical practices that straddled the house and the world outside, and in rooting personal identity in the house and family, individual men accessed authority both within and without the house.'[85] Similarly, women's household work connected both the home with the wider world and individual householders with external sites and communities – the legitimate domestic practice of letter-writing was central to this process. As Anne Laurence has described in relation to Irish households in the seventeenth century, 'Collective and individual identities coincided in the household, where servants and their masters and mistresses lived together in close proximity.'[86] For women of this era, the home was the defining space of intellectual thought and practice. Like letter-writing itself, the home was a multivalent space which encouraged the convergence of different 'spheres' of life. By seeing the practice of letter-writing and the space of the home as central to women's intellectual experience, a clearer picture can be drawn of how women came to engage with the life of the mind.

Sources

The qualitative detail evinced by letters of this period forms the key source material for this book. The social range of the correspondents encompasses women from aristocratic, gentry, professional and trade families. The geographic scope of this project has been dictated by the whereabouts of the collections and has come to include Yorkshire, Derbyshire, Northamptonshire, Oxfordshire, Berkshire, Bedfordshire, Hampshire, Hertfordshire, East Sussex, Somerset and Greater London. In total, over thirty collections of correspondence were studied closely from a source base of around 5,000 individual letters. The research was therefore able to use a broad cross-section of correspondents as contextual evidence for letter-writing practices of the period, against which ten women letter-writers were explored in detail. This method of dealing with the primary source material elucidated complex and personalised relationships with letter-writing and the life of the mind within a framework that attended to broader epistolary and intellectual cultures of the period. This could not have been achieved by an approach that either focused on quantitative evidence of participation in intellectual life or attended too narrowly to individual examples.

Archival research, by its nature, resists the researcher's intention as much as it meets their needs. For this book, the search terms were kept deliberately broad and any familiar letters written by women within the period were considered of possible interest. This way of working offered the opportunity to locate evidence of female learning in collections that had no connection with existing intellectual or literary histories. In some cases, a substantial collection of letters was researched because the letter-writer's intellectual interests had been acknowledged in scholarship, but the letters themselves had not been thoroughly explored. In other cases, a gnomic catalogue entry citing a woman's name within family papers was enough to prompt a look. Thus, the main examples discussed here emerged from a long search through the catalogues of national libraries and local record offices and from leads provided by existing scholarship. The resulting collection of letter-writers, gathered together for the first time in this book, represents the most substantial examples of engaged letter-writing identified by this process. The particular demands of the archive, therefore, had an important influence on the selection of correspondents presented here.

Some of the collections used in this study have survived in the archive because of their intellectual content, but many others were not kept for that reason at all. Some were kept because of the letter-writer's relationship to an important man or because she had an illustrious family heritage. But there are many examples of correspondence by non-elite women who had no connection with anyone of note, intellectual or otherwise. This makes it tempting to speculate about this correspondence as the tip of the iceberg of women's intellectual letter-writing. Whilst one should not overstate the case, the wealth of examples of childhood letter-writing, where adult epistolary habits were inculcated, does shed light on the broad seedbed for female intellectual letter-writing in this period. This must be taken into account when considering the extant examples of adult achievement in this arena. Furthermore, it was women who largely directed these early forays into epistolary literacy in both their sons and daughters – taking an active role in producing the next generation of engaged citizens.[87] Evidence of youthful or lifelong intellectual endeavour in surviving family papers is, by its very nature, limited and scattered. But the range of examples that have been located and explored here suggests wide participation in considered and cerebrally engaged

Representativeness of sources ↑

letter-writing. The question of how representative these letter-writers were of their gender, class, region or time is a difficult one. Some letters survive over other letters on account of a series of historically contingent choices and accidents, and an encounter with an eighteenth-century letter entails an acknowledgement of more than one historical framework of privilege. All of the women studied here are perhaps anomalous in the sense that their letters have survived in the historical record. Some of them were, no doubt, unusually prolific and engaged letter-writers for their time. However, all of them give an insight into the particular social conditions of their class, gender and circumstances and, with careful contextualisation, these women can represent the experiences of other similar women. By using the depth of qualitative detail offered by individual examples with the breadth of a large contextual source base, wider historical conclusions can be drawn.

The ten letter-writers who take centre stage in this book are Anne Dormer (Oxfordshire), Mary Evelyn (Greater London/Surrey), Jemima, Marchioness Grey, Catherine Talbot, Mary Grey (primarily Bedfordshire and Oxfordshire), Elizabeth Elstob (Worcestershire), Jane Johnson (Buckinghamshire), Mary Clarke (Somerset), Ann Worsley and Eliza Worsley (Yorkshire). Anne Dormer (*c.* 1648–95), the daughter of a courtier and wife of an Oxfordshire gentleman, has been studied by historians for the evidence she provides of an unhappy marriage but has not been acknowledged as someone who was also a thoughtfully engaged reader and writer.[88] Seventeenth-century gentlewoman Mary Evelyn (*c.* 1635–1709) has come to notice in studies of her husband, the writer and diarist John Evelyn, and his milieu, but there is no extended study on her intellectual letter-writing.[89] Evelyn, the daughter of the baronet and diplomat Richard Browne, enjoyed an elaborate humanist education during her childhood in France and was regularly present at court during her adult life in England. The two most famous names, Elizabeth Elstob (1683–1756) and Catherine Talbot (1721–70), were known in their own lifetimes as a scholar and a literary talent respectively and have been discussed in studies and biographies of the early Bluestockings.[90] Elstob and Talbot are also unusual within the group because they never married.[91] Elstob was born into an affluent merchant family in the north, lived her young adulthood in the London household of her brother, a scholar and cleric, and later earned her own income as a provincial schoolmistress. Catherine Talbot was born into an important clerical family in Berkshire but to a mother who had just lost her husband (and with him her means). The Talbots were later taken into the Reverend Thomas Secker's household, who proceeded to occupy a series of important positions within the Church before becoming the Archbishop of Canterbury in 1758. Unmarried and dependent, Talbot may have benefited from an improved material environment over time, but she retained an ambiguous social status in eighteenth-century literary circles. Jemima, Marchioness Grey (1722–97) and her aunt Lady Mary Grey (1719/20–62) are two of the most elevated letter-writers considered here: titled, aristocratic and well connected. Jemima Grey had inherited her grandfather the Duke of Kent's barony of Lucas of Crudwell, and subsequently a grand estate – Wrest Park in Bedfordshire. Jemima Grey and, to a lesser extent, Mary Grey, have received some attention in Sylvia Harcstark Myers's 1990 volume *The Bluestocking Circle: Women, friendship and the life of the mind in eighteenth-century England*, but until now there has been no sustained study of their lives or letters. Both Jane Johnson (1706–59) and Mary Clarke (mid to late 1650s–1705) have been considered for their influence on the field of childhood education, but less so for their own creative and intellectual motivations. Jane Johnson was the wife of a vicar, Woolsey Johnson, and lived in Buckinghamshire, but the family fortunes benefited from Jane having jointly inherited an estate and Woolsey being a man of private means. Mary Clarke of Somerset was the daughter of a gentleman, the cousin of philosopher John Locke; in 1675 she married a politician, Edward Clarke. The Worsleys – a well-to-do Yorkshire family – are unknown to histories of female writing altogether.

This combination of the well-known, the partially explored and the completely unknown female letter-writer is placed in context by a wide range of everyday letter-writing of the period so that continuities between and departures from the typical and the atypical can be identified. These ten women all used their letters as a space to openly contemplate themes central to understanding gender and intellectual life in this period. The ideas and experiences they elaborated in depth were identifiable in a broader range of the researched letter collections but did not receive the concentrated discussion that these individuals devoted to them. These examples, therefore, offer an opportunity to explore gender and intellectual life by using the qualitative detail of women's own words and practices. These examples also corroborate a pluralistic view of the family and domestic life in the seventeenth and eighteenth centuries. Although women encountered many of the same demands and restrictions on their lives, and a lack of autonomy was a theme consistently evidenced by the sources, the characteristics of women's individual experiences were diverse and frequently at odds with contemporary characterisations of gendered norms. Responses to family life varied widely as did the personalities of family members. The social landscape changed dramatically as many women of the gentry moved, according to season, from country houses to city settings, in pursuit of better health or vitality of a social kind. Geographic remoteness from the major urban centres, or the sensibilities of an overbearing husband could equally render some women genuinely isolated.

The letter-writers analysed in this study illustrate clearly both the diversity of circumstances experienced by women of the middling sort, gentry and aristocracy in this period (which altered with advancing life stage) and their personalised responses to what have been considered tightly prescribed lives. However, each example clearly shows how different women energetically applied themselves to bending their circumstances in order to meet shared intellectual aspirations.

Material, spatial and textual: approaches to studying letters

The material

There was a distinct and influential relationship between the act of letter-writing and women's personal engagement with intellectual life between the years 1650 and 1750. The materiality of letter-writing as a practice and the status of the letter as an object played a critical role in this relationship. This book sets out to demonstrate not only that the content of women's letters in this period could be intellectual, but also that the interaction that took place between the *practical* and the *cerebral* in the process of letter-writing represented a significant dynamic in women's experiences of the life of the mind. The physical processes of letter-writing affected the emotional and intellectual engagement of the correspondent and vice versa. For those women with the leisure and economic security to write, correspondence culture gave them a chance to integrate the intellectual within the framework of everyday life.

Traditionally historians have put people before the material world, often seeing the tools of people's labour – be that the pitchfork or the pen – as mere instruments. However, scholarship which has drawn on anthropological approaches has influenced the study of history and, in particular, 'things' in history. For example, the field of material culture studies, as applied in historical research, has been revealing of the symbolic meanings of objects and their importance in the forming of past social identities. Over the last ten years, work on the study of the domestic interior by scholars such as Amanda Vickery and John Styles has illuminated the complex networks of meaning surrounding the 'social life' of domestic objects.[92] However, as Frank Trentmann argues, the question historians should ask is how interactions with things shaped people's 'materially embodied selves, practices and relationships'.[93] Pioneering work on 'material texts' and the material culture of letter-writing has also illuminated early modern actors' social practices. In particular, work by Peter Stallybrass, Dena Goodman and James Daybell has been instrumental in bringing the material into contact with the textual.[94] The research undertaken for this book has attended to the material evidence imparted by correspondence collections, such as signs of method of sending, quality of pen and ink, handwriting, and also to the social commentary on these physical aspects of letter-writing. Although much of the analysis naturally rests on the words people wrote in their letters, the material evidence presented by correspondence collections informed the conclusions drawn. This was especially important when, for example, comparing correspondence written by the same person to several different letter-writers or at different junctures in their lifecycle. Differentiation in terms of the letter-writers' intent often went unwritten on the page but was made clear by the courtesy of a wide margin or the precision with which handwriting was executed. As the letter-writers' relationship with the social practice of corresponding formed a part of their engagement with the life of the mind, these indications of epistolary practice were informative to the central questions of this study. At times, invaluable corroboratory evidence from the size of paper, the extent to which it had been filled, the correctness of the handwriting or the clumsiness of execution threw crucial light upon the state of mind or circumstances of the letter-writer.[95] Moreover, there were frequent indications that contemporary letter-writers 'read' their letters for these insights in conjunction with the message written on the page. For example, a seventeenth-century letter-writer, Mary Evelyn, scolded her friend, Ralph Bohun, for his careless approach to correspondence, telling him: 'not to lay so much wax on them as to temper the fidelity of the post, who may Imagine all you write to be secrets, and that once in my life I may make a seasonable present, if you can but secure me of a safe conveyance, I will send you a seale to save y[r] fingers from burning'.[96] This comment acknowledged that, by contemporary standards, signs of the author's intention were implicit in the material presentation of letters. This evidence was read alongside the written message and communicated information about the letter-writer's state of mind and circumstances at the time of writing.

If the letter itself betrayed material evidence of its construction and intention, then pens and pots of ink and pounce are also revealing of contemporary investment in correspondence culture. This can be extended to the desks and tables upon which women wrote and the bureaus and boxes in which they locked away received missives. At this time, the material culture of correspondence was proliferating and specially designed women's writing desks began to appear in top-end furniture catalogues. Even after the purpose of the initial exchange of letters had been achieved, correspondence itself could take on alternative meanings as collected memorabilia. Letters from friends, family and associates were often neatly filed away for posterity, whilst some correspondents took to copying out their own letters, for record or example. In their own lifetimes, letter-writers might reread old correspondence at intervals to remind themselves of past friendships or lost loved ones, or to relive days gone by; this process converted the letter from message to collated record, open to reinterpretation. Yorkshire gentlewoman, Ann Worsley commented on this practice of keeping and rereading old letters when she wrote to her brother in 1737: 'his Letters to me are charming, I sometimes lock my self up to read some, … but Alas when shall I be able to read em without Crying & tendering me too much.'[97] For Ann Worsley, at least, a collection of old letters provided emotional reading and studying them an activity she would conduct from the privacy of a locked room. Even within the lifetimes of the correspondents themselves, then, letters could take on alternative meanings: starting life with the immediacy of a recently posted message and, later, becoming part of a lifetime's collected memorabilia, steeped in sentimental significance.

The letter had a many-layered status: firstly as constructed object, then as dispatched token, and finally as treasured keepsake. Of course, not all letters attained all three of these meanings, but many did and these material life stages most likely helped negotiate their place in a modern day archive. Chapter 3 will develop further the question of letter-writing as a social practice, showing that far from being an inert tool in the hands of a creative individual, the practice of correspondence acted upon the writer herself, informing her thought processes and modes of expression in dynamic ways.

The spatial

Seventeenth- and eighteenth-century letter-writers frequently evoked the spaces they wrote in and discussed how these spaces affected their intellectual activities. A quiet place and spare time in the day were prerequisites for serious study and, consequently, comment on personal privacy, household workload, sociability and solitude were all common in the letters of intellectually motivated women of this period.[98] The closet, for example, was an important and legitimate space for female private study across the period.[99] Despite the abundance of scholarly interest in the domestic sphere, the role of the home as a space in which intellectual endeavour was undertaken has been largely overlooked; as though the domestic sphere and intellectual life operated within entirely separate chapters of human experience. Whether the result of traditional disciplinary division or the false assumption that closeted female lives were devoid of intellectual opportunity, this is still a significant oversight. This book considers the spaces of the home as integral to the development of the life of the mind and as sites of knowledge production. Much as the academic institution might influence the young scholar, the home played a role in the life of the mind of its inhabitants, especially those who lacked alternative, exterior spaces for study and conversation.

The domestic, then, was much more than a static backdrop to life and its features, location, requirements and inhabitants had an important impact on the mental lives of women.[100] Letters linked home and household with other spaces or networks of exchange. Women's descriptions of the spaces they inhabited brought them closer to absent friends. Mental proximity was the next best thing to physical closeness and this was sometimes achieved by letters that provided visual images of the participants sitting by desk or fireside. Space was also psychological, and the extremes of solitude or absence of privacy affected letter-writers' emotional health. These findings echo Virgina Woolf's proviso, written two hundred years later, that 'a woman must have money and a room of her own if she is to write'.[101] Ultimately, time and space influenced personal autonomy and, above all else, it was some personal autonomy, the loss or attainment of it, which mediated women's engagement with the life of the mind.

The textual

The tendency to categorise writing, especially when it is seen through the lens of literature, reaps certain rewards but also imposes particular frameworks. The themes of this book have been heavily mined by literary historians interested in women's production of texts, be they manuscript or print. However, the understanding of the letter as a highly multi-functional written form, both pragmatically straightforward and expansively creative, means that categories common in literary criticism have not been employed here. Although the letter certainly did function as a text for contemporary and future readers of correspondence, it was also a tool of everyday life used by a broad cross-section of society for extremely diverse – and often prosaic – purposes.

This book contends that letters moved easily between genres, modes and conventional forms, acting – by turn – as familiar, literary, domestic or intellectual texts. Moreover, as Jennifer Summit has suggested, letter-writing was 'perhaps the defining genre of the household', one which allowed the coexistence of the material and the textual; the everyday and the intellectual.[102] Although it is important to unpack the letter's multiple meanings, focusing on its significance as a text can also serve to inhibit our understanding of the letter's pluralistic status. For example, sometimes letters were a written 'performance', an opportunity to project alternative selves to distant acquaintances, but often they were not.[103] Many straightforward letters focusing on the communication of local news exist in the archive alongside others that draw clearly on literary models and many do a combination of both. Likewise, the use of genre as a model to categorise letter-writing has its pitfalls, as many letters exhibit the characteristics of a range of genres and at the same time had the practical functions of message relaying and arrangement-making.[104]

Whilst historians must rely, to a certain extent, on categories such as manuscript, print and life writing, it is also important to see the overlap between these definitions and to recognise the connectivity between such products as notebooks and printed works, letters and political pamphlets. As the eighteenth-century print industry found ever greater opportunities to sell its wares, printed pocket books were bought in their thousands, providing a space for personal notes and reflections framed by the printed boundaries of a generic format. This was an explicitly mixed-media example, but the infiltration of forms and styles developed in one medium were often transferred or echoed in another. However, whilst letter-writing had an important relationship with print – which has been explored in great depth in relation to the epistolary novel or the advice manual – it was not a defining one. The study of letters necessarily confuses clear distinctions between life writing, letter-writing, writing for communication and reflective writing because letters can be many or all of these things. The women letter-writers in this study certainly used letters as a flexible medium for their self-education, relationship building and intellectual development amongst very many other purposes.

The next chapters delve into correspondence collections found in English archives. From childhood letters home, eager to impress, to the reflective letter-writing of older age, women's paths to intellectual life and their personal experiences of the life of the mind are explored in full. These letter-writers are situated firmly in their contexts of home, family and work – amongst the scattered possessions of their closets – in order to ground mental space in the physical environment. Part I of the book focuses on women's paths to learning from childhood to adulthood and their realisation of a life of the mind. In particular, Chapter 1 considers the skills and resources women needed to engage with a life of the mind and discusses how early experiences moulded adult expectations. Chapter 2 explores in detail what it meant to be an 'intellectual woman' in this period through the examples of two extremely scholarly letter-writers and considers how women's lifecycles affected their own creative production and the subsequent reception of their work. In Part II, the book turns to the material and spatial realities of letter-writing, first – in Chapter 3 – by discussing the relationship between epistolary writing and thinking, and secondly, by looking at the role of the home and the psychology of domestic space in women's letter-writing in Chapter 4. In Part III, Chapter 5 traces connections between the intellectual and the emotional through a discussion of epistolary relationships, concepts of perfect friendship and the use of letter-writing as a form of self-help. Finally, Chapter 6 draws together the main conclusions of this study and places its findings within longer-term historical processes of continuity and change. Throughout, the letters themselves occupy the foreground and illuminate their writers' uses of correspondence for cerebral and emotional gains.

Notes

1 S. M. Fitzmaurice, *The Familiar Letter in Early Modern English* (Amsterdam: John Benjamins, 2002), p. 1.

2 R. Perry, *Women, Letters and the Novel* (New York: AMS Press, 1980); T. F. Berg, *The Lives and Letters of an Eighteenth-Century Circle of Acquaintance* (Aldershot: Ashgate, 2006).

3 R. Earle (ed.), *Epistolary Selves: Letters and letter-writers, 1600–1945* (Aldershot: Ashgate, 1999); C. Brant, *Eighteenth-Century Letters and British Culture* (Basingstoke: Palgrave Macmillan, 2006); J. How, *Epistolary Spaces: English letter-writing from the foundation of the Post Office to Richardson's Clarissa* (Aldershot: Ashgate, 2003).

4 M. M. Dowd and J. A. Eckerle, *Genre and Women's Life-Writing in Early Modern England* (Aldershot: Ashgate, 2007); P. Coleman, J. Lewis and J. Kowalik (eds), *Representations of the Self from the Renaissance to Romanticism* (Cambridge: Cambridge University Press, 2000).

5 D. Cressy, *Literacy and the Social Order: Reading and writing in Tudor and Stuart England* (Cambridge: Cambridge University Press, 1980). For a discussion of methods

of measuring historical literacy rates, see R. A. Houston, *Literacy in Early Modern Europe: Culture and education, 1500–1800* (Harlow: Longman, 1988), pp. 116–29.

6   According to R. A. Houston, literacy rose most rapidly in the southern counties of England during the reigns of Elizabeth I and James I (1558–1625) but in the North the most notable growth in rates took place between 1660 and 1720, see *Literacy in Early Modern Europe*, p. 152.

7   Figures for 1720 from Cressy, Literacy and the Social Order, pp. 129, 176.

8   L. Stone, 'Literacy and Education in England, 1640–1900', *Past and Present*, 42 (1969), pp. 69–139.

9   J. Eales, 'Female Literacy and the Social Identity of the Clergy Family in the Seventeenth Century', *Archaeologia Cantiana*, 133 (2013), pp. 67–81.

10 Margaret Spufford has uncovered some of the limited sources on schooling in rural areas, but the picture remains murky, see *Small Books and Pleasant Histories: Popular fiction and its readership in seventeenth-century England* (London: Methuen, 1981).

11 Whilst spelling had not become entirely systematised in this period, letter-writers who showed the most internal consistency in their spelling were also those who had benefited from an extensive childhood education. Gil Skidmore has noticed phonetic spelling in Quaker women's manuscript letters, noting that 'none of this detracted from women's qualifications for the [Quaker] ministry and nor did it mean that they were not educated in other ways'. See *Strength in Weakness: Writings of eighteenth-century Quaker women* (Oxford: Altamira Press, 2003), p. 12.

12 S. Whyman, 'Letter Writing and the Rise of the Novel: The epistolary literacy of Jane Johnson and Samuel Richardson', *Huntington Library Quarterly*, 70 (2007), p. 604.

13 Whyman, 'Letter Writing and the Rise of the Novel'.

14 See S. Whyman, *The Pen and the People: English letter-writers, 1660–1800* (Oxford: Oxford University Press, 2009).

15 Linda Pollock's analysis of seventeenth- and eighteenth-century diarists shows that they were interested in the educations of their daughters as much as their sons, although differences still applied: see L. A. Pollock, 'Rethinking Patriarchy and the Family in Seventeenth-Century England', *Journal of Family History*, 23 (2000), pp. 3–27.

16 See E. Arizpe and M. Styles, *Reading Lessons from the Eighteenth Century: Mothers, children and texts* (Shenstone: Pied Piper, 2006).

17 M. Cohen, ' "Familiar Conversation": The role of the "familiar format" in education in eighteenth-century England', in M. Hilton and J. Shefrin (eds), *Educating the Child in Enlightenment Britain: Beliefs, cultures, practices* (Farnham: Ashgate, 2009), pp. 99–116.

18 J. Pearson, *Women's Reading in Britain 1750–1835* (Cambridge: Cambridge University Press, 1999), pp. 1–2.

19 See F. Molekamp, *Women and the Bible in Early Modern England: Religious reading and writing* (Oxford: Oxford University Press, 2013), especially pp. 1, 11. See also S. Mandelbrote, 'The English Bible and Its Readers in the Eighteenth Century', in I. Rivers (ed.), *Books and Their Readers in Eighteenth-Century England: New essays* (London: Leicester University Press, 2001), pp. 35–78.

20 See Pearson, *Women's Reading*, pp. 49–64; informative books might include history, geography and household arts, whereas poetry and drama were expected to provoke an imaginative engagement.

21 A classic text on this topic is Perry's *Women, Letters and the Novel*, others include: E. Bergen Brophy, *Women's Lives and the 18th-Century English Novel* (Tampa: University of South Florida Press, 1991) and R. Ballaster, 'Women and the Rise of the Novel: Sexual prescripts', in V. Jones (ed.), *Women and Literature in Britain, 1700–1800* (Cambridge: Cambridge University Press, 2000), pp. 197–216.

22 See J. A. I. Champion, 'Enlightened Erudition and the Politics of Reading in John Toland's Circle', *Historical Journal*, 49 (2006), pp. 111–41 at p. 138 for the importance of reading practices for non-elite intellectuals, and see I. Jackson, 'Approaches to the History of Readers and Reading in Eighteenth-Century Britain', *Historical Journal*, 47:4 (2004), pp. 1041–54 for the instrumental role of reading in processes of historical change.

23 J. Fergus, *Provincial Readers in Eighteenth-Century England* (Oxford: Oxford University Press, 2006), p. 59.

24 See, for example, B. Cunningham and M. Kennedy (eds), *The Experience of Reading: Irish historical perspectives* (Dublin: Rare Books Group of the Library Association of Ireland and Economic and Social History Society of Ireland, 1999).

25 N. Tadmor, "In the even my wife read to me': Women, reading and household life in the eighteenth century', in J. Raven, H. Small and N. Tadmor (eds), *The Practice and Representation of Reading in England* (Cambridge: Cambridge University Press, 1996), pp. 162–74 at p. 165.

26 Tadmor, 'In the even my wife read to me', pp. 165–70. In total, in Thomas Turner's diary over seventy different books were recorded.

27 See, for example, S. Colclough, 'Procuring Books and Consuming Texts: The reading experience of a Sheffield apprentice, 1798', *Book History*, 3 (2000), pp. 21–44. The value of this work is highlighted by Ian Jackson in his valuable review of the field, 'Approaches to the History of Readers', p. 1048.

28 The term 'Enlightenment' has its origins in the eighteenth century and, in particular, with Emmanuel Kant's famous essay: 'Beantwortung der Frage: Was ist Aufklärung?' [Answering the Question: What is Enlightenment?], *Berlinische Monatsschrift* [*Berlin Monthly*] (1784). However, it is a term that has been used to describe such a diverse array of societal shifts and developments that, for some, it has become too encompassing to be meaningful. For further discussion, see A. Pagden, *The Enlightenment: And why it still matters* (Oxford: Oxford University Press, 2013); G. Garrard, *Counter-Enlightenments: From the eighteenth century to the present* (London: Routledge, 2006); J. Israel, *Enlightenment Contested: Philosophy, modernity, and the emancipation of man, 1670–1752* (Oxford: Oxford University Press, 2006) and R. E. Norton, 'The Myth of the Counter-Enlightenment', *Journal of the History of Ideas*, 68:4 (2007), pp. 635–58.

29 A host of scholarship has shown this to be the case, examples include H. L. Smith (ed.), *Women Writers and the Early Modern British Political Tradition* (Cambridge: Cambridge University Press, 1998); P. McDowell, *The Women of*

Grub Street: Press, politics and gender in the London literary marketplace, 1678–1730 (Oxford: Clarendon Press, 1998); C. Hesse, 'Women Intellectuals in the Enlightened Republic of Letters: Introduction', in S. Knott and B. Taylor (eds), *Women, Gender and Enlightenment* (Basingstoke: Palgrave Macmillan, 2005), pp. 259–64; J. Daybell, *Women Letter-Writers in Tudor England* (Oxford: Oxford University Press, 2006); and J. Wallwork and P. Salzman (eds), *Early Modern Englishwomen Testing Ideas* (Farnham: Ashgate, 2011).

30 Here are just a few of the titles dealing with similar themes, but for the period 1750 onwards: H. Guest, *Small Change: Women, learning, patriotism, 1750–1810* (Chicago: University of Chicago Press, 2000); A. Vickery (ed.), *Women, Privilege and Power: British politics, 1750 to the present* (Stanford, Calif.: Stanford University Press, 2001); S. Morgan (ed.), *Women, Religion and Feminism in Britain, 1750–1900* (Basingstoke: Palgrave Macmillan, 2002); M. Hilton, *Women and the Shaping of the Nation's Young: Education and public doctrine in Britain, 1750–1850* (Aldershot: Ashgate, 2007); and M. Daly Groggin and B. Fowkes Tobin (eds), *Women and Things, 1750–1950: Gendered material strategies* (Farnham: Ashgate, 2009).

31 Scholars working on the 'Cultures of Knowledge' project (2009–14) based at the University of Oxford have used digital methods to bring together and interpret large bodies of early modern correspondence.

32 Voltaire, Samuel Hartlib and Hans Sloane, amongst others, have all received sustained attention as 'men of letters' whose epistolary contacts were scattered across the globe.

33 See L. Hunter, *The Letters of Dorothy Moore, 1612–64: The friendships, marriage, and intellectual life of a seventeenth-century woman* (Aldershot: Ashgate, 2004) for a discussion of Moore, a valued correspondent of Hartlib, and also L. Hunter 'Sisters of the Royal Society: The circle of Katherine Jones, Lady Ranelagh', in L. Hunter and S. Hutton (eds), *Women, Science and Medicine 1500–1700: Mothers and sisters of the Royal Society* (Stroud: Sutton, 1997), pp. 178–97. See C. Pal, *Republic of Women: Rethinking the Republic of Letters in the seventeenth century* (Cambridge: Cambridge University Press, 2012), which documents the transnational network of seventeenth-century women intellectuals who were active in the fields of philosophy, faith, science and learning.

34 As James Daybell's work has shown, as early as the fifteenth and sixteenth centuries a wide range of women used letters for literary, political, social and religious purposes: J. Daybell (ed.), *Early Modern Women's Letter-Writing, 1450–1700* (Basingstoke: Palgrave, 2001).

35 L. O'Neill, *The Opened Letter: Networking in the early modern British world* (Philadelphia: University of Pennsylvania Press, 2015).

36 Sylvia Harcstark Myers also used this term in the title of her seminal work on the Bluestockings: *The Bluestocking Circle: Women, friendship, and the life of the mind in eighteenth-century England* (Oxford: Clarendon Press, 1990); however, she never actually defines the phrase and seems to have chosen it simply to denote intellectual interest and engagement.

37 See H. Arendt, *The Life of the Mind*, vols 1–2 (London: Secker and Warburg, 1978).

38 Arendt, *Life of the Mind*, vol. 1, p. 5.

39 J. Gregory, 'Writing Women in(to) the Long Eighteenth Century', *Literature and History*, 11:1 (2001), pp. 83–4.

40 See S. H. Mendelson (ed.), *Margaret Cavendish* (Farnham: Ashgate, 2009), S. Clucas (ed.) *A Princely Brave Woman: Essays on Margaret Cavendish, Duchess of Newcastle* (Aldershot: Ashgate, 2003), C. Wayne White, *The Legacy of Anne Conway (1631–1679): Reverberations from a mystical naturalism* (Albany: State University of New York Press, 2008), S. Hutton, *Anne Conway: A woman philosopher* (Cambridge: Cambridge University Press, 2004), P. Sheridan (ed.), *Catherine Trotter Cockburn: Philosophical writings* (Peterborough, ON: Broadview Press, 2006), M. Atherton (ed.), *Women Philosophers of the Early Modern Period* (Indianapolis: Hackett Publishing Company, 1994).

41 This approach is also proposed by A. Lawrence-Mathers and P. Hardman (eds) in *Women and Writing, c. 1350–c. 1650: The domestication of print culture* (Woodbridge: York Medieval Press in association with The Boydell Press, 2010), p. 4.

42 B. A. Carroll, 'The Politics of "Originality": Women and the Class System of the Intellect', *Journal of Women's History*, 2 (1990), pp. 136–63 at p. 136.

43 Pearson, *Women's Reading*, p. 43. Also see James Raven on how the experience of reading might be 'more textual creation than passive reception': 'New Reading Histories, Print Culture and the Identification of Change: The case of eighteenth-century England', *Social History*, 23:3 (1998), pp. 268–87 at p. 270.

44 See L. K. Kerber, *Toward an Intellectual History of Women* (Chapel Hill: University of North Carolina Press, 1997), especially p. 19, and H. L. Smith, 'Women Intellectuals and Intellectual History: Their paradigmatic separation', *Women's History Review*, 16:3 (2007), pp. 353–68.

45 See, in particular, E. Eger, *Bluestockings: Women of reason from Enlightenment to Romanticism* (Basingstoke: Palgrave Macmillan, 2010).

46 Earle, *Epistolary Selves*, p. 1.

47 H. Dragstra, S. Ottway and H. Wilcox (eds), *Betraying Our Selves: Forms of self-representation in early modern English texts* (Basingstoke: Macmillan, 2000), p. 11.

48 'Scribal publication', or the circulation of hand-written texts, was an established part of early modern literary culture and a channel through which the work of many women writers reached its audience. For an earlier history of this practice, see J. Stevenson, 'Women Writing and Scribal Publication in the Sixteenth Century', in P. Beal and M. J. M. Ezell (eds), *English Manuscript Studies, 1100–1700*, vol. 9 (London: British Library, 2000), pp. 1–32.

49 Brant, *Eighteenth-Century Letters*, p. 9.

50 For a discussion of the letter as both public and private see J. Brewer, 'This, That and the Other: Public, social and private in the seventeenth and eighteenth centuries', in D. Castiglione and L. Sharpe (eds), *Shifting the Boundaries – Transformations of the language of public and private in the eighteenth century* (Exeter: Exeter University Press, 1995), pp. 1–21.

51 See S. Crangle, Epistolarity, Audience, Selfhood: The letters of Dorothy Osborne to William Temple', *Women's Writing*, 12:3 (2005), pp. 433–52.

52 J. Habermas, *The Structural Transformation of the Public Sphere: An enquiry into a category of bourgeois society* (Cambridge, Mass.: MIT Press, 1991). See also P. Spacks,

Privacy: Concealing the eighteenth-century self (Chicago: University of Chicago Press, 2003), especially p. 3, D. Goodman, 'Public Sphere and Private Life: Toward a synthesis of current historiographical approaches to the Old Regime', *History and Theory*, 31:1 (1992), pp. 1–20, and L. Klein's discussion of the meanings of 'public' and 'private' in relation to gender in the eighteenth century: 'Gender and the Public/Private Distinction in the Eighteenth Century: Some questions about evidence and analytic procedure', *Eighteenth-Century Studies*, 29:1 (1995), pp. 97–109.

53 See Whyman, *Pen and the People*, pp. 46–71 on the post.

54 How, *Epistolary Spaces*, p. 2.

55 See D. Goodman, *Becoming a Woman in the Age of Letters* (London: Cornell University Press, 2009).

56 K Dierks, *In My Power: Letter writing and communications in early America* (Philadelphia: University of Pennsylvania Press, 2009), pp. 4–5; his use of italics.

57 See M. Bigold, 'Letters and Learning', in R. Ballaster (ed.) *The History of British Women's Writing, 1690–1750* (Basingstoke: Palgrave Macmillan, 2010), pp. 173–86 and Eger, *Bluestockings*.

58 For letter-writing as representation of the self, see Earle, *Epistolary Selves*, especially S. Whyman, ' "Paper visits": The post-Reformation letter as seen through the Verney archive', pp. 15–36 and Toby L. Ditz, 'Formative Ventures: Eighteenth-century commercial letters and the articulation of experience', pp. 59–78.

59 See, for example, E. Tavor Bannet, *Empire of Letters: Letter manuals and transatlantic correspondence, 1680–1820* (Cambridge: Cambridge University Press, 2005); D. Raftery, *Women and Learning in English Writing, 1600–1900* (Dublin: Four Courts, 1997). Vivien Jones has also discussed early feminist history's reliance on conduct literature as a source for understanding the repression of women, see 'The Seductions of Conduct: Pleasure and conduct literature', in R. Porter and M. Mulvey Roberts (eds) *Pleasure in the Eighteenth Century* (Basingstoke: Macmillan, 1996), pp. 108–32.

60 Anon., *Polite Epistolary Correspondence: A collection of letters, on the most instructive and entertaining subjects* (London, 1751).

61 Anon., *The Accomplished Letter-Writer; Or, Universal Correspondent. Containing familiar letters on the most common occasions in life* (London, 1779).

62 For the relationship between prescriptive literature and contemporary practice, see R. Chartier, *Cultural History: Between practices and representations* (Cambridge: Polity in association with Blackwell, 1988).

63 See L. C. Mitchell, 'Entertainment and Instruction: Women's roles in the English epistolary tradition', *Huntington Library Quarterly*, 66:3/4 (2003), pp. 331–47 at p. 332, which shows the high degree of overlap in content between volumes that claimed originality. Clare Brant has also noted the differences that existed between letters as presented in advice manuals and the letters that eighteenth-century people sent and received, see *Eighteenth-Century Letters*, pp. 39–40.

64 Abbé d'Ancourt, *The Ladys Preceptor: Or, a letter to a lady of distinction upon politeness* (London, 1743), p. 59.

65 d'Ancourt, *Ladys Preceptor*.

66 d'Ancourt, *Ladys Preceptor*, p. 60.

67 See N. Phillips, *Women in Business, 1700–1850* (Woodbridge: Boydell Press, 2006); H. Barker, *The Business of Women: Female enterprise and urban development in northern England, 1760–1830* (Oxford: Oxford University Press, 2006).

68 Jones, 'Seductions of Conduct', pp. 111–12.

69 See Dierks, *In My Power*, especially p. 5.

70 See K. Parker (ed.), *Dorothy Osborne: Letters to Sir William Temple, 1652–54: Observations on love, literature, politics, and religion* (Aldershot: Ashgate, 2002), C. Hintz, *An Audience of One: Dorothy Osborne's letters to Sir William Temple, 1652–1654* (London: University of Toronto Press, 2005) and a short but illuminating piece by Carrie Hintz, 'A Second Reference to Marin le Roy de Gomberville's *Polexandre* in Dorothy Osborne's Letters', *Notes and Queries*, 46:3 (1999), pp. 339–40.

71 See G. Dow, 'A Model for the British Fair? French women's life writing in Britain, 1680–1830', in D. Cook and A. Culley (eds), *Women's Life Writing, 1700–1850: Gender, genre and authorship* (Basingstoke: Palgrave, 2012), pp. 86–102.

72 BL, Add. MS 78539: Mary Evelyn to Ralph Bohun, 21 May c. 1668. Vincent Voiture (1597–1648) was a French writer whose works Evelyn would have read in the original French rather than in translation, works such as: *Les Lettres de Mr. de Voiture* (Amsterdam, 1657).

73 Brant, *Eighteenth-Century Letters*, p. 10.

74 See A. Kugler, *Errant Plagiary: The life and writing of Lady Sarah Cowper, 1644–1720* (Stanford, Calif.: Stanford University Press, 2002); the texts that Cowper drew upon and subverted were largely prescriptive, including sermons, conduct literature and periodicals.

75 S. Walker, 'Prescription and Practice in the Visual Organization of Correspondence', *Huntington Library Quarterly*, 66:3/4 (2003), pp. 307–29.

76 A. Goldgar, *Impolite Learning: Conduct and community in the Republic of Letters, 1680–1750* (London: Yale University Press, 1995), p. 2.

77 Goldgar, *Impolite Learning*. Dena Goodman has confirmed this essentially social dimension to the Republic of Letters in 'Pigalle's Voltair nu: The Republic of Letters presents itself to the world', *Representations*, 16 (1986), pp. 86–109.

78 Pal, *Republic of Women*, where she proposes that social status was a more fundamental barrier to intellectual community than gender.

79 Bigold, 'Letters and Learning', p. 176. There are many famous examples of female patronage of female talent in eighteenth-century England, such as the poet Ann Yearsley and her patron Hannah More, but the example of Elizabeth Elstob discussed here in Chapters 2 and 5 is also revealing of the importance of female networks and aristocratic patronage in the support of women's intellectual work.

80 See M. Bigold, *Women of Letters, Manuscript Circulation, and Print Afterlives in the Eighteenth Century* (Basingstoke: Palgrave Macmillan, 2013).

81 S. Mendelson, 'Neighbourhood as Female Community in the Life of Anne Dormer', in S. Dragstra and S. Broomhall (eds), *Women, Identities and Communities in Early Modern Europe* (Aldershot: Ashgate, 2008), pp. 153–64.

82 Of course London took up a more central role during periods lived in the city, but on the whole, landed English men and women maintained close connections with the

metropolis throughout the year through commerce, politics and sociability; see, for example, A. Vickery, *The Gentleman's Daughter: Women's lives in Georgian England* (London: Yale University Press, 1998).

83 R. Sweet, *Antiquaries: The discovery of the past in eighteenth-century Britain* (London: Hambledon and London, 2004).

84 See L. Hannan, 'Collaborative Scholarship on the Margins: An epistolary network', *Women's Writing*, 21:3 (2014), pp. 290–315.

85 K. Harvey, *The Little Republic: Masculinity and domestic authority in eighteenth-century Britain* (Oxford: Oxford University Press, 2012), p. 169.

86 A. Laurence, 'Real and Imagined Communities in the Lives of Women in Seventeenth-Century Ireland: Identity and gender', in in S. Tarbin and S. Broomhall (eds), *Women, Identities and Communities in Early Modern Europe* (Aldershot: Ashgate, 2008), pp. 13–27 at p. 16.

87 See J. J. Popiel, *Rousseau's Daughters: Domesticity, education, and autonomy in modern France* (Lebanon: University of New Hampshire Press, 2008) and Hilton, *Women and the Shaping of the Nation's Young*.

88 See S. Mendelson and M. O'Connor, ' "Thy Passionately Loving Sister and Faithfull Friend": Anne Dormer's letters to her sister Lady Trumbull', in N. J. Miller and N. Yavneh (eds), *Sibling Relations and Gender in the Early Modern World* (Aldershot: Ashgate, 2004), pp. 206–15, and M. O'Connor, 'Representations of Intimacy in the Life-Writing of Anne Clifford and Anne Dormer', in Coleman *et al.*, *Representations of the Self*, pp. 79–96.

89 See 'Nuptial Love', in F. Harris, *Transformations of Love: The friendship of John Evelyn and Margaret Godolphin* (Oxford: Oxford University Press, 2002), pp. 64–90 and F. Harris, 'The Letterbooks of Mary Evelyn', in P. Beal and J. Griffiths (eds), *English Manuscript Studies, 1100–1700*, vol. 7 (London: British Library, 1998), pp. 202–15. Frances Harris has briefly addressed Mary Evelyn's intellectual motivations in a chapter 'Living in the Neighbourhood of Science: Mary Evelyn, Margaret Cavendish and the Greshamites', in Hunter and Hutton, *Women, Science and Medicine*, pp. 198–217.

90 Harcstark Myers, *Bluestocking Circle* and briefly in Eger, *Bluestockings*.

91 Three out of ten women remained unmarried, Eliza Worsley being the third.

92 J. Styles and A. Vickery (eds), *Gender, Taste, and Material Culture in Britain and North America, 1700–1830* (London: The Paul Mellon Centre for Studies in British Art, 2006). For women and material culture, see J. Batchelor and C. Kaplan (eds), *Women and Material Culture, 1660–1830* (Basingstoke: Palgrave Macmillan, 2007); Daly Groggin and Fowkes Tobin, *Women and Things*.

93 F. Trentmann, 'Materiality in the Future of History', *Journal of British Studies*, 48:2 (2009), pp. 283–307 at p. 290.

94 See, for example, M. de Grazia, M. Quilligan and P. Stallybrass (eds), *Subject and Object in Renaissance Culture* (Cambridge: Cambridge University Press, 1996); Goodman, *Becoming a Woman*; J. Daybell and P. Hinds (eds), *Material Readings of Early Modern Culture: Texts and social practices, 1580–1730* (Basingstoke: Palgrave Macmillan, 2010).

95 See K. Dierks, 'Letter Writing, Stationery Supplies, and Consumer Modernity in the Eighteenth-Century Atlantic World', *Early American Literature*, 41:3

(2006), pp. 473–94 and A. Brodie, 'Correspondence: The materiality and practice of letter-writing in England, 1650–1750' (unpublished MA dissertation, V&A/RCA, 2002).

96 BL, EP, Add. MS 78539: Mary Evelyn to Ralph Bohun, 13 March 1668/9.

97 WYAS, NH 2822/17: Ann Worsley to Thomas Robinson, c. June 1737.

98 See Spacks, *Privacy*.

99 K. Lipsedge, '"Enter into thy Closet": Women, closet culture, and the eighteenth-century English novel', in Styles and Vickery, *Gender, Taste, and Material Culture*, pp. 107–22; A. Laurence, 'Women Using Building in Seventeenth-Century England: A question of sources?' *Transactions of the Royal Historical Society*, 13 (2003), pp. 293–303; T. Chico, *Designing Women: The dressing room in eighteenth-century English literature and culture* (Lewisburg, Pa.: Bucknell University Press, 2005); and C. Christie, *The British Country House in the Eighteenth Century* (Manchester: Manchester University Press, 2000), pp. 71–3.

100 For the domestic duties undertaken by gentlewomen see R. Baird, *Mistress of the House: Great ladies and grand houses, 1670–1830* (London: Weidenfeld and Nicolson, 2003) and Vickery, *The Gentleman's Daughter*.

101 V. Woolf, *A Room of One's Own* (London: Hogarth Press, 1929), p. 4.

102 J. Summit, 'Hannah Wolley, the Oxinden Letters, and Household Epistolary Practice', in N. E. Wright, M. W. Ferguson and A. R. Buck (eds), *Women, Property, and the Letters of the Law in Early Modern England* (Toronto: University of Toronto Press, 2004), p. 202.

103 See Dragstra *et al.*, *Betraying Our Selves*.

104 See Emily Hodgson Anderson on the benefits of moving across categories of genre when studying women writers in this period: *Eighteenth-Century Authorship and the Play of Fiction: Novels and the theater, Haywood to Austen* (London: Routledge, 2009), pp. 2–3.

PART I

Women and learning

1

Getting started

The paths by which seventeenth- and eighteenth-century English women came to the task of intellectual thought were varied. Small details of personal histories interacted with larger dynamics of culture and society and created highly individualised contexts for intellectual work. Indeed, life stories betrayed the pervasive influence of a society which was both hierarchical and patriarchal on scholarly aspiration. In childhood, girls' and boys' educations diverged and for most young women home, rather than school, was the place of learning. Nevertheless, a domestic education was not necessarily an inadequate education and the practice of conversation and letter-writing were a mainstay of female learning.[1] When children left home, letters of advice were sent by concerned parents, offering encouragement for continued self-development and establishing habits of familial epistolary contact.[2] In adulthood, women were unable to join an intellectual club, society or institution. Instead, the circumstances of critical importance to their personal achievement were likely to be marriage, family, friendship and geography. The routes that women took to self-education and erudition are revealing of the opportunities and obstacles at work for women of this period. This chapter explores how women got started in the pursuit of a life of the mind and considers the skills and resources they needed to participate fully in the world of ideas.

Contemporary advice manuals can make for depressing reading – illustrating, as they most often do, the crushing restraints placed on female lives. However, a reading of this literature does pose the question: if women were not in fact slaves to conformity how did they gain the skills to become intellectual participants in their adult lives? Unfortunately, the answers to this question lie in separate fields of historical enquiry: the history of education (which consistently refers to childhood experiences) and the history of intellectual life (which dwells exclusively on adult efforts). Letter collections can illuminate both of these arenas, but rarely do they trace the entire educational and intellectual track record of a particular individual. Nevertheless, an examination of the expectations placed on young women – in educational terms – is revealing as to the origins of adult approaches to intellectual self-development. Some women excelled in their early studies and forged a strong commitment to the continuation of this practice. Others rebelled against unfavourable familial attitudes to their book learning. Opportunities for intellectual attainment were abundant for the few, ignored by some, utterly denied to others and hard won by the rest.

Literacy and self-education

When a woman sat down to write a letter, she may have had several concerns on her mind. Was she writing to a social equal, a family member or a mere acquaintance? Would she need to worry about the clarity of her script or the way she spelled her words? For the well educated, fluent written literacy was taken for granted – a tool used to display wit, clarity of thought and a stylish turn of phrase. In reading letters of this period, the disparities in the training women received are apparent on the page. Those who benefited from the most exalted of educations wrote in a flowing hand and with a careful continuity in spelling and sentence structure. Others boldly dispatched clumsily drawn letters of the alphabet, rolled into words, inconsistently spelled but resonant of the spoken word. In most cases, this is the only evidence available of lessons taken in youth. Women learned their epistolary skills by writing letters to parents, relatives and siblings away at school.[3] Perhaps some letter-writers were poor students but remained eager communicators in adult life, overlooking errors in order to make themselves understood. Other women's awkward epistles were no doubt the results of an inadequate textual education, sacrificed in favour of perfecting other household arts.

As James Daybell has argued for an earlier generation of women, letters provide revealing source material for understanding female literacy in a period before women entered mainstream schooling and higher education.[4] Letters not only convey societal attitudes towards female learning, but letters penned by women provide direct evidence of women's writing skills. It has been shown that manuscript writing demonstrated a much greater degree of variation in spelling in this period than did printed text.[5] Contractions, phonetic spellings and the retention of older spellings were common features of letter-writing in particular.[6] In fact, Gillian Weir's detailed analysis of the orthographic systems at work in the correspondence of Lady Katherine Paston (1578–1629) identifies personal spelling systems in operation alongside standardised forms.[7] Weir demonstrates that, even in the early decades of the seventeenth century, standardised spellings were evident in correspondence and attributes this to the increasing access to printed texts enjoyed by letter-writers (male and female) of the era. Interestingly, Weir's analysis also shows that men as well as women penned unorthodox spellings and that even women who shared the same education, in this case three Paston sisters, developed their own personal orthographies.[8] Despite variation in spelling remaining common into the early eighteenth century, educated writers tended to develop their own systems and remain largely consistent within these frameworks. When letter-writers used several different spellings of a given word it seems likely that they were – through education or temperament – less influenced by the standardised forms that appeared in print culture.

Childhood education for girls was not generally intended to prepare them for a lifetime of academic pursuit, but the roles of wife, mother and social participant required a certain degree of training. Letters, diaries and account books can give us glimpses of what an education at home might have entailed. The sources can show us bills for dancing teachers, notes about the progress of a daughter's embroidery or early attempts by children to imitate formulaic model letters in very neat handwriting. Although John Locke had argued that intellectual inequality between men and women was a function of society, rather than a biological fact, it was commonly assumed that the mind had a sex and the virtues of 'masculine reason' were contrasted with the intellectual deficiencies of 'feminine feeling'. Women were there to 'soften' social intercourse rather than to debate, contradict or expound. The education of girls and young women therefore involved something of a balancing act. Encouraging an excess of confident 'masculine reason' in women would contravene a social code of modest femininity, but a complete lack of understanding made for dull wives, inadequate mothers, irreligious citizens and unbearable guests. Ultimately, stupid women would bring up Godless children, perhaps to such an extent that even a boarding school or governess might fail to save them from impertinence and idleness.

The prominent seventeenth-century writer, Mary Astell, pointed out that whilst accruing a good education was important for women, showing this off was probably unwise.[9] As always, there were competing guidelines for life, moral and practical, emanating from various sources. The prolific French author, François Fénelon,[10] was being translated into English and he offered parents advice on how best to educate their daughters. Fénelon was, of course, joined in this endeavour by philosophers such as John Locke and Jean-Jacques Rousseau. Published literature provided readers with both the tools to educate young women and also advice against doing so. However, the letter-writers studied here demonstrated high levels of literacy, engagement with reading and a strong urge to write. Jane Johnson, an eighteenth-century vicar's wife, mother and home educator, is known to have read the work of John Locke, François Fénelon and Charles Rollin and incorporated their findings in the methods she devised to teach her children.[11] But Johnson was also an innovator, creating her own tailor-made educational tools with which to inspire a love of learning in her children. Where competing guidelines for educating girls and young women existed, mothers and teachers were selective along personal lines, generating educations for the young which were inflected with their own familial and social influences.

Expectations of intellectual life

Myra Reynolds's 1920 work, entitled *The Learned Lady in England, 1650–1760*, identified the Tudor age as a time of particular female intellectual freedom and a flowering of talent. Her precursor, the seventeenth-century writer Bathsua Makin, had also bemoaned the loss of humanism and progressive educational practices of the Tudor age, and considered the late seventeenth century to be a particularly low point for female educational opportunity. The early eighteenth-century letter-writer, Jemima, Marchioness Grey, also claimed that her 'Want of Genius … is through no Fault of my own' because 'le Genie depends entirely upon the Disposition of the Air at the time of one's Birth & Education; which is the reason why a considerable number of Great Men in most of the Arts appear (generally speaking) in the Same Age'.[12] However, women's motivations and talents, as demonstrated in epistolary form, provide clear evidence of educationally ambitious generations of women living in the late seventeenth and early eighteenth centuries, long after Queen Elizabeth I received her famously full humanist education and some time before Elizabeth Montagu gathered her coterie of gifted women in the Bluestocking circle.

Women's expectations of learning were naturally influenced by their upbringing, although, there is not always a straightforward relationship between positive and negative experiences of education in childhood and adult outcomes for the life of the mind. When the Northamptonshire scholar and politician Sir Justinian Isham put pen to paper in 1642, he did so to address his four daughters on how they should endeavour to live their lives, and elaborated several common expectations for seventeenth-century women. He made it clear that his advice should 'not be expected [to be] any generall or exact Treatise of a cõpleate [complete] Woman', of the kind found in published manuals, 'but only a briefe mention of what is most Necessary relating cheifely to your selfes as my Children'.[13] Liberally quoting from the scriptures, Sir Justinian Isham mapped out guidelines to pious life for his daughters, making it clear that their allegedly lesser intellectual abilities (as the 'weaker' sex) need not damage their relationship with God:

> although your Sex is not so capable of those stronger abilities of the Intellect, to make you so learned & knowing as men ought to be; yet be sure to keepe your Hearts upright and your Affections towards God unfained & there is no doubt That will be more acceptable unto him then all the Wisdome of the whole World besides.[14]

His expectation for them, as thinking young women was considerably diminished by the fact of their gender. Clearly he did not expect them to become intellectuals. In his eyes, the negotiation of the marriage market provided a more compelling imperative for the young woman. He, therefore, advised them on how best to equip themselves for this challenge:

> And this lett mee tell you, though a faire Fortune & a faire Face will never want suitors to them; yet cannot say whether they have oftener availed, or betrayed their Owners. However, I am sure the internall Graces of the Minde will be your Best & Surest Portion, both unto your selves and unto men of such discretions as I beleeve you would willingly give your selves unto.[15]

For Justinian Isham, 'the internall Graces of the Minde' referred principally to a good understanding of Christian scripture and the incorporation of its strictures. Another father, writing to his daughter in 1726, confirmed the importance of combining general learning with specifically religious instruction. As a member of the Derbyshire-based Soresby family, who were husbandmen and yeomen, he had taught his daughter accounting 'which will allways distinguish among those of your Own sex'.[16] However, he insisted, 'since religion is the great refiner of reason', she should 'be devout and steady in the profession of itt, Attend constant[ly to] the Publick services of the church with serenity & Evenness of temper'. This was typical advice. In both Soresby's and Isham's advice to their daughters, little detail was given on the exact content of the education. However, both agreed with the popular view that some education (primarily of a religious nature) would better a

woman, but that too much was beyond her capabilities and might her-
ald her ruin. Certainly, religious reading was highly encouraged in
women. As Femke Molekamp has highlighted for an earlier generation
of women: 'The Bible lay at the heart of early modern female reading
culture' and 'Devotional reading structured the day of people in this
period (of women in particular) as well as guiding their beliefs and
behaviours'.[17] Published sermons were commonly mentioned in wom-
en's letters of the seventeenth and eighteenth centuries and it has been
shown that women were often left religious reading in wills.[18] However,
it was still accepted by many that excessive learning would put at risk a
woman's development into the model of pious femininity. This view was
persistent in the long term and can be detected throughout the period
studied here.

A century after Isham put pen to paper on the subject of his
daughters' transition into adulthood, three teenage girls were hastily exchanging letters that suggested a different outlook for young
womanhood. These girls were Jemima Campbell (1722–97),[19] Mary
Grey (1719–61)[20] and Catherine Talbot (1721–70).[21] Mary Grey (later
Mary Gregory) and Jemima Campbell (later Jemima, Marchioness
Grey) were aunt and niece respectively, but as they were close in
age they were raised more as siblings. Catherine Talbot has gained
scholarly attention as a member of the Bluestocking circle and she
maintained correspondences with other high-profile women of that
eighteenth-century coterie.[22] However, her friends Jemima Campbell
and Mary Grey have largely escaped notice as intellectual women.[23]
Their letters, on the other hand, have survived in significant numbers
and testify to years of intellectually challenging conversation. When
the three friends first met as teenage girls, an important aspect of their
bond lay in their shared reading. In 1738, Jemima Campbell wrote to
Talbot, to comment on their mutual progression into bookishness: 'We
shall be such meer Book-Worms that t'will be absolutely impossible
to travel even from hence to London without contriving to get some
Shelves put up on the coach, & so turn it into a Library'.[24] It seemed
that Jemima Campbell had been exposed during her childhood to
more positive influences on female learning than many young women
of her era. Campbell was certainly privileged and her friend, Catherine
Talbot, at this time in her early teens, was already considered something of a child prodigy. Talbot's childhood poetry had been read and
circulated in Bath and her name often takes its place amongst those of
Elizabeth Carter, Elizabeth Montagu and Hester Thrale as an example
of eighteenth-century female literary talent. However, where Talbot's

name has been preserved on the contents pages of historical works on female intellect, her two friends remain largely unacknowledged by intellectual histories.[25] By exploring the letter-writing of these women it will be shown that the absence of publication and the presence of children are the only major differences between Campbell and Grey's life stories as compared with their publicly recognised friend, Talbot.

A key figure in these young girls' lives was the Reverend Thomas Secker. He had taken Catherine Talbot's mother, Mary, into his household when he married Catherine Benson, as Mary Talbot had been residing with Benson since her husband's death in 1720.[26] The Talbots lived in his household until Secker's death in 1768. Catherine Talbot's acquaintance with Secker was both long term and genuinely supportive, although biographies of Talbot have also attributed his influence to inhibiting her self-confidence and creativity.[27] During her childhood, it was Secker who encouraged Talbot in her studies and supervised her broad education which included classical, English, French and Italian literatures, alongside history, the arts, astronomy and scripture. However, the combination of Talbot's role as his housekeeper and personal secretary and Secker's powerful personality and public standing may have encouraged Talbot's insecurity about her worth and deference to Secker's authority.[28]

Catherine Talbot came into contact with Jemima Campbell and Mary Grey when they moved into a family residence close to Secker's home at the rectory of St James's, Piccadilly. In the late 1730s, Thomas Secker wrote some short letters to his young neighbours, Jemima Campbell and her companion Mary Grey. They were written in a tongue-in-cheek style and included mock formal invitations to tea alongside light-hearted requests for their presence at breakfast. Despite the familiar and jocular tone of the correspondence, Secker occasionally attempted to put the girls in their place. Seemingly concerned at their precocious characters, he gently teased them about their self importance:

> if you are desirous to come to me, I will receive you in a private room unless you chuse to be with the rest of the company and we shall have time to drink Tea together. Tomorrow morning I can neither come to you nor permit you to come to me. This is treatment Ladies which possibly you may not have been used to. But I assure you I treat others with much greater freedom, who yet never pretend to resent it, as you may immediately be witnesses your selves, if you please. And I hope this may be a lesson to you of due submission to the superior sex. I remain my good charges,
> Your loving Guardian.[29]

The girls did not entirely heed the reprimand at the end of this message. Mary Grey grew up to marry an Oxford academic, Dr David Gregory,[30] and her correspondence reveals a solid self-possession throughout her life. David Gregory was an innovator, reforming the Oxford curriculum to offer students four years of study across classics, poetry, history, logic, mathematics, philosophy and divinity.[31] The Grey–Gregory marriage was mutually beneficial. Mary Gregory's lofty social connections to court circles enhanced her husband's political influence, while Gregory's university position kept his wife in touch with the academic world.[32] Jemima Campbell's letters, likewise, do not betray any qualms about engaging with subjects of traditional male learning. She too had a husband, Philip Yorke, who was committed to the pursuit of learning and he also operated in circles of writers and critics that included women. Whilst at Cambridge, Philip and his brother Charles had embarked on the writing of *Athenian Letters*, a project that married their literary and classical interests.[33] Notably, Catherine Talbot was one of the several authors of this text, which was printed for private circulation in two volumes in 1741 and 1743. Philip Yorke maintained his interest in the intellectual world by becoming a Fellow of the Royal Society and the Society of Antiquaries in 1741 and 1744 respectively, and embarking on a series of scholarly projects.[34] Yorke was also an avid collector of historical documents and, given the scarcity of earlier antiquarian finds, he was likely to have been most successful in amassing examples of sixteenth- and seventeenth-century manuscripts.[35] In addition to Yorke's interest in English history, his name appeared in several prefaces to literary works, highlighting his connections to a range of contemporary writers.[36] By marrying the intellectual Philip Yorke, Jemima Grey[37] was able to broaden her letter-writing circle to include other like-minded women and men.[38] Furthermore, Yorke himself was sympathetic to Grey's self-educational endeavours and the intellectual sociability that took place at the Yorke residences included both men and women.[39]

Despite the close relationship between these three women, their lives diverged over time. Jemima Campbell married young, at seventeen, and was thrust into the upper echelons by the title and estate she inherited at that time. Mary Grey would live more modestly once married, but she gave birth to three wayward sons and a daughter and was fully embarked on child-rearing years before her niece had given birth to the first of two daughters in 1751. Meanwhile, Talbot remained unmarried – through, it seems, a lack of financial security rather than choice. This circle of acquaintance provides an important illustration of self-educational practices and intellectual engagement amongst women of this period.

Whilst Talbot's name has survived the test of time and her abilities of the mind have gained the notice of critics and historians, her two friends' contributions to the world of ideas remain obscure. However, the letters between these three women show them to have all been embarked on a programme of study which would have been considered ambitious for young men of their time.

In order to illuminate women's own expectations of intellectual life, the Grey circle's early years of correspondence have been reviewed for subject content. This analysis reveals how the women initially engaged with intellectual life and Chapter 2 will examine the strategies they used to maintain a foothold in the world of ideas, despite the changing life circumstances they experienced in middle age. These examples are also illustrative of the ways in which women's lives rarely fitted a model of consistent intellectual output, especially when motherhood made its demands on their time and energies. The women were at their most intellectually active in the early 1740s when they were in their twenties. However, as the 1740s gave way to the 1750s, the passage of time was reflected in the changing styles of the women's letter-writing. During the 1740s Jemima Campbell was married (becoming Marchioness Grey) but childless, Mary Grey married in 1743 (becoming Mary Gregory) and swiftly had four children, and Catherine Talbot remained single. In the 1750s Mary Gregory continued her life as wife and mother, Jemima Grey had two daughters (in 1751 and 1756), and Catherine Talbot continued living as an unmarried woman in the Secker household. The first half of the 1740s was a key period of intellectual activity for all three women. By 1761, Mary Gregory had died, leaving Jemima Grey to adopt her daughter. Cancer ended Talbot's life nearly a decade later, when she was forty-eight years old, and Jemima Grey outlived many of her friends by surviving to the age of seventy-four.

During the 1740s Jemima Grey and her husband, Philip Yorke, resided partly at Wrest Park, the childhood home which she had shared with Mary Grey, and Wimpole Hall, the Yorkes' Cambridgeshire estate. However, Catherine Talbot and Mary Grey continued living together, largely at Secker's home at Cuddesden, during the first years of this decade. Talbot and Grey wrote independently to Jemima Grey, but they frequently commented on the other's activities or attitudes and even wrote on the end of each other's letters. Mary Grey apologised on 17 August 1740 for her lack of letters as follows: 'I am ashamed to think how many letters I have had from you & how few I have wrote, but when Kitty did it for me I thought you no great loser & at the same time indulged Her scribbling fit & my own lazy one.'[40] Likewise, Talbot wrote for Mary Grey when she was away from home, 'With how little pleasure have I viewed the rising sun this morning tho' drest in every Picturesque or Poetical Beauty, whose setting Beams will usher poor Lady Mary into detestable London: Her last Commands were that I should say to You every thing she would have said herself upon this occasion.'[41] Several letters were jointly written. In this manner, the intimacy that had been established between the three women was maintained, despite Jemima Grey's marriage and departure from their immediate company. As Mary Grey wrote on 10 August 1740: 'I should have said twenty things to You when we parted Dear Lady Grey, but perhaps it was more expressive to say none of them.'[42] In this first letter, marking their friend's departure, Grey wrote a chaotic mix of her own and Talbot's news:

> When I got out of the Coach my Friend Mr Hobdie welcomed me with so merry an Air I could almost have wished Him hanged says Kitty [Talbot] there she breakfasted with the Chevalier Benson, & by what I can find was very bad company both there & all the way home, Where she did not arrive till Eleven, but before I continue Her story I must bring my own down to that time.[43]

Grey detailed the minutiae of their lives since Jemima Grey had left, as if this information somehow maintained her presence in their lives, or theirs in hers. The expectation for frequency of contact between the separated women was high, as Mary Grey finished her first letter saying, 'I expect a letter from you at Dinner time with great impatience' and put pen to paper again herself the next day.[44] Their correspondence remained very frequent throughout this decade.

Mary Grey wrote to Jemima Grey, during this period, in long letters, reeling off every detail of her and Talbot's lives, saying of herself: 'You see how naturally I write to you by my letters being like my conversation sans fin to you I own the truth of this charge & assure you that it is with some concern that I am forced to leave you tho it is on the Sixth Side'.[45] Jemima Grey's letters also flowed conversationally across the page, and the two women discussed at length their joint memories of Wrest Park, and the plans which the newly married couple had for future improvement to the house and gardens. Talbot's letters to Jemima Grey were stylistically the most considered but she also took solace in writing to her friend: 'For your sake I wish I was in a more entertaining Humour, but I am really quite stupefied with a thin dull Thursday, & should never have done yawning I believe if I had not enliven'd my self a Little by taking up the Pen & thinking of You.'[46] At times, Talbot exhibited a concern over the superficiality of most letter-writing, including her own:

How insipid is all this [comment on people she has met recently] –
methinks I could write you a much prettier letter, a much more interesting one, & not bound myself merely to fill up a proper quantity of
Paper with that sort of Chit Chat that ceremoniously keeps a conversation from absolutely dropping, & May very well be called a Silence
Audible.[47]

Despite this rather damning appraisal of the correspondence, 'Chit
Chat' was not in fact the mainstay of the letters exchanged during
the 1740s.

Amongst these years of correspondence, there was a strong vein
of intellectual exchange between the three women. As in childhood, an
important aspect of their mutual bond lay in their shared reading and
engagement with cultural life. They tracked their own 'Joint History'
through the books they had shared.[48]

L^{dy} Carpenter tells me she hears poor Old Rollin[49] had finished his
Roman History before he died. I shall be glad if it's true: – but are you
not very sorry for Him? I have been used to love & esteem him so long,
& he has given me so much Entertainment, … Besides I have another
Obligation to him far superior to all the Others: for to him I owe the
Happiness of the greatest part of my Life, since He in a manner began
our Acquaintance. Had it not been for Rollin, we should perhaps never
have known enough of each Other to enjoy the Pleasures of Friendship,
but might have been just so much acquainted as to Curtsy cross a
Room, have each Others Name down in a long List of Visits instead of
at the Bottom of a Hundred Letters.[50]

This connection was maintained throughout their adult lives, by not only
suggesting reading for one another, but taking pleasure in reading the
same books at the same time. The texts that they read created a tangible
link between their mental worlds, so that, although physically separated,
their thoughts during moments of private contemplation came to embody
their friendship. Jemima Grey wrote to Talbot on 7 September 1742:

I am much pleased we have sympathised so much without knowing it;
& that you too are studying Clarendon.[51] He has been my Study ever
since I came here, but as I have a great deal of Time & do nothing else,
I shall dispatch it quicker than you, … Alas! why should our Eyes travel
over the same Pages & yet be at such a distance from One Another's!
Why must we see the same Words, & not be able to see what we wish so
much for each Other! Could I join in your Morning & Evening *Lectures*
together, & go on with Clarendon with you after Supper, how happy
would it make me.[52]

Like her husband, Philip Yorke, Jemima Grey was interested in the history of the previous century and all three women read the Earl of Clarendon's history of the Civil War and Commonwealth period with its moderate royalist perspective on events. As Paul Seaward has emphasised, Clarendon's *History* was 'the most sophisticated and finely balanced history yet written in English' and incorporated 'a forensic dissection of character and issue, and a sense of the depth of individuals' moral responsibility for their actions'.[53] Clarendon had been intimately involved in the political events of his time and his account could, therefore, lay claim to the authority of first-hand experience. Jemima Grey certainly counted Clarendon amongst the great writers and intellects of his age. The Grey circle's reading of Clarendon allowed them to engage with a witness testimony concerning the political upheavals of the seventeenth century and compare this with other writings on this period.

Grey's letters also demonstrated her need for shared intellectual endeavour, the reading they undertook simultaneously not only represented their bond but also allowed them to exchange and discuss their responses to the text. These women seemed determined not to abandon the ambitious self-educational practices they had established together as girls. Amongst the catalogue of visits, breakfasts, tea-taking and dinners, Mary Grey described how she and Talbot spent their time:

> Why, from breakfast to Dinner Kitty reads & I work [embroider] or perhaps she draws or works whilst I read a sermon & Homers Odyssey, upon which we speedily intend to publish notes not being at all satisfied with those already wrote we have read Nine books & I think the Eighth is our favourite of all those that are to come enough to judge if it will be so of the whole from four to six in the afternoon we retire again, to our Italian & digressions, to writing if either of us is so disposed or to Hanyer's History at six we either go out or walk in the Gallery till tis dark.[54]

This catalogue of scholarly endeavours – punctuated by the mainstay of needlework – was taken a step further by Catherine Talbot, who entered into closer analysis of her reading with Jemima Grey. Talbot commented at the end of a long disquisition on her reading letters by French authors: 'I do not much wonder at your not being very fond of Petrarch, because I am only fond of several particular Sonnets, & I think the Sonnet way of writing in general very tiresome. Tasso's is less so because being less stupidly constant he has a greater variety of subjects.'[55] Again, this letter illustrates the intellectually challenging nature of the reading undertaken by Talbot and Grey. The works they cited would have been considered vital reading for educated men, but Catherine Talbot, Jemima Grey and Mary Grey routinely read literature of this kind. Indeed, Jemima Grey wrote to Mary Gregory in 1745 expressing surprise when she found that her male company had not read texts she had read several times:

> After finishing the Odyssey we have after Supper taken the Arcadia, some of the Gentlemen had never read it, & I am always amused by it. The Characters are mighty well drawn, the Story's well carried on, the Speeches sometimes excellent, & at other Times such horrid Quaintnesses, & such poor Wire-drawn Similies, it makes one laugh but puts one out of Patience.[56]

The titles they mention may have rested on the well-stocked library shelves of their respective households or, perhaps, brothers, friends and relations helped secure new material that lay outside familial collections. Whether these women regarded the books as their own is not clear, but their strong engagement with the authors and works sings from the page and the frustrations attendant to a scarcity of new reading seemed rarely to have intruded on their studies.

Along with classics from bygone eras, the women also discussed contemporary work and revealed their dependence on newspapers for much of their news about the latest publications, as Jemima Grey wrote to Catherine Talbot in the early 1740s:

> You asked in your last Letter for some Account of *Pamela in High Life*;[57] that which is come out is not by the Author of Pamela, but by Somebody who says he understands High Life much better; as I suppose you have seen in the Papers for they have been advertising against One Another a great while. If you take in the Daily Advertiser you will be fully satisfied about this Book, for there is a Quotation in it this Day, which I suppose is put in by the Antagonist, & which I thought was only meant as a Ridicule but it is a literal & indeed a most extraordinary One. That, & just turning over the Book have left me no more Curiosity about it, for it is writ in the same low Manner & with all the Particularities of the Other, without any interesting Story to carry you on or to make you pardon them.[58]

This comment demonstrates that the three friends followed the debates of their day about popular literature, in this case about a widely celebrated, yet controversial, epistolary novel. Their interest in reading did not stop at works of serious reputation, but incorporated popular, contemporary fiction.

Aside from literature, current affairs filled the pages of many of the letters in this collection. Jemima Grey seemed to be the primary source of news, as she wrote to Catherine Talbot on 17 June 1742: 'You desire a Letter of News my dear Miss Talbot, so to begin in the very Newest-fashion'd Stile.'[59] Her letter described news from Europe – of the King of Prussia signing preliminaries of peace with the Queen of Hungary – and then 'having gone round Europe tis Time I think to look at Home' and revealed the latest parliamentary news from London.[60] Jemima Grey ended her letter with the warning, 'So never complain any more that I don't write News – but don't expect that I should write such Letters often, for I intend this to satisfy you for a great while.'[61]

This large collection of letters reveals the three young women entering eagerly into the debates of their age and, moreover, feeling it necessary to form an independent opinion on the basis of their wide reading. On 24 November 1743, Jemima Grey called on her two friends to accept the challenge of commenting on a packet of information concerning King Charles I that she had read and would send to them. She anticipated that they would strongly disagree with what it contained, but in the interests of broadly surveying available information on the subject, felt it necessary that they absorb contrary views to their own.

> M[r] Birch brought a great Pacquet with him last Monday, that it was agreed ought to be communicated to you both, though he fears he shall incur your Displeasure by it; since they were all Materials for a strong Abuse upon King Charles the First, & some Remarks might possible be drawn from them upon my Lord Clarendon's Partiality for not mentioning them ... Now Ladies, what do you say? Are not you at all stagger'd in your Opinion of your Heroe? or don't you believe any of these Facts? One or Other must be the Case.[62]

Here Grey revealed that the women held partisan views on historical issues, but were also keen to interrogate the sources in order to ascertain their validity. Clarendon was an important figure in the Grey circle's canon of great writers. Moreover, their joint reading of his work had played a role in cementing their friendship. Clarendon's *History* was not published until 1702, thirty years after the text had been put together by the author, in part due to the political controversy surrounding Clarendon and his writings.[63] Once published, Clarendon's text sustained a prolonged attack from John Oldmixon, who disputed its accuracy and accused a circle of high Tories at Christ Church, Oxford of interfering with the text to suit their political ends.[64] Whilst many years had passed since Clarendon's text had found itself under intense scrutiny, the 1740s witnessed another scandal over the veracity of a text. As Paul Baines has discussed in his work on eighteenth-century forgery, the 'Casket Letters' of Mary, Queen of Scots, found themselves the subject of a series of quasi-legal challenges as their authenticity was called into question.[65] By engaging with material produced by the critics of Clarendon, the women not only betrayed an empirical approach to their studies but showed that they were in touch with the concerns of their time about the reliability of the textual record. They stood at barely one hundred years distance from the history that they studied and accounts of regicide, Interregnum and Restoration were still allied to political and religious territory firmly occupied and defended by the 'great men' of early eighteenth-century public life. By tackling these debates, and considering the validity of the available evidence, the Grey circle demonstrated an intellectual verve that extended beyond the traditional parameters of female learning.

At this time in their lives, all three women were able to devote a significant amount of time to private study. From Catherine Talbot's and Mary Grey's accounts of their time, it is clear that they applied themselves diligently to their books. Even letter-writing, at times was considered a distraction from their reading, as Talbot pointed out to Jemima Grey: 'Among all your Fiddle Faddle Employments Dear Lady Grey I do not think you will be at all peevish at the interruption of a letter from Cuddesden, & in return I can leave my more quiet engagements here with less regret for writing to You than for any other hindrance I could name.'[66] Even Mary Grey, the least prone to dramatic confessions concerning her scholarly vocation, wrote from Windsor in August 1741: 'I hope on Wednesday to begin to live, at present I only breathe, for then I expect my Table & Books.'[67] The strength of this sentiment showed that Mary Grey believed, at this stage in her life, that intellectual endeavour was inseparable from her life more generally. Again, Talbot mentioned the conflict between corresponding and concentrating on her other work: 'I really cannot help writing to you today merely because it is Post Day, tho' King David [the Bible story] & my Embroidery wait impatiently by the Fire Side, & I have not much spare time for them before Church.'[68] The women of the Grey circle engaged with a wide range of literature, but incorporated within their schedule the more traditional female reading material of sermons and spiritual works. Whilst they devoured challenging texts, they also regularly picture themselves with needlework in hand and involved in traditional patterns of sociability. For all their academic energy, the Grey circle were no lonely group of cloistered women, tucked away with candle and books. They saw their intellectual work as an integral part of their daily life, which fitted alongside other roles and responsibilities. The letters exchanged by the women when they were in their twenties rarely acknowledged any conflict in their lives concerning the pursuit of learning. Considering the time each devoted to this activity, it seems likely that they were unhampered by critical family members or a domestic scenario that was hostile to female learning on either practical or ideological grounds. This example demonstrates that, despite the many volumes of published literature that lined the shelves of booksellers' shops describing the proper parameters of women's roles in society, real women contravened such prescripts. Moreover, they did so without betraying any concern about their 'unconventional' engagement with books and ideas, seeing these activities – instead – as theirs to own and enjoy. However the Grey circle had apparently excellent access to the materials and people that fed their intellectual exploration. The discussion will now move to consider this crucial prerequisite for engaging with a life of the mind: access to sources of information for study.

Access to information

Women's experiences of childhood education varied widely, from the location of the schoolroom (within or without the home) to the scope of the studies undertaken. Aside from formal educational scenarios such as school or lessons with a governess, access to books had a major influence. Reading was the primary method of self-education, and so the range of reading matter available to an individual largely governed their engagement with the wider world. As in childhood, the vagaries of circumstance played an important role for adult women. Many letters from this period described their attempts to gain access to the books and information of interest to them. Men, by and large, had easier access to the world of knowledge and women often needed their help in obtaining reading material or up-to-date news from the seats of government and learning. However, the period witnessed a huge growth in circulating and subscription libraries, offering individuals the option to borrow as well as to buy books.[69] Moreover, new forms of reading material also proliferated, including periodicals such as the *Spectator* (1711–14), the *Gentleman's Magazine* (1731–1907) and the *London Magazine* (1732–85) and daily and weekly newspapers.[70] Some of these periodicals explicitly addressed a female audience and, as a generation of scholarship has shown, women were active participants in a multivalent 'public sphere'.[71] As Markman Ellis and others have discussed, women were not absent from key 'public' spaces, such as the coffee house, that hosted contemporary debate.[72] Likewise, as Uriel Heyd has demonstrated, newspapers reached an encompassing readership in the eighteenth century, generating new engagements with text by men and women and helping to shape readers' understandings of the society they lived in.[73]

Whilst these serialised forms of reading provided valuable opportunities for women to connect with, and participate in, public debates, access to books remained important for more serious study. For example, Lady Isham wrote to her husband on 3 February 1699 to say:

> I find that my S[r] Just thinks of me often and is kinder than I cou'd have expected & knows what will please me most in sending me Books w[ch] no dispute I shall like very well and take much diversion in reading them, nor have I been without some impatience to see what they were (much more than if it had been a new fashioned Head) but the Carrier is gon by & left nothing, all my hopes is he will bring it a Munday.[74]

Nearly half a century later, Elizabeth Robinson (later Elizabeth Montagu) wrote to her friend, Anne Donnellan, commenting on England's premier poet, Alexander Pope, and his recently published volume of letters.[75] Robinson's letter implied that it would be relatively easy to obtain a copy, and there is no mention of having to ask a favour or enlist the help of a man to achieve this.

> I hear Mr Popes Letters which he has just publishd are extreamly good I intend to send for 'em for I am an admirer of his Letters they are not full of Compliment Point, turn, & the Quirks & Quiddities of wit like the French, good sense Elegant wit & warm Friendship is all expressed in them but because they are not Inspired with the Poetick fire of the Verse people think them vastly Inferior to his Poetry.[76]

Here the twenty-two-year-old Elizabeth Robinson demonstrated that she followed authors whose work she found interesting and was confident in assessing their merits and stating her personal opinions about their style and content. Her later fame as 'Queen of the Bluestocking' underscores both the favourable circumstances she enjoyed and her personal dedication to intellectual achievement.

In the 1740s, Catherine Talbot sometimes had to employ the help of male friends in accessing literature. She wrote to her friend, Jemima Grey, asking if her father-in-law could help to obtain some information about the works of a famous female author of the previous generation: Margaret Cavendish, Duchess of Newcastle. At this time, Grey was newly married to Philip Yorke, whose father was the Lord Chancellor and possessed of a sizeable library at Wimpole Hall in Cambridgeshire, where the married couple were regular visitors. Talbot requested: 'Pray ask Mr Yorke if my Ld Chancellor has not got in his Library the Works of a Duchess of Newcastle who lived & writ in the times we are reading of,

& if he knows what sort of Character they bear, & especially her History of her Husbands Conduct.'[77] Talbot's specific interest in the Duchess of Newcastle also suggests that, as a woman engaged in a high level of self-education, she was interested in women of previous generations who had aspired to intellectual achievement. The implication that Jemima Grey's husband was willing and able to help with Talbot's request also points to the favourable social conditions under which the Grey circle operated.

Likewise, in the 1730s and 1740s the Anglo-Saxon scholar, published author and schoolmistress, Elizabeth Elstob (1683–1756), often struggled to get hold of texts on account of her living in a market town in Worcestershire. She used her correspondence with another provincially located contact, the antiquary George Ballard (1705/6–55), to gain access to books and texts. For example, in May 1736 Elstob acknowledged the loan of a book, but apologised for 'Not having had leisure to read through the Annals of Dunstaple, which you were so kind as to lend me.'[78] She assured her friend 'that the Books shall be return'd with my thanks, as soon as I have read them over, and likewise the Beautiful Specimen of the Ingenious Mr Parry's writing, which I took upon with as much delight, as I have formerly view'd the works of Raphael Urban, or Titian, it being as excellent in its kind.'[79] Four months later, Elstob managed to return the books: 'I have at last sent your Books with many thanks, and beg pardon for keeping them so long, which I hope you will grant, knowing how little time I have at present to Read.'[80] Her response to their content reveals that she was still engaged with her subject and that she possessed a drive to dig deeper into available sources for further information. In the same letter, Elstob commented: 'I am apt to Fancy I have met with two of our Family, that is Maurice de Elnestorva, and John, the one mention's p. 280 and other 444 in the Annals of Dunstaple, 'tis probable cou'd I see the old writings belonging to the Family I might there find them.'[81] Similarly, on Christmas Eve of the same year Elstob wrote: 'I have just run over Rob: de Avesburys Chronicle for the use of which you have my thanks.'[82] Interestingly, Elstob did not even have access to her own published works, and so she asked her friend Ballard: 'can you put me in a way how to procure my Saxon Grammar it is for my Honourable Friend Mr Hastings, who is desirous to see one. I have employ'd our Bookseller to get me one but without success.'[83] Specialist books were relatively hard to obtain in Worcestershire, and Ballard's parcels of reading material were therefore gratefully received. In return, Elstob sent Ballard antiquarian curiosities she had collected, dubbing them a 'Bundle of trifles'.[84] In this realm also, Elizabeth Elstob's in-depth knowledge of history helped her to identify objects of interest to Ballard.

> I am using my endeavours to procure you some old Coins, I have sent you two or three. The small ones I can make nothing of, and shou'd be glad of your judgement, who understand them so well. I at first thought them no older than the time of the Great Rebellion, when many had the Liberty of Coining their own Money as I have been told. But observing Crowns on one side I alter'd my opinion, well knowing their aversion to that Regal Ornament, and to the Persons that wore them. The other I believe is a Genuine Roman Coin by the Metal, but not being well acquainted with the Faces of the Caesars I can say nothing of it.[85]

These examples show that where local resources could not provide the necessary objects of study, correspondence networks could facilitate women's access to important material.

Some women, of course, were fortunate enough to have extensive collections of books in their own homes.[86] In 1648 a younger member of the Isham family of Lamport Hall wrote, on the back of a letter from her aunt, a list of 'My own Bookes' suggesting that in her case she even considered some of the household volumes as specifically her possessions.[87] Similarly, Sir Justinian Isham wrote: 'A note of my Sister Ishams books in my hand' and proceeded to list many religious titles, alongside a French ABC.[88] Nevertheless, whether women owned several books or none, access to a variety of reading material was the key to effective self-education. Moreover, if the female reader had an eye to becoming a more refined participant in cultural life, opportunities to read the latest and most discussed contributions from contemporary writers, poets and playwrights were also crucial. Otherwise, an ancient guide to the French language and some traditional works on the Christian faith did little to broaden the horizon.

An illustrative example of a woman's use of male contacts to gain access to information is found in the letters of gentlewoman Mary Clarke (c. 1655–1705), of Chipley in Somerset, in the later seventeenth century.[89] In Clarke's case, the man was her husband and the information she sought concerned the distinctly male sphere of parliamentary politics. Edward Clarke entered Parliament as MP for Taunton in 1690 where he remained until his death in 1710 and, during this time, the couple experienced long periods of separation while Parliament sat.[90] Mary Clarke meandered from the business of the estate, family news, remedies for sickness and amusing anecdotes concerning the children to direct requests for lists of how MPs had voted in Parliament that week. The fact that Parliament kept her husband away from home for large portions of the year may well have stimulated Clarke's interest in that subject. Or maybe she had correctly judged her husband-to-be best placed to update her on parliamentary politics over other possible lines of enquiry. On 27 October 1691, Clarke thanked her husband for the votes, which he had detailed in his last letter, and asked for further details about the key players: 'I wase very Glad to heare of your Good health and returne you my thanks for it as alsoe for this by the Last post with the votes, pray in the next Letts know whats become of the discovery my Ld Bellemount[91] wase Like to make.'[92] The information which Mary Clarke read in her husband's letters allowed her to follow the politics of her day, informed with up-to-the-minute news. She also commented on how she felt about political life. At intervals Clarke summed up her general feelings about current affairs and exposed her view that the age was one of great change and uncertain outcomes:

> I thanke you for ye Kings Speech whearein I find he thinkes the prosperity or ruen of the Kingdom depends on thiss sitting of parlement, thearefore I hope you will Looke aboute you and make what dispatch you Can and I pray God derectt you all for the best but I phancy alittle of our Good and bad fortune depends on the minnisters of state to as well as on the parlement and I doupt nott but as the K[ing] Considers one he will the other, and take Care as he has done hitherto; to have all his afaires mannaged for his one and his subjects Good and safty.[93]

When she did feel strongly about what she had heard, she responded sharply with seemingly little concern for maintaining an image of retiring feminine modesty. On 28 April 1690, Clarke mocked the recent decisions made in Parliament: 'by the Constant votes you send me I find that thiss parlement dose such Exterordinary things that I intend If my mind dose not alter and I come to towne while it sitts to put in a Bill to inable me to be att 2 places att once which would be very Convenent for me' (Figure 1).[94]

During this month alone, Parliament had addressed issues as diverse as paving and cleaning the streets of London, discouraging the importation of thrown-silk and preventing papists from disinheriting their Protestant heirs. But by far the most extraordinary actions by Parliament in the last two years had been in relation to the new monarchs, King William and Queen Mary. On 9 April 1690 (nineteen days prior to Clarke's letter), the Commons read a Bill from the Lords recognising the King and Queen.[95] This action related to the turbulent recent

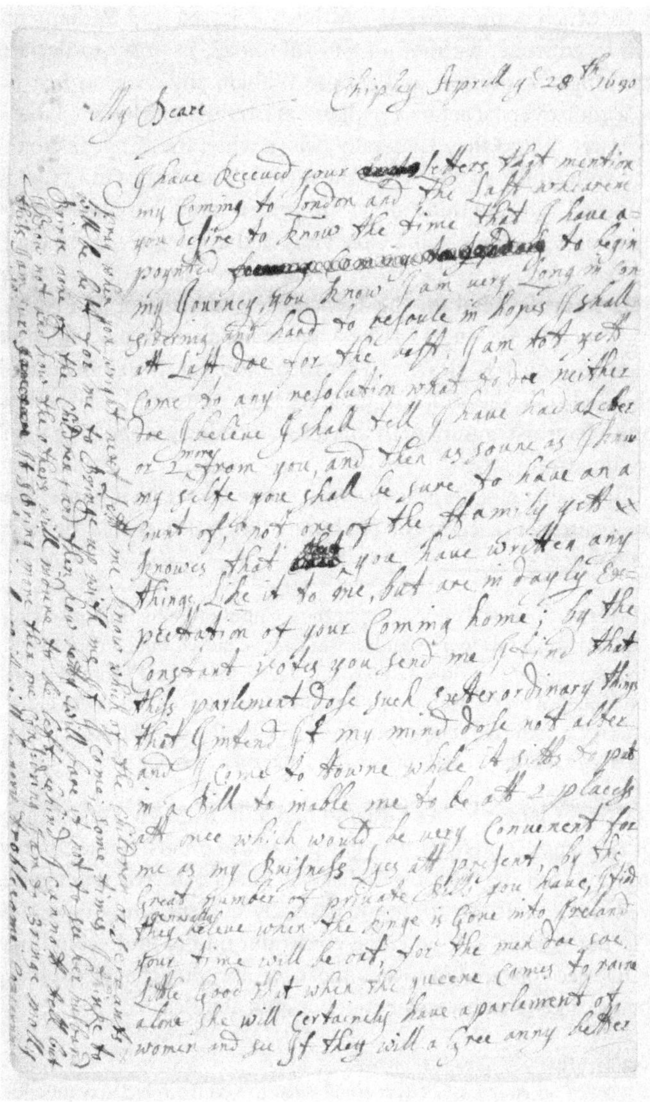

Figure 1: A letter written by Mary Clarke and addressed to her husband, Edward Clarke, on 28 April 1690, courtesy of The South West Heritage Trust: Somerset Archives and Local Studies, DD\SF/7/1/31.

years in which King James II had been deposed and Parliament had chosen to convene, without a royal summons, in order to declare the former king's 'abdication' and choose William and Mary as his successors – a controversial act by a parliament. In the same letter Clarke went on to assert: 'I find they Generally beleve when the Kinge is Gone into Ireland your time will be out, for the men doe soe Little Good that when the queene Comes to raine alone she will certainly have a parlement of women and see If they will a Gree anny better.'[96] Here, Clarke may well have been referring to the divided vote in the House of Commons on whether to bring a Bill for the 'General Naturalizing of all Protestants' in April 1690.[97] Although Clarke's statement about replacing the male MPs for women was clearly a rhetorical flourish, it demonstrated the uninhibited style she adopted in letters to her husband. Clarke was not making a feminist argument in this letter, but she was applying her critical eye to current affairs.

This challenging sentiment was echoed later that same year, as Clarke again marvelled at the seemingly illogical decisions being made by the political elite.

> [I received] yours alsoe y^t brought the a Count of Ld Torringtons being aquited Came safe to my hands it was strange newes, but I have Larnt to wonder att nothing now neither would it surprise me If I should heare he is made a prevey Counceller for now I Looke upon it he is in a Good way to be preferred If possoble for it is noe matter now what the Dutch thinke of it if the K[ing]s presens will make a menes for all.[98]

Mary Clarke's letters to her husband had a disarmingly honest tone and she often demonstrated her firm grasp of world events. Rather than using apology and self-deprecation to disguise her considered statements, she allowed her conviction to be unabashedly evident. Only once did she refer to her gender, as a potential constraint on her understanding, and this reference appeared more as a means to abruptly change subject matter than as a genuine assessment of her own abilities:

> My Deare
> I receved all your Last Letters sinc I writt to you from Nettlecombe for which I thanke you but wase soery to find you wase under such mallancoly Aprehensions and doe hertily wish that all peaple would make it theyr Buisness to indevor to prevent our misfortunes in time that we may not be surprised the next summer as we wase the Last and not have our Gunns to be Cleanned when we should be discharging them, me thinkes it should Concern us as much to preserve the Lives and

fortunes of those that are alredy protestants as to take Care to bringe
up Little new protestants before we know what will become of these,
but stay, I shall say to much by and by of what I dont understand, and
thearefore I will now come to the subiectt of toppnotts.[99]

By way of comparison, the letters of Clarke's contemporary, Amabel
Grey, who was the eldest daughter of Henry Grey, Duke of Kent, have
survived to illustrate her correspondence with her brother in 1690. In the
spring of that year, she too reported on the main political upheavals that
had caught Clarke's attention. In May she told her brother that at social
gatherings: 'wee talk daily of the parlements rising & the Kings goeing
into Ireland'.[100] By June, she could inform him that 'I have very little news
to send you but the good news of the Kings being safe landed in Ireland
on the 15 of this month he rid the same night to Belfast & gave order for
the rendevous of the army so I belive it will not be long before we shall
hear of some action'.[101] In Amabel Grey's case, her brother was abroad,
whilst she was living in London in close proximity to government. Unlike
Mary Clarke, Amabel Grey was able to participate in London social circles, where parliamentary men or those in the king's service were heard
relaying the latest news from the seat of government. In these circumstances, Amabel Grey found herself better positioned to access the latest
news from the home front than her brother.

Clarke, on the other hand, was in no position to be well informed
about London affairs. Her life as a mistress of a household in the rural
West Country made her determination to educate herself in politics all
the more surprising. In her support, Clarke's husband facilitated her
interest in politics and fed her the information which she craved. Clarke's
letter-writing as a whole reveals a busy woman who was left largely alone
to manage a household, her children and her husband's business concerns. Despite this full schedule, she actively pursued her interest in current affairs and any potential conflict between household or wifely duties
and her extra-curricular interests went unacknowledged. In Clarke's case
her husband was supportive of her and his help, in conjunction with her
ability to access the required information, allowed her greater freedom
than others.

Evidence of women like Mary Clarke, who pursued her intellectual
interests alongside her roles as wife and mother, becomes more common
in women's letter-writing of the eighteenth century. For one, the proliferation of printed material in eighteenth-century society made access to
varied reading more commonplace and, increasingly, women might find
new reading material via several routes, be that a circulating library, a

bookseller, a periodical or a newspaper. Likewise, the 1700s saw women writers entering the publishing market in unprecedented numbers. This trend was connected with the birth, and subsequent popularity, of the novel, and the perceived female market for this written form. Of course, it is important to avoid too easy assumptions that all trends are mutually reinforcing, and there was no automatic correlation between change in cultural life and the quotidian particulars of women's lives. However, the growing number of women's names on the spines of books, and the explosion in printed media in general, must have affected literate women's relationships with reading and writing, especially in the early 1700s.

Although transformation was uneven, and illiteracy still hampered many women, opportunities for female self-education were growing during this period. This trend made a significant difference to those who were privileged enough to be able to pursue an intellectual life. Although most women would not publish their ideas, many did express intellectual intent through their informal letter-writing. Epistolary networks of acquaintance could, in turn, support scholarly projects. In some cases, letters could be read to wider audiences, allowing them in the first instance a level of semi-public dissemination. An examination of intellectual life through letters demands the patience to see intellectual material as it appears in amongst many other themes, anecdotes and epistolary conventions. The often haphazard jumble of topics which streamed from the pen can be bewildering. Moreover, letters lack the material permanence of print media and rarely represent a sustained and consistent line of argument across a range of individual epistles. Written on different days and for different readers – a corpus of letters is a correspondingly heterogeneous body of work. Having considered the origins and prerequisites of intellectual life in this chapter, we will now move to fully fledged female intellectuals and their relationship with letter-writing and the life of the mind.

Notes

1 Cohen, ' "Familiar Conversation" ', pp. 99–116.
2 See Brant, *Eighteenth-Century Letters*, pp. 60–92.
3 See 'The epistolary academy' in Chapter 3 for a full discussion of childhood letter-writing as a method of learning how to perform socially in person and on the page.
4 J. Daybell, 'Interpreting Letters and Reading Script: Evidence for female education and literacy in Tudor England', *History of Education: Journal of the History of Education Society*, 34:6 (2005), pp. 695–715.

5   M. J.-M. Soenmez, 'English Spelling in the Seventeenth Century: A study of the nature of standardisation as seen through the MS and printed versions of the Duke of Newcastle's "A New Method …"' (unpublished PhD thesis, Durham University, 1993).

6   N. E. Osselton, 'Informal Spelling Systems in Early Modern English: 1500–1800', in N. F. Blake and C. Jones (eds), *English Historical Linguistics: Studies in development* (Sheffield: The Centre for English Cultural Tradition and Language, University of Sheffield, 1984), pp. 123–37. Different strategies in print and manuscript have also been found for morphology and syntax, as well as for spelling, see for example I. Tieken-Boon van Ostade, '"You was" and Eighteenth-Century Normative Grammar', in K. Lenz and R. Möhlig (eds), *Of Dyuersite & Chaunge of Language: Essays presented to Manfred Görlach on the occasion of his 65th birthday* (Heidelberg: C. Winter, 2002), pp. 88–102.

7   G. Weir, 'Orthography in the Correspondence of Lady Katherine Paston, 1603–1627' (unpublished MPhil thesis, University of Glasgow, 2010).

8   These orthographies might be subject to change over time and Weir sees correspondents being influenced in their spelling choices by other letter-writers.

9   M. Astell, *A Serious Proposal to the Ladies, for the Advancement of their True and Greatest Interest* (London, 1694).

10 F. Fénelon, *Instructions for the Education of a Daughter Done into English, and Revised by Dr. Hickes* (London, 1713); F. Fénelon, *The Accomplish'd Governess: Or, short instructions for the education of the fair sex* (London, 1752).

11 Arizpe and Styles, *Reading Lessons*, p. 6.

12 BLA, LP, L 30/9a/3, fo. 89: Jemima Grey to Catherine Talbot, 3 Oct. 1742.

13 NRO, IP, I.C.3415.

14 NRO, IP, I.C.3415.

15 NRO, IP, I.C.3415.

16 DRO, D331/12/26/1: a father to a daughter, 11 May 1726.

17 Molekamp, *Women and the Bible*, pp. 1, 11. See also H. Brayman Hackel and C. E. Kelly (eds), *Reading Women: Literacy, authorship, and culture in the Atlantic World, 1500–1800* (Philadelphia: University of Pennsylvania Press, 2008).

18 See, for example, Eales, 'Female Literacy', pp. 70–1; and K. J. Hayes, *A Colonial Woman's Bookshelf* (Knoxville: University of Tennessee Press, 1996), pp. 6–7 which details similar practices in America.

19 J. Collett-White, 'Yorke, Jemima, *suo jure* Marchioness Grey (1722–1797)', in *ODNB*; www.oxforddnb.com/view/article/68351; J. Godber, *The Marchioness Grey of Wrest Park* (Bedford: Bedfordshire Historical Record Society, 1968). ✗

20 See Godber, *The Marchioness*, pp. 11–14.

21 R. Zuk, 'Talbot, Catherine (1721–1770)', in *ODNB*; www.oxforddnb.com/view/article/26921.

22 In particular Elizabeth Carter (1717–1806). See Harcstark Myers, *Bluestocking Circle*; R. Zuk, *Bluestocking Feminism: Writings of the Bluestocking Circle, 1738–1785*, vol. 3 (London: Pickering & Chatto, 1999); C. B. Rasmussen, '"Speaking on the Edge of my Tomb": The epistolary life and death of Catherine Talbot', *Partial Answers: Journal of Literature and the History of Ideas*, 8:2 (2010), pp. 255–75.

23   Archivist James Collett-White, of the Bedfordshire and Luton Archive, has made efforts to publicise the wealth of women's writing evident in the Lucas Papers, besides his entry for Jemima, Marchioness Grey in the *ODNB*. see Collett-White, 'Yorke, Jemima'.

24   BLA, LP, L 30/9a/3, fo. 61: Jemima Campbell to Catherine Talbot, *c.* 1737/8 [copy].

25   A notable exception – and the only one I have found – being Harcstark Myers, *Bluestocking Circle*, pp. 61, 65–8, 209.

26   Rev. Edward Talbot died in December 1720 and his daughter, Catherine, was born the following May.

27   Myers, *Bluestocking Circle*, p. 64.

28   See Zuk, 'Talbot, Catherine'.

29   BLA, LP, L 30/9/84/2: Thomas Secker to Jemima Campbell, before 1737.

30   As a young man, David Gregory became in 1724 the first professor in history and modern languages at the University of Oxford.

31   E. T. Bradley, 'Gregory, David (1695/6–1767)', rev. S. J. Skedd, in *ODNB*; www. oxforddnb.com/view/article/11458.

32   Bradley, 'Gregory, David'; through her husband Mary Gregory kept abreast of developments at the university, see for example: BLA, LP, L 30/9/50/1–43: Mary Gregory to Jemima Grey, 1750–7.

33   S. L. Barczewski, 'Yorke, Philip, Second Earl of Hardwicke (1720–1790)', in *ODNB*; www.oxforddnb.com/view/article/30246.

34   Barczewski, 'Yorke, Philip'.

35   Godber, *The Marchioness*, pp. 31–2.

36   For example, the poet Edward Young dedicated one part of his *Night Thoughts on Life, Death and Immortality* (London, 1742) to Yorke; likewise the critic Thomas Edwards made a dedication to Yorke in his *Canons of Criticism* (London, 1750), see Godber, *The Marchioness*, pp. 24, 31 and J. A. Dussinger, 'Edwards, Thomas (*d.* 1757)', in *ODNB*.; www.oxforddnb.com/view/article/8558.

37   After her marriage to Philip Yorke, Jemima retained the title of Marchioness Grey in her own right.

38   For example, Jemima Grey maintained a thoughtful correspondence with Yorke's sister, Elizabeth Anson, see BLA, LP, L 30/9/3, fos 1–116: Elizabeth Anson to Jemima Grey, 1748–59.

39   Barczewski, 'Yorke, Philip'; see also the quotation on p. 45, which comments on the 'lectures' that took place at Wrest Park. Also, on 8 July 1745, Jemima Grey describes after dinner reading in mixed company, commenting that the gentlemen present had, to her surprise, not read *Arcadia* (probably referring to the late sixteenth-century text by Sir Philip Sidney), BLA, LP, L 30/9a/1–3, fos 49–51: Jemima Grey to Mary Gregory.

40   BLA, LP, L 30/9/53/3: Mary Grey to Jemima Grey, 17 Aug. 1740.

41   BLA, LP, letter 448: Catherine Talbot to Jemima Grey, 7 Oct. 1742 [modern transcript].

42   BLA, LP, L 30/9/53/1: Mary Grey to Jemima Grey, 10 Aug. 1740.

43   BLA, LP, L 30/9/53/1: Mary Grey to Jemima Grey, 10 Aug. 1740.

44 BLA, LP, L 30/9/53/1: Mary Grey to Jemima Grey, 10 Aug. 1740.

45 BLA, LP, L 30/9/53/2: Mary Grey to Jemima Grey, 11 Aug. 1740.

46 BLA, LP, letter 447: Catherine Talbot to Jemima Grey, 14 Oct. 1742 [modern transcript].

47 BLA, LP, letter 3354: Catherine Talbot to Jemima Grey, 29 June 1744 [modern transcript].

48 BLA, LP, letter 448: Catherine Talbot to Jemima Grey, 7 Oct. 1742 [modern transcript].

49 Charles Rollin (1661–1741), a French historian, who published his *Ancient History* in the 1730s and later his *Roman History* in 1741.

50 BLA, LP, L 30/9a/3, fos 75–76: Jemima Grey to Catherine Talbot, Sept. 1741 [copy].

51 Edward Hyde, first Earl of Clarendon (1609–74), English historian and states-man whose published works included *History of the Rebellion and Civil Wars in England: Begun in the Year 1641* (Oxford, 1717), see P. Seaward, 'Hyde, Edward, First Earl of Clarendon (1609–1674)', in *ODNB*; www.oxforddnb.com/view/article/14328.

52 BLA, LP, L 30/9a/3, fo. 87: Jemima Grey to Catherine Talbot, 7 Sept. 1742 [copy].

53 See Seaward, 'Hyde, Edward'.

54 BLA, LP, L 30/9/53/3: Mary Grey to Jemima Grey, 17 Aug. 1740.

55 BLA, LP, letter 3356: Catherine Talbot to Jemima Grey, 15 June 1744 [modern transcript].

56 BLA, LP, L 30/9a/1, fo. 51: Jemima Grey to Mary Gregory, 8 July 1745 [copy].

57 This referred to one of a number of publications, reflecting upon themes in Richardson's best-selling epistolary novel, *Pamela* – a genre that included J. Kelly, *Pamelas Conduct in High Life* (London, 1741), as well as E. Heywood, *Anti-Pamela* (London, 1741).

58 BLA, LP, L 30/9a/3, fos 67–8: Jemima Grey to Catherine Talbot, *c.* 1741 [copy].

59 BLA, LP, L 30/9a/3, fo. 77: Jemima Grey to Catherine Talbot, 17 June 1742 [copy].

60 BLA, LP, L 30/9a/3, fo. 78: Jemima Grey to Catherine Talbot, 17 June 1742 [copy].

61 BLA, LP, L 30/9a/3, fo. 80: Jemima Grey to Catherine Talbot, 17 June 1742 [copy].

62 BLA, LP, L 30/9a/1, fos 18–22: Jemima Grey to Mary Grey and Catherine Talbot, 24 Nov. 1743 [copy].

63 See Seaward, 'Hyde, Edward'.

64 Seaward, 'Hyde, Edward'.

65 See P. Baines, *The House of Forgery in Eighteenth-Century Britain* (Aldershot: Ashgate, 1999), p. 39.

66 BLA, LP, letter 447: Catherine Talbot to Jemima Grey, 14 Oct. 1742 [modern transcript].

67 BLA, LP, L 30/9/53/15: Mary Grey to Jemima Grey, 30 Aug. 1741.

68 BLA, LP, letter 450: Catherine Talbot to Jemima Grey, Dec. 1742 [modern transcript].

69 See J. Raven, 'From Promotion to Proscription: Arrangements for reading and eighteenth-century libraries', in Raven *et al.*, *Practice and Representation of Reading*, pp. 175–201.

70 See I. Italia, *The Rise of Literary Journalism in the Eighteenth Century: Anxious employment* (London: Routledge, 2005), M. Ellis, 'Coffee-Women, *The Spectator*

and the Public Sphere in the Early Eighteenth Century', in E. Eger, C. Grant, C. O Gallchoir and P. Wharburton (eds), *Women, Writing and the Public Sphere, 1700–1830* (Cambridge: Cambridge University Press, 2006), pp. 27–52; and E. Lorraine de Montluzin, *Daily Life in Georgian England as Reported in the Gentleman's Magazine* (Lewiston, NY: Edwin Mellen Press, 2002).

71 See, for example, Eger *et al.*, *Women, Writing and the Public Sphere*; and D. Norbrook, 'Women, the Republic of Letters, and the Public Sphere in the Mid-Seventeenth Century', *Criticism*, 46:2 (2004), pp. 223–40.

72 Ellis, 'Coffee-Women', pp. 27–52.

73 U. Heyd, *Reading Newspapers: Press and public in eighteenth-century Britain and America* (Oxford: Voltaire Foundation, 2012).

74 NRO, IP I.C. 4213: Lady Isham to Justinian Isham, 3 Feb. 1699.

75 An edition of Pope's *Letters* was published in 1737, but in 1740 a series of Pope's works were published; his *Letters* may have been among these. For a critical edition, see H. Erskine-Hill (ed.), *Alexander Pope: Selected letters* (Oxford: Oxford University Press, 2000).

76 BL, PP, Add. MS 70493, fo. 33: Elizabeth Robinson to Anne Donnellan, *c.* 1740–1 [copy].

77 BLA, LP, letter 446: Catherine Talbot to Jemima Grey, 21 Oct. 1742 [modern transcript].

78 Bodl., Ballard 43, fo. 23: Elizabeth Elstob to George Ballard, 9 May 1736

79 Bodl., Ballard 43, fo, 23: Elizabeth Elstob to George Ballard, 9 May 1736.

80 Bodl., Ballard 43, fo. 27: Elizabeth Elstob to George Ballard, 12 Sept. 1736.

81 Bodl., Ballard 43, fo. 27: Elizabeth Elstob to George Ballard, 12 Sept. 1736.

82 Bodl., Ballard 43, fo. 31: Elizabeth Elstob to George Ballard, 24 Dec. 1736.

83 Bodl., Ballard 43, fo. 25: Elizabeth Elstob to George Ballard, 15 June 1736.

84 Bodl., Ballard 43, fo. 42: Elizabeth Elstob to George Ballard, 18 June 1737. Through Ballard, Elstob became acquainted with important antiquaries, such as William Brome (a Herefordshire antiquary, 1664–1745), who was aware of her early published work and the quality of her scholarship.

85 Bodl., Ballard 43, fo. 9: Elizabeth Elstob to George Ballard, 16 Nov. 1735.

86 See p. 133, for more on private libraries.

87 NRO, IP I.C. 4829: 'SS' to her niece, 27 May 1648.

88 NRO, IP I.C. 5111, *c.* 1648.

89 S. H. Mendelson, 'Clarke, Mary (d. 1705)', in *ODNB*; www.oxforddnb.com/view/article/66720.

90 M. Goldie, 'Clarke, Edward (1649/51–1710)', in *ODNB*; www.oxforddnb.com/view/article/37290.

91 For Richard Coote, first Earl of Bellamont (1636–1701), politician and colonial governor, see R. C. Ritchie, 'Coote, Richard, First Earl of Bellamont (1636–1701)', in *ODNB*; www.oxforddnb.com/view/article/6247. Mary Clarke's reference to Bellamont indicates that she was keen to remain up-to-date with topical political news.

92 SARO, SEP, DD\SF/7/1/31, fo. 22: Mary Clarke to Edward Clarke, 27 Oct. 1691.

93 SARO, SEP, DD\SF/7/1/31, fo. 12: Mary Clarke to Edward Clarke, 11 Oct. 1690.

94 SARO, SEP, DD\SF/7/1/31, fo. 8: Mary Clarke to Edward Clarke, 28 April 1690.

95 'House of Commons Journal Volume 10: 9 April 1690', *Journal of the House of Commons: vol. 10: 1688–93* (1802), pp. 372–3. Online at www.british-history.ac.uk/report.aspx?compid=29004; accessed: 30 Sept. 2012.

96 SARO, SEP, DD\SF/7/1/31, fo. 8: Mary Clarke to Edward Clarke, 28 April 1690.

97 On 10 April votes had been split seventy-seven yeas and eighty-two noes on this issue, see 'House of Commons Journal Volume 10: 10 April 1690', pp. 373–4. However, many other votes cast this month in the Commons resulted in closely matched results on each side.

98 SARO, SEP, DD\SF/7/1/31, fo. 20: Mary Clarke to Edward Clarke, 17 Dec. 1690.

99 SARO, SEP, DD\SF/7/1/31, fo. 19: Mary Clarke to Edward Clarke, 13 Dec. 1690.

100 BLA, LP, L 30/8/31/1: Lady Amabel Grey to Henry Grey, Lord Ruthyn, 23 May 1690.

101 BLA, LP, L 30/8/31/4: Lady Amabel Grey to Henry Grey, 19 June 1690. For the military context, see J. Childs, 'The Williamite War, 1689–91', in T. Bartlett and K. Jeffery (eds), *A Military History of Ireland* (Cambridge: Cambridge University Press, 1996), pp. 188–210.

2

Becoming an 'intellectual'

Becoming a woman intellectual in early modern England was no straightforward task. Financial dependence, lack of personal autonomy, marriage and motherhood could all bring pressures to bear on practices of self-development. However, it was from within these circumstances that women found ways to engage with the life of the mind. Moreover, the forms intellectual engagement took were informed by their domestic contexts and the patterns of exchange framed by letter-writing. This chapter explores the cultures of knowledge in which women made their mark. Female intellectual networks, opportunities for cross-gender exchange and amateur circles of scholarship all existed outside traditional centres for intellectual production. These opportunities are considered in the context of other factors that affected female learning: the development of an intellectual identity, the changing demands of the lifecycle and the ramifications of public scrutiny of female achievement. These opportunities and obstacles for female intellectual engagement in this period will be explored through the qualitative detail offered by a series of examples of learned women.

Intellectual identities

Much as writing is a self-affirming act, correspondence – with its promise of a reader and the possibility of exchange – was an identity-forming experience. An individual's identity was, of course, highly relational and early modern letter-writers negotiated their roles and relationships within complex frameworks of belief, experience and interaction.[1] Moreover, as Udo Thiel has explored, 'interest in the issues of self-consciousness and personal identity is certainly characteristic and even central to early modern thought'.[2] This was particularly true for the work of the philosopher John Locke who, as Raymond Martin and John Barresi have highlighted, 'was the first to propose an empirically grounded *psychology* of personal identity'.[3] Whilst philosophers were tackling issues of consciousness and the self, the eighteenth-century social world was also deeply concerned with the stability of identity.[4] In particular, the notion that individuals might have multiple identities undermined the security of an ordered and hierarchical society. Nevertheless, modern scholars of the eighteenth-century 'self' have accepted a pluralistic understanding of identity in this era. For the purposes of this chapter's discussion, Joan Wallach Scott's description of the operation of personal identity is a helpful one: she says 'most commonly, you [as a woman] will skate across the several identities which will take your weight'.[5] Of course, the act of writing added yet another layer to the process of articulating personal identity and, as Adam Smyth has suggested, forms of life writing did not necessarily privilege distinction in terms of the individual. Instead – he argues – commonplace books: 'reveal the degree to which a compiler's identity might be constructed through a process of alignment with other figures, narratives and events; through a pursuit of parallels; through an interest in sameness, not difference'.[6] In a similar vein, Anne Kugler's analysis of Sarah Cowper's diary entries reveals that personal identity could be constructed through compiling, reconstructing and subverting other authors' texts.[7] However, in some letter-writing the individual appeared very present. As Sara Crangle has observed of seventeenth-century letter-writer Dorothy Osborne's correspondence with her husband-to-be, William Temple:

> As a couple, Osborne and Temple participate in a single epistolary pact, but they are also individuals within it. As such, Osborne is not only a writer to Temple, but reader of her own text: letters represent an opportunity to construct and review her own person, both for the man she adores, and for her own purview.[8]

In surviving letter collections, the development and negotiation of female intellectual identities are certainly evident, and on studying these sources it becomes apparent that there was no one model of the woman intellectual in this period.

In the second half of the seventeenth century, Mary Evelyn (*c.* 1635–1709) conducted several intellectual correspondences with male friends. She had grown up in France, where her father, Sir Richard Browne, had been a representative of King Charles I. As a child, Mary Browne had been the fortunate beneficiary of an extensive humanist education, unusual for girls and young women of this period. She was fluent in French and English, proficient in Italian and trained in mathematics, among other subjects, although she did not have the facility of either Latin or Greek and had to read ancient works in translation. However, this childhood experience of education moulded Mary Browne's subsequent adult commitment to private study.

At age thirteen, in June 1647, Mary Browne married the famous diarist and thinker, John Evelyn (1620–1706), who was at this time twice her age. On account of her young age, Mary Evelyn only made the journey to John Evelyn's house, Sayes Court in Deptford, five years later, in 1652. The Brownes were very keen for Mary Evelyn to be allowed to continue with her studies under her new circumstances as wife and mistress of a household. Indeed, the emphasis placed on Mary Evelyn's hitherto scholarly existence seemingly concerned John Evelyn in regard to his wife's potential lack of interest in home economics. On 16 September 1648 he had furnished her with a hand-written manual to domestic life, claiming that the skills detailed within could only add to her already impressive repertoire of accomplishments: 'if you grow as proficient therein, I dare pronounce you the most Accomplished creature of your Sex'.[9] As it happened, Mary Evelyn took the responsibilities of her role as wife, and later mother, very seriously and became renowned not only for her intellect but also for her skills in the still-room.[10]

Mary Evelyn did maintain a life of the mind in adult life, but did not engage with publication as an outlet for her ideas. Via letters to her son's tutor, Ralph Bohun, Evelyn wrote for a coterie of Oxford academics who appreciated her eloquent analysis (in letter form) of literature and the arts. The physician and cleric Doctor Bathurst (1620–1704) was the point of contact with this group and his circle included Royal Society luminaries such as Robert Boyle. Throughout the earlier years of their correspondence, in the 1660s, Bohun made it clear that he desired to show Mary Evelyn's letters to a wider circle of academics: 'I received your excellent letter, & assure you, it was so well approved at D^{ctr} Bathursts, yt I am promisd absolution if I can steal away ye rest, wch they infinitely desire to see.'[11] Mary Evelyn rarely acknowledged this process, but religiously sent her best wishes to Doctor Bathurst, showing her approval of the circulation of her letters in this public forum. Moreover, at this time Mary Evelyn was keeping copies of chosen examples of her letters to others. These letter books, discussed in detail by Frances Harris, were modest in their presentation, but revealing of the value Evelyn placed both on her own letter-writing talent and in particular epistolary friendships.[12] The letter books, taken alongside the evidence of Evelyn's surviving correspondences, give an insight into this seventeenth-century woman's complex relationship with letter-writing and intellectual life.

Despite side-stepping the aspiration of publishing, Mary Evelyn still placed herself within the context of contemporary creative work. When Ralph Bohun nick-named her 'Madame Balzac', she claimed that her 'ambition aspires not to the fame of Balzac', but explained that this modesty was because 'I do not admire his style, nor emulate the spirit of discontent which runns through all his letters'.[13] Jean-Louis Guez de Balzac had been credited with introducing a new clarity to French prose and had demonstrated this through a series of exemplary letters, designed to showcase a new streamlined style.[14] The comparison drawn with Mary Evelyn confirmed that her letter-writing paid particular attention to epistolary style. Balzac was not the only writer criticised in this letter, as Evelyn undermined 'Doctor Donne', the public servant and celebrated poet,[15] whose most famous words were written in *Devotions upon Emergent Occasions* in 1624: 'who had he not bin really a learned man, a libertine in witt, and a courtier, might have ben allowed to write well, but I confesse in my opinion with those qualifications he falls short in his letters of the praises some give him.'[16] It was Evelyn's eloquent and authoritative criticisms of literature and the arts in letter form that had won her the audience of Dr Bathurst's circle.

On 3 February 1668, Mary Evelyn sent Bohun her assessment of the recently published *History of the Royall Society*.[17] The Royal Society was an institution of the age and Evelyn mixed in social circles with the academics who were making the society's reputation.[18] Some of the Oxford academics for whom Mary Evelyn wrote were members of the Royal Society and she was correspondingly complimentary about the content of this published History (Figure 2):

> though it needs not my suffrage to make it passe for an admirable piece both for witt and eloquence, force of Judgment, and evennesse of style; yet suffer me to do my selfe the right to acknowledge I never liked anything more; not only because it is written in the defence of worthy and learned men, or of a cause which promises so many future advantages; but that his notions are conveyed in so just, easy, and polite expressions, in knewn and yet not vulgar english.[19]

Here, Evelyn's discussion engaged with the contemporary debate concerning a suitable written style for the writing of science, showing that Evelyn was conversant with the issues debated by the early society.[20] At the end of this letter, Evelyn wrote 'Now I am silent, and must wish when you and my selfe have any works in print, wee may have no greater

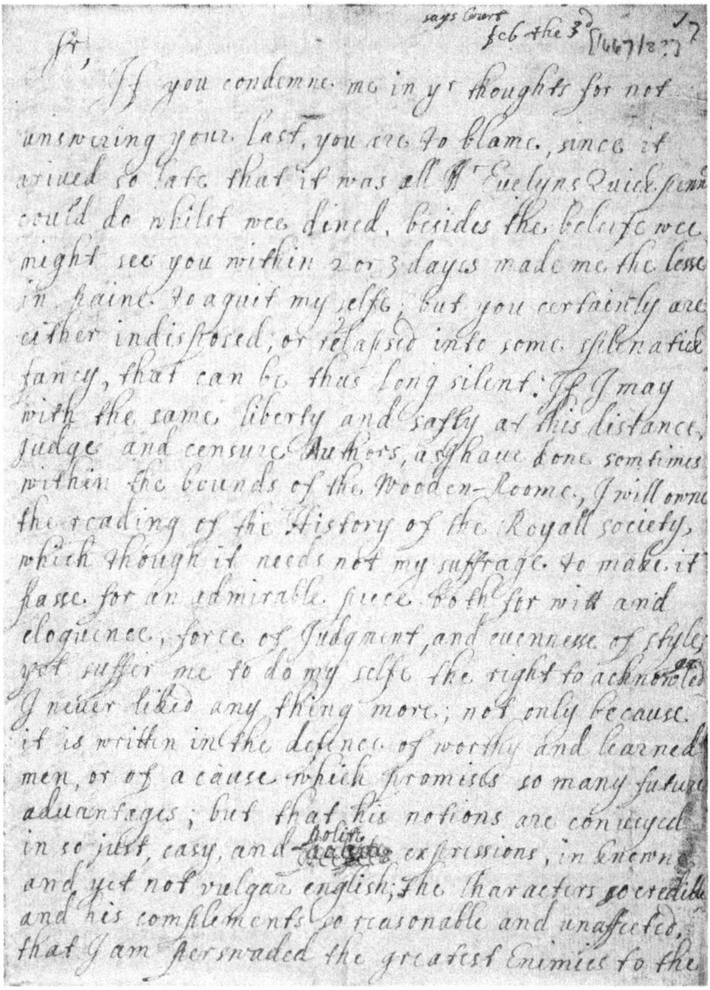

Figure 2: A letter written by Mary Evelyn and addressed to her friend, Ralph Bohun, on 3 February 1668, © The British Library Board (Add. MS 78539).

faults layd to our charge'.[21] This comment was ambiguous; it lightened the tone of the previous critical analysis but it also placed Evelyn and Bohun alongside the scholarly published authors of the day, in ability if not in ambition. This comment was consistent in tone with Mary Evelyn's other intellectual letters of this period. For the most part she adopted an identity of personal detachment, a position from which she could apply her cool, reasoning mind to other people's works of creative expression. However, at times, convention dictated that she should disavow the quality or impact of her own writing, so she did so. For example, in one letter Evelyn denied the wider interest of personal correspondence altogether:

> I wonder at nothing more then at the ambition of printing letters; since if the designe be to produce witt and learning, there is too litle scope for the one, and the other may be riduced to a lesse compasse then a sheet of guilt paper … Businesse, Love, accidents, secret displeasures family intrigues, generally make up the body of letters and can signifie very litle to any besides the persons they are addressed to; and therefore must loose infininitly by being exposed to the unconcerned.[22]

This comment could be read as Evelyn stressing a modest evaluation of her letter-writing, but more probably it expressed her own indecision over the purpose of her writing at that time.

Evelyn's high standard of education and academic talent did not lead to a straightforward relationship with intellectual life in adulthood and she increasingly found her intellectual identity in conflict with her other identities of wife and mother. Evelyn pursued a life of the mind through thoughtful epistolary exchange with a small group of chosen confidants. When her audience of one (Ralph Bohun) became several academics, Evelyn consented to the arrangement. However, it is clear that she questioned the intellectual validity of short written pieces delivered in letters. No doubt, Evelyn acquiesced to the situation because she enjoyed exercising her mind and receiving semi-public approval for her writing. Ultimately, Mary Evelyn could see no advantage in raising the profile of her work, or herself, higher than this informal arrangement and even this gave her room for doubt.

Mary Evelyn never either openly nor, it seems, seriously entertained the idea of herself as a published author. In fact she heavily criticised the Duchess of Newcastle for, as she saw it, crashing about in the world of print without the requisite talent to support such a public display. Evelyn, by contrast, successfully transmitted an intellectual identity which was rooted in a cerebral, domestic retreat, but at the same time she cast a critical eye over play, book and poem to the applause of a small and learned audience. However, whilst Evelyn's projection of herself as an insightful critic was at times extremely masterful; at others it became painfully self-limiting. Evelyn's lack of resolution over her sense of identity as a wife, mother and intellectual ultimately curtailed the extent to which she could fully develop her life of the mind. Early in her marriage, she had discussed with her husband the possibility of establishing a scholarly community; her vision of life in this community was cloistered and contemplative.[23] Evelyn did succeed in balancing several life roles simultaneously for some years. However, her view of intellectual life as best pursued from the quiet confines of retreat goes some way to explain her objection to the manner in which she herself was able to engage with intellectual matters: amidst the competing tasks of rearing children, directing servants, entertaining guests and provisioning the household.

Evelyn's experience of conflicting identities is less apparent in the self-confident letter-writing of the young Grey circle. Even when the demands on their time from children and household emerged, they rarely acknowledged any competition between their various roles. In the same letter that Jemima Grey blamed the age she was born in for the lack of intellectual talent surrounding her and, indeed, her own, she conversely seemed wholly at ease with herself as an intellectual. Claiming that the stars under which she was born were to blame for the 'Trifling Insignificant Age' in which she lived, she stated that had they 'produced me in the same Age as a Milton, a Shakespere, a Pope, A Newton, *a Clarendon*, or any Other Great Men you please to add, I should without doubt have been equal to any of Them'.[24] Lightening the stridency of this claim, Grey continued to joke: 'O Sad! who can help these Misfortunes! All the Use I can make of this Discovery is to warn you for the future never to wonder when my Letters or Myself are Dull; but to consider the time of my Birth, as I intend to do when I feel any particular Degree of Stupidity'.[25] The levity of Grey's discussion of these issues expressed the relative self-confidence with which she and her friends dealt with issues concerning their own intellectual identities. The letters of Mary Evelyn and the Grey circle, separated in time by nearly eighty years, reveal very different responses to the notion of female, intellectual identity. Nevertheless, the letters acted in both cases as a space to perform, discuss and negotiate the contested identity of the learned woman. In so doing, the act of letter-writing both explored and constructed the life of the mind for women like Mary Evelyn and Jemima Grey.

The 'learned lady' and the amateur intellectual

Here, the discussion turns to a collection of letters written by eighteen women to the professional tailor and stay-maker, self-taught antiquary and prolific correspondent, George Ballard (1706–55). The letters are now contained in a bound volume in the Bodleian Library with a frontispiece

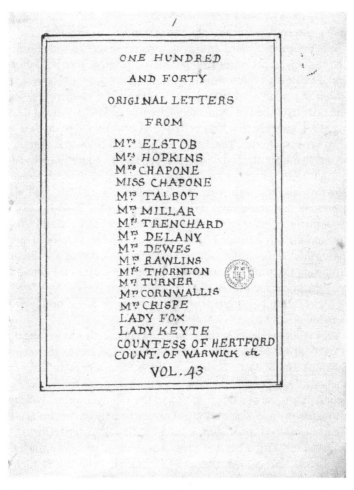

/

ONE HUNDRED

AND FORTY

ORIGINAL LETTERS

FROM

M.ʳˢ ELSTOB
M.ʳˢ HOPKINS
M.ʳˢ CHAPONE
MISS CHAPONE
M.ʳ TALBOT
M.ʳ MILLAR
M.ʳ TRENCHARD
M.ʳ DELANY
M.ʳ DEWES
M.ʳ RAWLINS
M.ʳˢ THORNTON
M.ʳ TURNER
M.ʳ CORNWALLIS
M.ʳ CRISPE
LADY FOX
LADY KEYTE
COUNTESS OF HERTFORD
COUNT. OF WARWICK etc

VOL. 43

Figure 3: George Ballard's letter book containing 140 original letters from female contacts, including Elizabeth Elstob, courtesy of The Bodleian Libraries, The University of Oxford, MS Ballard 43, fo. 1r.

listing the names of the letter-writers within (Figure 3). The names consisted of Ballard's female friends and supporters of his subscription publication, *Memoirs of Several Ladies of Great Britain*, which went to press in 1752. The most substantial contribution to this collection of 140 letters is the correspondence penned by Anglo-Saxon scholar and schoolmistress, Elizabeth Elstob (1683–1756). Having been claimed by feminist historians as an example of female achievement in the face of patriarchy, Elstob's legacy has likewise been examined for its significance in the emerging field of eighteenth-century Anglo-Saxon studies.

When George Ballard struck up a correspondence with Elizabeth Elstob she was in her fifties and had been separated from her scholarly research for nearly twenty years.[26] The first half of these letters were written from the small market town of Evesham in Worcestershire, where Elstob had established an elementary school for girls and earned a modest living as a schoolmistress. This period in Elstob's life sat in marked contrast to her earlier years. Elstob had been born in Newcastle-upon-Tyne to a merchant family and, from the beginning, education played an important role for Elstob who was taught Latin by her mother. However, by the time she was eight years old her parents were both dead and it was decided that she should move south to join the household of her uncle – the prebendary of Canterbury Cathedral, the Reverend Charles Elstob and his wife Matilda Elstob. Whilst Elstob has often been quoted as saying that her uncle did not encourage female learning, she did make gains during her time in Canterbury, learning French to the extent that in 1708 she published her translation of Madeleine de Scudéry's *Discours de la Gloire*.[27] Elstob dedicated this, her first sole-authored print publication, to her aunt.[28]

As a young woman in the early 1700s, Elizabeth Elstob joined her brother William's household in London – he had become the rector of St Swithin's and St Mary Bothaw's and the Elstobs lived in Bush Lane in the City. Despite William Elstob's appointment, he too was engaged in scholarly projects in this period and the siblings worked collaboratively on their Anglo-Saxon studies, drawing heavily on the contacts that William Elstob had made during his education at Oxford. During this time, Elizabeth Elstob became proficient in eight languages, including Latin, Greek, Hebrew, German and Old English. With this facility, she was more than capable of tackling the demands of Anglo-Saxon itself and engaging with the scholarly texts and debates that would aid her research.

Through her brother, Elizabeth Elstob was introduced to the community of Anglo-Saxon scholars at Oxford. In fact, it is likely that the Elstobs made many trips from their London home to the Bodleian Library to consult the manuscript collections. At this time, the study of Anglo-Saxon language and literature was relatively new and the field had not yet been integrated into university curricula, nor was there a dedicated professor of the subject at either Oxford or Cambridge.[29] Nonetheless, the study of Anglo-Saxon was particularly attractive to antiquaries of this period because it connected closely with contemporary concerns. For one, scholars sought to locate the origins of the modern English state in

Anglo-Saxon records and, further to this, they saw in their studies the opportunity to demonstrate that 'the pre-Conquest church was the true progenitor of the reformed Church of England' and, therefore, that Catholicism had come about through undesirable post-Conquest developments in Europe.[30] For Protestant English men and women, these were powerful arguments and made the study of ancient language and text a significantly political act. In these early but exciting days of Anglo-Saxon studies, Elizabeth Elstob not only came into contact with a dynamic set of scholars but she became one of them. As Mechthild Gretsch has emphasised, 'these scholars apparently saw no difficulty in admitting a young woman into their province of study and treating her as an equal'.[31] Not only was Elstob given access to the university's manuscript collections, but her work was championed by one of the most respected antiquaries of the era, George Hickes.[32] It was in these circumstances, at the beginning of the eighteenth century, that Elizabeth Elstob made important advances in the study of Anglo-Saxon language and literature and propelled her findings into print.

Many claims have been made for Elizabeth Elstob as a pioneer and promoter of women's intellectual achievement, but there are some particular aspects of her work that have caused disagreement amongst scholars. For example, the fact that Elstob chose to translate the Saxon into the vernacular rather than Latin has been cited as evidence of her interest in a female readership, a population who lacked training in classical languages. Norma Clarke has argued that by using Modern English instead of Latin, 'Elstob was making a conscious polemical point. The argument for the vernacular tradition over the classical was of obvious use to women. The established institutions of learning, the church and the universities, excluded women and rooted scholarship in classical training'.[33] However, Gretsch has refuted this claim, arguing instead that there was an established tradition of translating Old English into Modern English – a tradition that 'comprised texts of paramount religious importance' confirming Elstob's wish to emphasise 'the importance of Ælfric's homily for understanding the origin and development of the English church'.[34] Whether or not Elstob stood outside the prevailing norms in producing a Modern English translation of the text, the fact that the Saxon words were readable by all literate men and women was certainly significant – if only in confirming the author's belief that this scholarship had contemporary relevance and a potential readership outside the universities.

Elizabeth Elstob's life was one of two contrasting halves and the change occurred in 1715 when her brother, William, died. Elstob was thirty-one and the consequences of this loss were sudden and dramatic.

Without the financial stability brought by her nearest relation, Elstob fell on hard times and her whereabouts for several subsequent years is unknown.[35] The loss in the same year of her other academic supporter, George Hickes, rendered Elstob's ability to continue her studies even more unlikely. In this same year Elstob published her *Rudiments of Grammar for the Anglo-Saxon Tongue*, but her larger project – an edition of Ælfric's *Catholic Homilies* – lay incomplete.

So it was with this history that Elizabeth Elstob came into contact with the antiquary, George Ballard, in the mid-1730s. In one of Elstob's first letters to her new friend Ballard, she claimed that 'Not having had for near twenty years the Conversation of one Antiquary' she was out of touch with the world of ideas (Figure 4). Whilst it was Elstob's situation in Evesham in Worcestershire that was, in part, the cause of her isolation, it was also what brought her into contact with George Ballard's local network of women who were concerned with the pursuit of antiquarian knowledge.[36] Decades after she had been forced to part with the Anglo-Saxon manuscripts she wished to study, Ballard acknowledged Elstob as the intellectual woman who had gained recognition for her scholarly works. Whilst Elstob's importance has been recognised by historians, the correspondence between Ballard and Elstob is revealing of wider cultures of knowledge in this period. Ballard was a man of trade; Elstob was bankrupted at an early stage of her scholarly career and thereafter relied on her skills to earn a living through teaching. The surviving correspondence provides valuable evidence of the potential for individuals on the margins of intellectual life to form supportive networks of scholarly exchange.

In George Ballard, Elstob had met a fellow enthusiast. As he worked on a book celebrating 'learned ladies', Ballard saw a suitable candidate for that title in Elstob. However, the exchange went further than this – Ballard often enquired after Elstob's knowledge of a learned woman he wished to write about and, likewise, he shared his latest findings with her. On 15 June 1736, Elstob wrote: 'I do assure you S[r] that this last Favour of your accurate account of the Learned M[rs] Margaret Roper[37] will be esteem'd by me as a choice curiosity for which I return you a thousand thanks.'[38] A year later, Elstob offered Ballard her thoughts on the seventeenth-century poet Katherine Philips: 'I was always a great admirer of M[rs] K. Philips's charming performances, and am intirely of your opinion that the Dialogue between Lucasia, and Rosania comes behind none of the rest.'[39] She also asked Ballard for information for herself: 'I shou'd be glad to know what the Manuscript was which you saw in Queens College Archives by that perhaps I may be able to find out

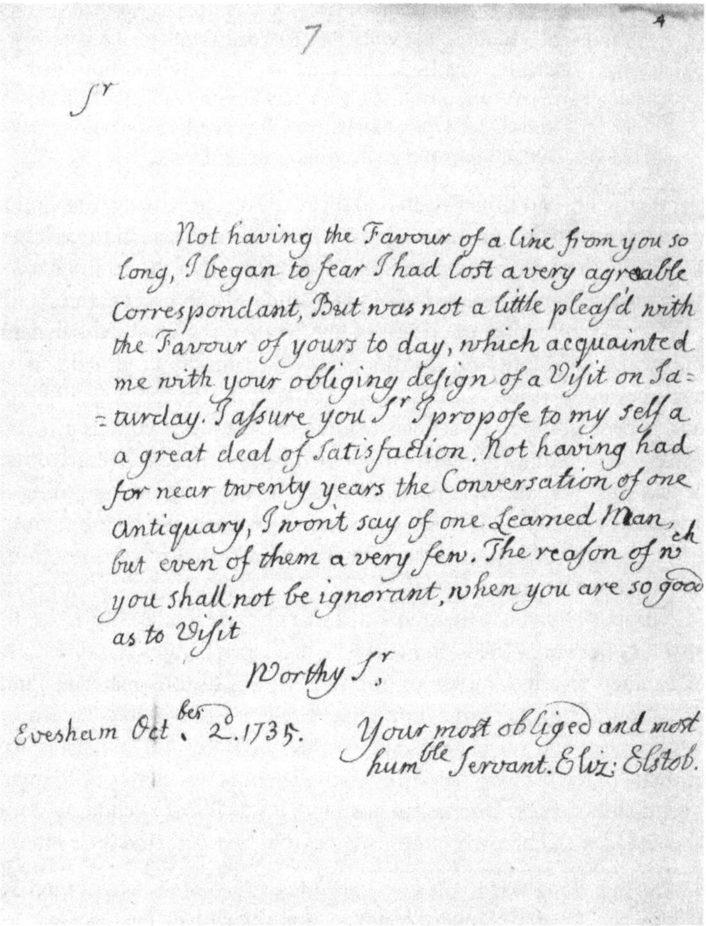

7

Sr

Not having the Favour of a line from you so
long, I began to fear I had lost a very agreable
Correspondant, But was not a little pleas'd with
the Favour of yours to day, which acquainted
me with your obliging design of a Visit on Sa-
-turday. I assure you Sr I propose to my self a
a great deal of satisfaction. Not having had
for near twenty years the Conversation of one
Antiquary, I won't say of one Learned Man,
but even of them a very few. The reason of wch
you shall not be ignorant, when you are so good
as to Visit

Worthy Sr,

Evesham Octber 2. 1735.   Your most obliged and most
                            humble servant. Eliz: Elstob.

Figure 4: A letter written by Elizabeth Elstob and addressed to her friend, George Ballard, on 2 October 1735, courtesy of The Bodleian Libraries, The University of Oxford, MS Ballard 43, fo. 7r.

how it came [there] which at present I can't guess.'[40] Ballard passed on many requests from fellow antiquaries and scholars for Elstob's perusal, but it was not always possible for her to meet their expectations, as she explained on 24 December 1736:

I shou'd readily comply with his [Mr Knight's] request, cou'd I send him any thing that I thought worth his Learned Fathers acceptance, but you know where I am placed, is out of reach of any Manuscripts, so that I can transcribe nothing but what that Learned Gentleman has seen already. I return his thanks for the sight of the inscription from that valuable peice of Antiquity. The Characters are undoubtedly Runick, but the little knowledge I once had in that Language, by a long disuse is almost lost, so that I dare not give any judgement upon it.[41]

Despite the limited time Elstob had for reading and writing, the circulation of historical source material was a prominent theme in these letters.

Elizabeth Elstob's letters to Ballard also show that she retained a very clear sense of herself as an intellectual. When Elstob had taken up work in Worcestershire after the death of her brother, she changed her name. This switch in identity on Elstob's part was primarily pragmatic, as she owed money to printers in London; however it also symbolically separated her former life as a scholar from her subsequent work as a schoolmistress. She remarked, early in her correspondence with Ballard, that she was still: 'very much concern'd to find the Language of our Ancestors so much neglected'.[42] Despite the serious obstacles to Elstob's continued study, the correspondence with Ballard revealed Elstob's continued self-identification as a scholar.

Elizabeth Elstob benefited intellectually and materially from this epistolary network. The writer and wife of a vicar, Sarah Chapone,[43] used her contacts to advocate for an improvement in Elstob's material conditions. On the fringes of this immediate circle of letter-writers lay women with financial and social clout, such as Mary Delany and, her sister, Ann Granville (later D'Ewes). As Ann Granville wrote, in a letter to Margaret Cavendish Bentinck, Duchess of Portland, it was Elstob's scholarly standing coupled with her lowly circumstances that first attracted their interest:

> The first thing which rais'd my curiosity to enquire after Mrs Elstob was her Saxon Grammar ... she delivers her reasons for this work very nobly in an English Preface to the whole from which (though I by no means presume myself a judge of Learning) I conceiv'd a great Veneration for her understanding. ... I omit giving any further account of this or any work of hers, because I think 'tis very likely some time or other you may hav seen them ... I then made some enquiries after her, but was inform'd she was dead, last summer by meer accident I heard that she was living in low circumstances and taught an English school at Evesham in Worcestershire as that place is but five miles from me, I soon took an opportunity to go thither where I found her mistress of a little school.[44]

Granville's letter went on to stress that Elstob's role provided 'no more than the base supports of Life ... she frequently dines upon a toasted peice

of bread'. Granville commented on the 'Loweness of her spirits and tenderness of her constitution' and bemoaned that 'a woman of her Learning
& great abilities [is] in so forlorn a condition'.[45] Granville also 'took the
freedom to enquire into her reasons for burying her self alive in a little
Illiterate Market Town, where no one Person had y[e] least apprehension of
her distinguishing Quallity's'.[46] Clearly this letter was designed to prompt
the duchess into action, but Granville's description of her 'discovery' of
Elstob is also revealing of the way in which Elstob's value as a female
scholar was understood by other women of her time. The result of this
advocacy was that the Duchess of Portland offered Elstob a position as
governess in her household in that same year. A letter dated 8 November
1738, from Elstob to Portland (delivered to the duchess by Mary Delany)
documents this development. Elstob took the opportunity to explain her
views on the education of young women (see Figure 5):

> You are very sensible Madam how much the Education of our Youth
> especially that of the Females is neglected ... those who spend their
> whole time and thoughts on cultivating and improving the minds of
> those committed to their care, in the most material parts of Education,
> and the most lasting, shall hardly be allow'd a mean subsistence. This
> I am sure I have sufficiently experienc'd for many years.[47]

Elstob then reassured her future employer that she could be trusted
to perform her role well with respect to the duchess's children:

> My first care shall be to instill sweetly into the minds of my Young ones
> the Principles of Religion and Virtue. The younger they are the better
> before they are corrupted by any bad example. At the same time I shall
> endeavour to teach them to read spell and speak their own Language
> well, and as soon as they are capable, will instruct them in the Rules of
> English Grammar Etymology &c. and then make them acquainted with
> the Histories of our own and other Countreys, and such other useful
> and Good Books, as shall be thought proper for their improvement.[48]

Elizabeth Elstob lived out the rest of her life in the Portland household.

Many other connections of mutual support for intellectual achievement exist within the pages of Ballard's letter book, including names both
familiar and unfamiliar to the histories of the early eighteenth century.
Some, such as Mary Delany, performed a role that sat within a traditional
model of patronage, but others were relatively powerless individuals who
chose to support Ballard's work in smaller ways, according to their own
means. Ultimately, Ballard's extensive work in his field would be recognised when he was appointed clerk of Magdalen College, Oxford, giving him an annuity and proximity to the Bodleian's valuable collections.

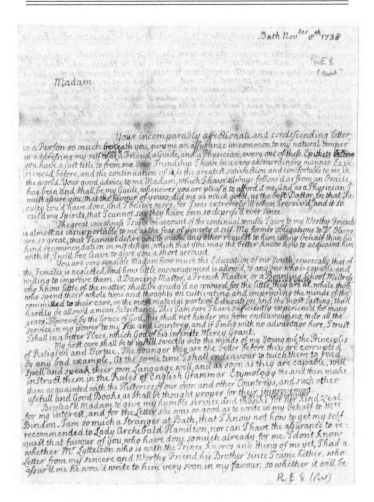

Figure 5: A letter written by Elizabeth Elstob and addressed to Margaret Cavendish Bentinck, Duchess of Portland, courtesy of the Manuscripts and Special Collections, The University of Nottingham, Portland Papers, PwE8.

His social background excluded him from higher seats within the universities, but – like Elstob – his dedication and the quality of his work won him friends able to manoeuvre on his behalf for a situation more conducive to study. In the 1730s, Ballard's chosen topic of research heralded the later eighteenth-century flurry of interest in the clever women in Elizabeth Montagu's Bluestocking circle. Ballard's project, as it is now manifested, as one large compendium of letters and another slim, printed text, exemplifies the wealth of informal scholarship undertaken by men and women in this period. All the eighteen women whose letters feature in Ballard's letter book were supportive in some way of his work of history.

So, what can Elstob and Ballard tell us about eighteenth-century cultures of learning? For one, their examples – and those of their acquaintances – speak to the existence of high-level scholarship in unusual places. From Ballard's tailor's shop in Campden, he amassed a collection of antiquarian artefacts, studied the histories of ancient peoples and became a recognised activist within a network of English antiquaries, most of whom hailed from more illustrious lineages. Elstob, on the other hand, was proud of her background, claiming noble family history, but struggled through want of financial independence. Even in her twenties, when Elstob was at her most intellectually productive, she had relied on the income and living provided by her brother's work. William Elstob, a keen scholar in his own right, had to take up clerical posts to fund his intellectual pursuits, a fact upon which some blamed his early demise. Nevertheless, both Elstob and Ballard achieved notice amongst the intellectual circles of the early eighteenth century. Ballard's network of acquaintance was impressive, now evident in his epistolary archive. Elstob's assurance that learning was her life's work seems formidable, even at this distance of time. Elstob's example also highlights the central place of letter-writing in connecting diffuse, diverse, but intellectually engaged English men and women. Despite being separated by only five miles, Ballard and Elstob were utterly dependent on correspondence to maintain their contact; they only met in person twice in twenty years. These letter-writers used their contacts to seek out others who were engaged with similar academic interests. This process rested, to a large degree, on the cultivation of an intellectual identity, even if this identity existed outside traditional institutions of scholarship or privileged circles of acquaintance.

Of the examples of female intellectual activity considered in this book, Elstob is one of the most well-known, primarily because she did publish her early research. Elstob's reputation has also been taken up by scholars interested in the Bluestockings, thus subsuming her intellectual endeavour within the framework of that female network. However, the cosseting effect of Bluestocking society was not a feature that Elstob would have recognised in her own life history. Undoubtedly she was gladdened by the attention she received from several supportive contacts in her later years, but they could not undo the decades that preceded their intervention and, despite their efforts, Elstob never returned to her studies. Nonetheless, Elstob's relationship with the intellectual world in her fifties and sixties is illustrative of the challenges other women faced. Unlike some of the other women letter-writers discussed here, Elstob did not marry or have children, but her teaching in a local school dominated her time and left her with limited energy or resources for other work. The association with Ballard may not have been an adequate substitute for Elstob's expectations of a life committed to research, but she was genuinely glad of the intellectual friendship it provided. Moreover, the network of sympathetic friends that Elstob was introduced to by Ballard did hold genuine opportunity for patronage. A fundamental change in Elstob's life circumstances was, in fact, never realised but the evidence of the potential provided by such epistolary networks, to connect intellectual talent with sympathetic patronage, is compelling.

Lifecycle and the intellectual biography

As previously discussed, women did not often have biographies which saw consistent and sustained intellectual output across the lifecycle. They have therefore been more difficult candidates for analysis in terms of intellectual history. Instead, it is more common to see fragmented periods of activity, punctuated by periods of silence, during times when other responsibilities came to the fore. Having traced the productive early years of the Grey circle's correspondence, we will move now to examine their mutual letter-writing during a period when two of the three women had families of their own.

In the letters written during the early 1740s, it was clear that Mary Grey, Jemima Grey and Catherine Talbot maintained their friendship and emotional closeness not only through their regular correspondence but, primarily, via a continued and meaningful exchange of ideas. A reading of the letters written between the three women during this decade reveals that dominant subjects were recent activities, descriptions of everyday life, discussion of reading material and contemporary culture, for example, the theatre and current affairs. Broadly speaking, Mary Grey spent the most time describing daily life and the rounds of visits, walks and social engagements which she and Catherine Talbot experienced. Talbot's letter-writing, on the other hand, moved between stylistic flourishes and serious discussion of literary works. Of the three women, she commented the least on the people she had met and on her social life, as she regarded this exercise largely as pointless 'Chit Chat'. Jemima Grey engaged with Talbot on the contents of the books which they had both read, but her letters also contained reports of current affairs and her own reviews of the plays she had seen in the London theatres. The 1740s, in this correspondence, were characterised by long letters, many of them, and an ever-present urgency to remain properly in touch with one another.

By the early 1750s this picture had begun to change. Mary Grey had become Mary Gregory and had children in the second half of the 1740s; Jemima Grey had followed her, with two daughters born in the 1750s. The letters exchanged between the two of them, now as wives and mothers, contained more discussion of childcare, ill-health and home improvement. Mary Gregory's letters became almost completely devoid of any direct discussion of reading material and, by 1757, her letters were routinely short, a departure from her lengthy epistles of the early 1740s. Where Jemima Grey's letters to Mary Gregory veered away from domestic matters, they tended to concentrate on current affairs over her earlier mainstay: the discussion of contemporary and classic literature. With diminished time for serious study, Grey had switched her attention to the quicker mode of newspaper reading, to glean news of the world outside. However, her own experience did extend to the theatre and high society life, and consequently these topics still made an appearance as she progressed towards middle age.

The correspondence between Jemima Grey and Catherine Talbot during the 1750s was of a different nature. Although they no longer kept such a close connection via their reading, this period provided other stimuli. In particular, Jemima Grey sent Talbot several travel journals which she had written to document her trips to East Anglia and a tour of the north and Scotland in 1755. Talbot's letters occasionally reminisced about their earlier years: 'By Accident my Dear Lady Grey I have got sole possession this Evening of the Great Parlour where we have passed so many winter hours by the cheerfull fire-side very happily, & I have been conversing so long with Old Ideas & Pleasing Rembrances that I can write about nothing else.'[49] As their lives were moving into middle age, and their letter-writing correspondingly changing, Talbot reviewed their lives to date. She seemed sensible of the great privilege, which they had enjoyed during their early life: 'We are neither of us children & we have lived to these years of discretion in the self same world that is by so many wise & good writers represented as a very wretched & unsatisfactory place, & yet all our years in it have been distinguished by real pleasures & sincere enjoyments.'[50] In general, the two women's lives appeared from their letters to be more wholly dominated by social obligations in the 1750s and many pages were taken up with accounts of meeting other people – a topic which Talbot had previously condemned as 'insipid'.

Pressure to make motherhood the main priority in life came not only from the women themselves, but also from exterior social pressure, as Grey described in the following anecdote:

> I really was ashamed of myself all the Evening ... everybody that met me in the Room even in the Midst of a Dance would ask me – *How my Daughter did?* What a Recollection to tell a fine gay dancing Lady she had a Chit at home in the Nursery! ... Well, well, I must make the best Use of this Year, that is certain! When she can Walk, I can't for shame think any more of Dancing.[51]

When asked by Talbot how she spent her time, Grey replied 'like most other Folks, Eat, Drink & Sleep, & perhaps Read'.[52] Had the same question been asked ten years earlier, the order of activities would surely have been reversed.

Catherine Talbot did not follow the conventional route of marriage and children and must, therefore, have felt the loss of the more intellectually committed content of her friends' letters in earlier years. However, the absence of children did not exempt Talbot from responsibilities altogether and she spent considerable amounts of her time running Thomas Secker's household until his death in 1768, only two years before her own. In the last two decades of her life, Talbot could not be persuaded to publish, but continued to exchange ideas with her close friends and advise others on their literary activities. For example, Talbot helped the poet and writer, Elizabeth Carter (1717–1806), in her translation of *Epictetus* (*c.* 1750). The two women had met through the antiquary, Thomas Wright, and formed a lifelong, intellectually supportive relationship. Talbot's private studies continued unabated and in the 1760s she succeeded in teaching herself German.[53] In the year of her death, 1770, Talbot's work, *Reflections on the Seven Days of the Week*, was published and her name became widely known.[54]

The letters of the Grey circle point to a culture that allowed women to learn and engage with literature. Aside from the changing trend apparent in the content of the letters over this period of twenty years, in general there is little direct comment about restrictions on scholarly endeavour, which is unusual for women intellectuals of this period. The women of the Grey circle had high expectations for themselves and, in their earlier years, seemed free to gratify this drive for self-development. However, it is true that the intellectual output of Grey and Gregory took a serious knock, if a temporary one, from the pressures of bringing up a family. Nevertheless, these letter-writers demonstrated that where restriction on female aspiration existed it did not obliterate women's motivations

BECOMING AN 'INTELLECTUAL'

to learn and when time became more limited, alternative and quickly accessible sources could be sought in order to maintain an active engagement with the wider world.

Mary Evelyn provides an earlier and more dramatic example of an intellectual history at odds with the rigours of the female lifecycle. Despite years of engaged letter-writing to Ralph Bohun, amongst other male confidants, by the early 1670s Evelyn's commentary on literary themes had become much less frequent. By way of excuse, she referenced her demanding schedule of responsibilities in the home. At this time, Mary Evelyn had four children, having lost a further four children and suffered at least three miscarriages. Her son, Jack, was a young man and her three daughters were still children requiring her attention.[55] For example, a subject that might have warranted an entire letter in earlier years, the John Dryden play, *The Siege of Grenada* (1670–1),[56] only received a few lines, the brevity explained by Evelyn's role as a mother:

> since my last to you I have seene the siege of Grenada, a play so full of Ideas, that the most refined Romance I ever read, is not to compare with it ... I do not quarrell with the Poet, but admire one borne in the decline of morality, should be able to feigne such exact virtue. ... this account perhaps is not sufficient to do M[r] Dreiden[57] right; yet is as much as you can expect from the leisure of one who has the care of a Nurcery.[58]

By 26 March 1672, Mary Evelyn sounded increasingly defensive about her time and capacity to write: 'I have had litle leasure to think of any thing but the meanes of gaining health and ease, I am perswaded you will excuse me if I have not decided in my thoughts which was the greatest Captaine Ceasar or Pompey.'[59] By citing the historically heavyweight figures of Caesar and Pompey,[60] Evelyn emphasised her position as a woman who was expected to care for children, keep the house and debate the merits of Roman statesmen in the course of an ordinary afternoon. At times these circumstances had worked for Evelyn, but at others they clearly generated tension. Evelyn began to write more frequently about her duties about the house and Bohun took to teasing her about the ever-present demands of the 'still-house'. In the letter that most immediately predated a dramatic declaration of intent from Mary Evelyn, she commented on the favourable aspects of Bohun's modest means and lifestyle. 'I am glad you passe yr time in a place that creates such variety of Ideas, an effect of perfect ease and entire satisfaction.'[61]

Bohun's complaints of meagre finances were sharply countered by the comparatively wealthy Evelyn, with the charge that his true wealth lay in his absolute freedom to pursue an intellectual career, which was of far greater value than material riches. Mary Evelyn, it seems, had not found 'perfect ease' or 'entire satisfaction' from her own life circumstances and craved Bohun's comparative freedom to indulge in intellectual pursuits unhampered, as he was, by domestic responsibility.

Despite her long-term unconventional correspondence with Ralph Bohun on literary themes, Mary Evelyn eventually reframed the parameters of this correspondence. In 1674, by way of explanation, she delivered a stinging appraisal of the limited domestic existence open to women and, on these grounds, rejected her own epistolary involvement in academic life. Mary Evelyn kept her resolve, after this date, her letters almost entirely revolved around family anecdotes and news from friends, whilst loftier subject matter was effectively banished:

> Do not think my silence hitherto has proceeded from being taken up by the diversities of the towne, the Esclat of the Court, Galantrie in clothes, … should I confesse the reall cause it is yr expectation of extraordinary notions of things wholly out of my way, Women were not borne to read Authors and censure the learned, to compare lives and Judge of virtues, to give rules of morality, and sacrifice to the Muses, wee are willing to acknowledge all time borrowed from family duties is misspent, the care of Childrens education, observing a Husbands commands, assisting the sick releeving the poore, and being serviceable to our friends, these are of sufficient weight to employ the most improved capacities amongst us and if sometimes it happens by accident that one of a thousand aspires a litle higher, her fate commonly exposes her to wonder, but adds litle of esteeme, the distaff will defend as well as the sword, and the needle is as instructive as the penne.[62]

[marginal note: echoing Fordhall gill.]

Evelyn's infant daughters, reaching an age where their education demanded her services (they were seven, five and three years old at this time), may well have prompted this reversal in policy. Evelyn herself was in her late thirties. Increasingly she had commented on her limited time for reading and writing: 'but you will excuse If I judge so unrefinedly, who have the care of piggs, stilling, cakes, salves, sweet-meats, and such usfull things.'[63]

However, Evelyn's finale suggests a more fundamental re-evaluation. Despite having made the letter her particular forte, she perversely claimed that 'the needle is as instructive as the penne.'[64] Of course, Evelyn was perfectly capable of using the rhetorical force of commonly held views on gender roles to explain her decision and these statements may not represent her whole thinking on the subject. Nevertheless, it was on the basis of domestic responsibility that Evelyn chose to anchor her withdrawal from intellectual letter-writing.

When Bohun finally responded to this upsetting termination of their intellectual exchange, he perceptively touched on this central discord. Bohun referred to the delay in his reply and assumed that Evelyn would understand his motivation: 'I suppose you know my resolution, & may divine ye cause why I did not [write sooner].'[65] Bohun apologised for having teased her about her household duties, but harked back to a time 'before children & stilhouses were so much in y^r thoughts.'[66] He realised that Evelyn wanted to 'be acknowledgd by all to be ye best wife, & daughter, ye most constant friend, ye kindest mistress to her domestic servants.'[67] Bohun employed familiar tactics, praising Mary Evelyn's astonishing abilities at juggling all her different roles, and performing each with equal conscientiousness. He insisted that, despite the perceived conflict of the competing demands on her attention, Mary Evelyn's intellect was not merely an adjunct to her person but an innate quality, with all the significance that implied: 'And tho all ye rest of ye shining perfections of her conversation or pen, may vanish into good-huswifery and ye management of Nursery affairs, yet this must still be inseparable from her.'[68] It was not clear whether Evelyn conceded this point, as she did not return to the subject again in her letters to Bohun.

There were two threads to Mary Evelyn's argument for turning her efforts away from her intellectual life. One was that as a woman she was unsuited to (and would be unappreciated by) the male academic arena. And secondly, her primary (and most time-consuming) responsibilities lay at home with her household and children. Anecdotally, it was the latter commitment that made the greater impression in the letters. Even in the early years Evelyn had expressed frustration with her lack of news to report: 'It is not an easy thing to spinne out a long letter without learning, businesse or intrigue, all which I pretend not to; either there is somthing so indifferent, and insignificant in my life, or at least things are so in my esteeme, that I know not which accident most worthy to be comunicated.'[69] Then towards the early 1670s her schedule appeared to get busier, causing her problems in reserving time for writing. She wrote to Ralph Bohun excusing herself:

> Do not impute my silence to neglect; had you seene me these tenne days continually entertaining persons of difficult humor, Age and sence, not only at meales, an afternoone, or the time of a civill visit, but from morning till night, you would be assured it was impossible for me to finish these few lines sooner, so often have I sett pen to paper, and ben taken off againe.[70]

Even her husband was impressed by the level of domestic work she had undertaken, and commented on it in his correspondence with Samuel Pepys: 'Never was any matron more buisy than my wife, disposing of our plaine country furniture ... She has a dairy and distaffs for *lac, linum, et lanam,*[71] and is become a very Sabine.'[72] In fact, the specific objection to women's involvement in intellectual life only appeared once, in her statement of intent to Bohun. Elsewhere in her letter-writing Evelyn had been critical of the manner in which one female intellect, the Duchess of Newcastle, engaged with intellectual life, but she had not quarrelled with the premise that women could aspire to a life of the mind. Although Evelyn never published, she did compose letters for an audience of the academic elite, so in a very real sense she herself participated in public intellectual life. It can be concluded, then, that the categorical statements issued in the milestone letter of 1674 did not represent the whole truth. Mary Evelyn was not a person who commented on life idly and her letters give the impression of being carefully drafted and the thoughts very heavily considered. However, this is not to say that Evelyn should have come to a final conclusion on her most personal dilemma. The question of female education, and women's pursuit of an intellectual life, caused heated and wide-ranging debate in her time. She was, ultimately, capable of choosing a course of action, and the letter to Ralph Bohun was the declaration of that decision. In her later years, it seems that, although Mary Evelyn remained someone with intellectual purpose, she resolutely constrained the means by which she might express this aptitude.[73] Evelyn continued with her private studies until her death in 1709, but ceased to express her ideas fully in letters to Ralph Bohun.

In Mary Evelyn's mid-life, the demands of home and family had proved time-consuming but, crucially, they had occupied an important position in her understanding of her role in life. The weight of this responsibility, it seems, had posed a serious challenge to Evelyn's sense of her intellectual self which, although never entirely defeated, was damaged by her decision of 1674. Mary Evelyn's attempts to occupy a role oscillating between the contemporary ideas (and ideals) of the masculine and feminine had failed. Nonetheless, she had found for a time some congenial male friends and she, in turn, had provided them with guidance, challenging discussion and support.

Female intellect, originality and the public domain

The examples so far discussed have demonstrated that women did participate in high-level learning even if they did not do so consistently through the lifecycle or often publish their work. But without the critical framework and broader public gaze brought by publication, how did women engage with the notion of original thought? As we have seen, Mary Evelyn was an accomplished critic of contemporary cultural production; the members of the Grey circle were firmly committed to a programme of self-education and were at ease with themselves as intellectually engaged women to the extent that issues concerning academic talent were usually dealt with humorously. But what did women think about the originality and innovation in their own thinking? The truth is it is difficult to say. Whilst Elizabeth Elstob was fully assured of the merit of her original research, most women letter-writers of this period steered away from categorical statements about the worth of their output. However, the comments women made about other women's intellectual merit can give an insight into the anxieties about promoting the value of private intellectual work in a more public domain.

Mary Evelyn, for all her ambivalence in relation to her own intellectual work, had a flair for criticism of the endeavours of others. In her letters to Bohun, the character of Margaret, Duchess of Newcastle (1623–73) received the most rounded condemnation of anyone. This letter was considered worth saving, because it was chosen for transcription into Evelyn's letter book. The letter entirely focused on the faults of this seventeenth-century celebrity and ridiculed her attempts to be taken seriously, academically and intellectually. Evelyn opened her letter by dubbing the Duchess of Newcastle 'the Mistresse both Universities court'.[74] The Duchess of Newcastle was a prolific writer, widely published at this time. In 1662 alone she had published *Orations*, *Plays*, *Sociable Letters* and *Philosophical Letters*. However, her phenomenal output did not escape criticism and she was also known for being a tireless self-publicist and seeker of fame.[75] She was dubbed 'Mad Madge' and scholars reassessing her contribution to intellectual life have had to work hard to undermine this image of Newcastle as a crank as opposed to a serious scholar. The topics upon which she wrote were wide ranging and her repertoire included poetry, plays, romantic fiction, autobiography, biography and philosophy and she is also credited with writing one of the earliest examples of science fiction: *The Description of a New World Called the Blazing World: and Other Writings* (1666).

Mary Evelyn's criticism of Newcastle seemed redoubled on account of her sex. Evelyn stressed her ostentatious ambition and narcissism: 'I was surprised to finde so much extravagancy and vanity in any person.'[76] She also extended her criticisms to encompass the duchess's attire and make-up, making her attempts to affect beauty and youth seem ludicrous: 'Her Habit particular, fantasticall, not unbecoming a good shape which she may truly boast off, her face discovers the facility of her sex in being yet perswaded it deserves the esteeme years forbid, by the infinite care she takes to place her curls and patches'.[77] Not only were the Duchess of Newcastle's appearance and mannerisms censured, but more substantially, her claim to fame: her intellect. This cultural target was a woman, who had published widely and participated confidently in a male-dominated field. In particular, she had dared to publish on 'Natural Philosophy', which as a science was considered a concretely male endeavour. At first glance, Mary Evelyn might have been expected to salute the duchess as a praiseworthy pioneer, but Evelyn's expressed conservatism in relation to airing her own work publicly affected her expectations of other women's endeavours. The anticipation of the vigorous criticism which women encountered, if they ventured into the public sphere of intellectual life, made Evelyn all the more cautious on behalf of ambitious women. As she commented about the Duchess of Newcastle, aspiring to greatness and publicly failing seemed infinitely worse for a woman than not having aspired at all: 'her discource ... is as Ayery empty whimsicall and rambling, as her Books, ayming at science difficulties and high thoughts, terminating commonly in nonsence Pathos and folly'.[78] Mary Evelyn described a social occasion at which she had the opportunity to witness the duchess 'Magnifiyng her owne generous actions statly buildings Noble Fortune, her Lords prodigious losses by the war, his power Valour witt' and complained that each time the duchess paused for breath there 'came in a fresh admirer' to sing her praises.[79] Evelyn went on to say: 'at last being weary I came out of my revery and concluded that the creature called a Chimera which I had hear off, was now to be seene, and that it was time to retire for feare of infection'.[80] This attempt to distance herself completely from the model of female intellectuality posed by the Duchess of Newcastle was striking. Evelyn further invoked the concept of 'originality', this time in a negative sense to further discredit her contemporary, saying: 'yet I hope as she is an Originall she may never have a Copie, never did I see a woman so full of her selfe, so amasingly vain and ambitious'.[81] This was a striking condemnation.

However, Mary Evelyn was not uniformly negative about the intellectual endeavours of women. To some extent it was the immodest mode of the Duchess of Newcastle's rise to fame that so little endeared her to Evelyn. Towards the end of her letter, she compared this kind of vain celebrity with someone she considered a real intellect: the poet Katherine Philips (1632–64).[82] Evelyn noted: 'what contrary miracles dos this Age produce This Lady and M[rs] Phelips, the one transporded [sic][83] with the shadow of reason the other possessed of the substance and insensible of her treasure, and yet men who passe for learned and wise not only put them both in equall balance.'[84] In these, Evelyn's concluding remarks, the core of the matter was revealed. It was the threat of harsh, public and predominantly hostile male judgement that Evelyn feared, despite her recognition of its faulty critique. Nevertheless, Evelyn's concerns over public reception of female intellectual talent did not prevent her from expressing candid, strongly worded and personal opinions in her letters to Ralph Bohun. Within these she focused on the content of the published work in order to assess intellectual validity, invoking the language of originality only in negative terms, to discredit someone who she saw as an ambitious eccentric, trespassing where she should not. An acute sense of the trap that public display could lay for women certainly complicated Mary Evelyn's view of herself as an intellectual and she crafted a careful image of quiet domestic retirement in her letter-writing in order to legitimise her incisive commentary. This was one strategy among many to deal with the difficulties of aspiring to the world of ideas from the context of life as a woman: be that as unmarried and financially dependent on paid employment or as a wife, mother and housewife.

The intellectual histories, told through letters, of the women discussed here illuminate a diffuse intellectual culture in England. It was one which allowed the intellectually marginalised to participate in the production and transmission of knowledge through epistolary networks. Where the pressures of life interfered with formal studies, high levels of female literacy combined with a growing availability of print media offered new possibilities. The world of ideas lay within reach. Earlier studies have already shown how the more informal social spaces of intellectual exploration in the burgeoning coffee-shop culture of later seventeenth-century London provided opportunities for men and a few daring women. Yet epistolary culture went much further still. It offered to all literate women as well as men a far more inclusive network of intellectual acquaintance. And it thereby opened doors to those physically and socially distant from the institutional and social centres of intellectual debate.

Notes

1 Dror Wahrman has offered a meta-analysis of identity in the long eighteenth century, whereby he tracks the gradual change over time from early modern corporate identity towards the individualised 'modern' self, see *The Making of the Modern Self: Identity and culture in eighteenth-century England* (London: Yale University Press, 2004).

2 U. Thiel, *The Early Modern Subject: Self-consciousness and personal identity from Descartes to Hume* (Oxford: Oxford University Press, 2011), p. 1.

3   R. Martin and J. Barresi, *Naturalization of the Soul: Self and personal identity in the eighteenth century* (London: Routledge, 2000), p. 11. See chapter 27 'Of Identity and Diversity' of Locke's *An Essay Concerning Human Understanding*, 14th edn (London, 1753), pp. 280–322 and especially sections nine and ten on 'Personal Identity' and 'Consciousness Makes Personal Identity'.

4   See P. Meyer Spacks, *Imagining a Self: Autobiography and novel in eighteenth-century England* (London: Harvard University Press, 1976), p. 25.

5   J. W. Scott, *Feminism and History* (Oxford: Oxford University, 1996), p. 31.

6   A. Smyth, *Autobiography in Early Modern England* (Cambridge: Cambridge University Press, 2010), pp. 5–6.

7   Kugler, *Errant Plagiary*.

8   Crangle, 'Epistolarity, Audience, Selfhood', p. 435.

9   BL, EP, Add. MS 78431: John Evelyn to Mary Evelyn, 16 Sept. 1648.

10 Harris, *Transformations of Love*, pp. 66–7.

11 BL, EP, Add. MS 78435, fo. 204: Ralph Bohun to Mary Evelyn, 16 Jan. 1673/4.

12 Harris, 'The Letterbooks of Mary Evelyn', pp. 202–15. Mary Evelyn's letter books are discussed more fully in Chapter 3, pp. 116–18.

13 BL, EP, Add. MS 78539: Mary Evelyn to Ralph Bohun, 21 May 1668.

14 Jean-Louis Guez de Balzac (1597–1654) published his *Lettres* in 1624.

15 See J. Stubbs, *John Donne: The reformed soul* (London: Viking, 2006).

16 BL, EP, Add. MS 78539: Mary Evelyn to Ralph Bohun, 21 May 1668.

17 T. Spratt, *The History of the Royal Society of London for the Improving of Natural Knowledge* (London, 1667). See also M. C. W. Hunter, *The Royal Society and Its Fellows, 1660–1700: The morphology of an early scientific institution* (Chalfont St Giles: British Society for the History of Science, 1982).

18 The Royal Society, founded in 1660, enjoyed the support of the restored monarchy, but with its new and experimental philosophy, the institution found itself challenged by the more traditional Aristotelian theories of religious academies.

19 BL, EP, Add. MS 78539: Mary Evelyn to Ralph Bohun, 3 Feb. 1668.

20 Harris, 'Living in the Neighbourhood of Science', pp. 198–217. See also L. Moessner, 'The Influence of the Royal Society on 17th-Century Scientific Writing', *International Computer Archive of Modern and Medieval English*, 33 (2009), pp. 65–87.

21 BL, EP, Add. MS 78539: Mary Evelyn to Ralph Bohun, 3 Feb. 1668.

22 BL, EP, Add. MS 78539: Mary Evelyn to Ralph Bohun, 21 May c. 1668.

23 See Harris, *Transformations of Love*, pp. 67–8. See also Pal, *Republic of Women*, pp. 4–5 on the difference between those seventeenth-century women intellectuals who worked alone, such as Margaret Cavendish, and those who worked in mutually supportive networks.

24 BLA, LP, L 30/9a/3, fos 89–90: Jemima Grey to Mary Grey and Catherine Talbot, 3 Oct. 1742 [modern transcript].

25 BLA, LP, L 30/9a/3, fo. 90: Jemima Grey to Mary Grey and Catherine Talbot, 3 Oct. 1742.

26 There is almost no mention of Elizabeth Elstob in the historical record from the time of her brother's death until 1735, when she begins to correspond with George Ballard.

The last of her letters to Ballard is dated 1753, two years before his death and three years before her own.

27 The original was published in French in 1671.

28 The translation was published in the same year that Elstob's Old English 'Athanasian Creed' was printed in William Wotton's *Conspectus breuis* – an abridged version of George Hickes's important work of Anglo-Saxon scholarship: *Thesaurus* (1703–5).

29 M. Gretsch, 'Elizabeth Elstob: A scholar's fight for Anglo-Saxon studies, part I', *Anglia*, 117:2 (1999), pp. 163–200 at p. 200.

30 Gretsch, 'Elizabeth Elstob, part I', pp. 166–9.

31 Gretsch, 'Elizabeth Elstob, part I', p. 200.

32 See T. Harmsen, 'George Hickes (1642–1715)', in *ODNB*; www.oxforddnb.com/view/article/13203.

33 N. Clarke, 'Elizabeth Elstob (1674–1752): England's first professional woman historian?', *Gender & History*, 17:1 (2005) pp. 210–20 at p. 217. Elstob's dates are incorrect in this article's title.

34 M. Gretsch, 'Elizabeth Elstob: A scholar's fight for Anglo-Saxon studies, part II', *Anglia*, 117:4 (1999), pp. 481–524, at p. 498.

35 Mechthild Gretsch suggests that Elstob's whereabouts must have been known to some of her former acquaintances because there is a reference to Humfrey Wanley sending five guineas to Elstob in 1719 as recompense for her transcript of *Textus Roffensis*, which she had presented to the Harleian Library in 1713.

36 For a fuller analysis of George Ballard's epistolary network, see Hannan, 'Collaborative Scholarship on the Margins', pp. 290–315.

37 Margaret Roper (1505–44) was the daughter of the Renaissance humanist, Thomas More, and a writer and translator in her own right.

38 Bodl., Ballard 43, fo. 25: Elizabeth Elstob to George Ballard, 15 June 1736.

39 Bodl., Ballard 43, fo. 38: Elizabeth Elstob to George Ballard, 8 April 1737.

40 Bodl., Ballard 43, fo. 38: Elizabeth Elstob to George Ballard, 8 April 1737.

41 Bodl., Ballard 43, fo. 31: Elizabeth Elstob to George Ballard, 24 Dec. 1736.

42 Bodl., Ballard 43, fo. 5: Elizabeth Elstob to George Ballard, 29 Aug. 1735.

43 Sarah Chapone (1699–1764) was an author and wife of a vicar who lived over the county border from Elstob in Gloucestershire. Chapone was a strenuous supporter of Elizabeth Elstob, writing persuasive letters to more influential women to help secure Elstob a more favourable position.

44 UNMSC, PP, PwE9: Ann Granville to Margaret Cavendish Bentinck, the Duchess of Portland, *c*. 1738.

45 UNMSC, PP, PwE9: Ann Granville to Margaret Cavendish Bentinck, *c*. 1738.

46 UNMSC, PP, PwE9: Ann Granville to Margaret Cavendish Bentinck, *c*. 1738.

47 UNMSC, PP, PwE8: Elizabeth Elstob to Margaret Cavendish Bentinck, the Duchess of Portland, 8 Nov. 1738.

48 UNMSC, PP, PwE8: Elizabeth Elstob to Margaret Cavendish Bentinck, 8 Nov. 1738.

49 BLA, LP, letter 2892: Catherine Talbot to Jemima Grey, 11 Oct. 1750 [modern transcript].

50 BLA, LP, letter 2892: Catherine Talbot to Jemima Grey, 11 Oct. 1750.

51 BLA, LP, L 30/9a/6, fos 40–41: Jemima Grey to Catherine Talbot, 11 May 1751.

52 BLA, LP, L 30/9a/6, fo. 102: Jemima Grey to Catherine Talbot, 28 Sept. 1752.

53 See Zuk, 'Talbot, Catherine'.

54 C. Talbot, *Reflections on the Seven Days of the Week* (London, 1770), which was a work of practical theology. It was published through the efforts of her friend Elizabeth Carter.

55 Mary had been born in 1665, Elizabeth in 1667 and Susanna, the youngest, in 1669.

56 This play, otherwise known as *The Conquest of Granada* (1670–1), was typical of the tragicomic Spanish intrigue plays of the period: see R. D. Hume, 'Diversity and Development in Restoration Comedy, 1660–79', *Eighteenth-Century Studies*, 5 (1972), pp. 365–97.

57 In the 1670s, the influential poet, literary critic and playwright, John Dryden (1631–1700), produced plays such as the Restoration comedies: *The Assignation* (1672) and *Marriage à la Mode* (1672), and a tragedy: *Amboyna* (1673).

58 BL, EP, Add. MS 78539: Mary Evelyn to Ralph Bohun, 27 Feb. 1671.

59 BL, EP, Add. MS 78539: Mary Evelyn to Ralph Bohun, 26 March 1672.

60 The reference was to the well-known figures of Julius Caesar and Pompey the Great, the politicians and military commanders in the late Roman Republic, who eventually vied for leadership of the entire Roman state: S. Sheppard, *Pharsalus 48 BC: Caesar and Pompey – clash of the titans* (Oxford: Osprey, 2006).

61 BL, EP, Add. MS 78539: Mary Evelyn to Ralph Bohun, 23 Nov. 1674.

62 BL, EP, Add. MS 78539: Mary Evelyn to Ralph Bohun, 4 Jan. 1673/4.

63 BL, EP, Add. MS 78539: Mary Evelyn to Ralph Bohun, 23 Nov. 1674.

64 BL, EP, Add. MS 78539: Mary Evelyn to Ralph Bohun, 4 Jan. 1673/4.

65 BL, EP, Add. MS 78435: Ralph Bohun to Mary Evelyn, 26 Jan. 1675/6. It appears that the letters between Evelyn and Bohun (stored in separate bundles under different shelf-marks) have been dated wrongly and that in fact the 26 January 1675/6 letter from Bohun was a direct reply to Evelyn's of 4 January 1673/4. There are further examples of letters that appear to match, but have been dated (subsequently) as different years.

66 BL, EP, Add. MS 78435: Ralph Bohun to Mary Evelyn, 26 Jan. 1675/6.

67 BL, EP, Add. MS 78435: Ralph Bohun to Mary Evelyn, 26 Jan. 1675/6.

68 BL, EP, Add. MS 78435: Ralph Bohun to Mary Evelyn, 26 Jan. 1675/6.

69 BL, EP, Add. MS 78539: Mary Evelyn to Ralph Bohun, 12 April 1668.

70 BL, EP, Add. MS 78539: Mary Evelyn to Ralph Bohun, 21 May 1668.

71 *Lac, linum, et lanum* meaning milk, linen and wool.

72 Sabines were an ancient people of central Italy, conquered and assimilated by the Romans in 290 BC. When Romulus founded Rome, he was said to have captured Sabine women to provide wives for the Roman population: John Evelyn, as quoted in G. de la Bédoyère (ed.), *Particular Friends: the correspondence of Samuel Pepys and John Evelyn* (Woodbridge: The Boydell Press, 1997), p. 271.

73 In later life Mary Evelyn corresponded regularly with two close female friends, Samuel Tuke's widow, Lady Mary, and Elizabeth Packer Geddes, but none of Evelyn's letters to these women survive, see Harris, 'The Letterbooks of Mary Evelyn', p. 214.

74 BL, EP, Add. MS 78539: Mary Evelyn to Ralph Bohun, c. 1667.

75 See Clucas, *A Princely Brave Woman*.

76 BL, EP, Add. MS 78539: Mary Evelyn to Ralph Bohun, *c*. 1667.

77 BL, EP, Add. MS 78539: Mary Evelyn to Ralph Bohun, *c*. 1667.

78 BL, EP, Add. MS 78539: Mary Evelyn to Ralph Bohun, *c*. 1667.

79 BL, EP, Add. MS 78539: Mary Evelyn to Ralph Bohun, *c*. 1667.

80 BL, EP, Add. MS 78539: Mary Evelyn to Ralph Bohun, *c*. 1667.

81 BL, EP, Add. MS 78539: Mary Evelyn to Ralph Bohun, *c*. 1667.

82 Discovered by Henry Vaughan, who dubbed her 'the matchless Orinda', in his *Olor Iscanus* (1651), Katherine Philips published two books in her lifetime: her *Poems* (1667) and Letters from Orinda to Poliarchus (1705) were published posthumously. Philips's poetry was considered to be refined and was compared favourably with the writings of her more controversial contemporary, Aphra Behn. On this, see P. Thomas, *Katherine Philips, 'Orinda'* (Cardiff: University of Wales Press, 1988).

83 The spelling 'transporded' is a variant of the word 'transported'.

84 BL, EP, Add. MS 78539, fo. 6: Mary Evelyn to Ralph Bohun, *c*. 1667.

PART II

Putting pen to paper

3

Writing and thinking

Letter-writing represented the most accessible form of written expression available to individuals during this period. Correspondence also provided crucial links between people who only met rarely in person. As a result, in many cases it is difficult to deduce whether women intended to use letter-writing to exercise their minds, or whether, conversely, the daily routine of corresponding provided a starting point for intellectual exploration. Either way, letter-writing represented a crucial space for female (and male) intellectual expression in this period.

Amongst the collections of letters explored in this book, there are many comments that refer directly to the link between letter-writing and exercising the mind. Women frequently used their letters as a forum to describe thwarted attempts to educate themselves and, ironically, the toll that dutiful letter-writing to relatives took on their freedom to write to preferred confidants. Anne Dormer, a seventeenth-century letter-writer of the upper gentry, sought refuge in her books so as 'to put some thoughts in my mind that looks reasonable to me' as she could 'hear nothing from my Ld that either entertaines or satisfies my mind'.[1] She wrote about this problem in letters to her sister. Sarah Cowper, a prolific diary-writer could have appreciated Dormer's complaint as she too felt trapped in an unhappy and frustrating marriage. Cowper was married to the lawyer William Cowper, and her social circle included eminent clergymen and influential wives of Whig politicians. Nevertheless, she complained that 'my very solitary being must ha' stupify'd me beyond hope of reviving' for lack of intelligent company.[2] Again, Cowper sought refuge from this intellectual isolation through epistolary contact with a close friend. It seems no accident that these feelings were expressed in letters.

In some cases, the prospects of self-expression offered by letter-writing proved a catalyst for intellectual exploration. Letter-writing started in childhood, as a tool in parents' strategies to educate and socialise their children. Once the childhood exercise had been converted into a lifelong epistolary habit, however, its scope broadened – laying open networks of acquaintance both geographically and socially distant from the correspondent. Here girls' experiences of childhood education through letter-writing will be explored in order to identify the origins of adult epistolary practice. This formative education through the 'conversation of the pen' informed adult relationships with letter-writing and the life of the mind.

The epistolary academy

Regardless of where a girl was educated, her parents' aspirations for her had an important influence on her opportunities to learn and the variety of subjects she might encounter. When a child was receiving an education away from home (formal or social), letters between parents and children were the main point of contact. These correspondences also helped younger children develop their literacy within a framework that trained them in an important social art. Anxious parents enquired after their children's progress, encouraged diligence and advised on how best to present themselves in the wider world. The letter of advice from parent to child is a common find, both in the archive and in print.[3] Indeed, letters such as those written in the 1750s by the Earl of Chesterfield to his son living in France 'on the Fine Art of becoming a Man of the World and a Gentleman' have been frequently cited as illuminating examples of the formative social education that elite parents gave to their offspring.[4] Children were expected to write often and their letters represented a hybrid: partly educational exercise in the adult skill of correspondence and partly genuine communiqué. The letters of Charles and Anne Petty, writing to their mother and aunt in the late seventeenth century, show the children ruling neat guidelines below and above their letters to keep the format of their missives in the expected order.[5] Parental letters of advice are also revealing as to early modern anxieties about politeness, prudence, education and duty. Mary Clarke, writing in 1690 to her absent husband reported the efforts of her precocious daughter, Betty, to persuade her father to buy her a watch:

> nothing would serve her but she would write to her Father by the very next post to desire him to by her one ... but we all perswaded her it would be to noe purpose for that he had soe many uses for his money that he would not doe it soe then she Considered she would write to you in French ... she pleased her selfe much with thiss piece of Craft but I tell her it will never take.[6]

When girls wrote to their parents they showed off the fruits of their education as an inducement to their parents' generosity. For example, the Collier daughters, when writing to their parents in Hastings in the 1730s, described their introduction into adult social life, which formed an important part of their education as young women. As the offspring of the local town clerk and practising solicitor, John Collier, the young women hoped to move in the polite social circles of the lower gentry and professional classes. Consistently, they described occasions when they had presented themselves well at a social gathering alongside requests for items of clothing that would allow them to move easily in that society. Their demonstration of learned social skills and accomplishments earned them the outward apparel of well-to-do adult social participants.

Children's letters home often followed learnt patterns. John Collier's letter to his father, written from school on 5 February 1730, exemplified this point:

Honoured Father
This is to let you know that I am in good health and hope you are Well I hear you will goe to London the Day after the Markett, and I hope you will bring my Books and Jemmy's Kings speech then, My Cold is Better than it was. Tell my Mamma I hope she'll come over to Battell [the village of Battle, near Hastings] Quickly, and My sister Molly too, M[rs] Thorpe and her Daughters Give their service to you and My Mamma, I Desire you to send me a Letter to let me know the News at Hasting, Tell my Mamma I desire her to send us some Hankerchiefs, I give my Duty to you and My Mamma and my Love to my sisters.
    I am your Dutiful Son
    John Collier[7]

Using the traditionally prescribed address: 'Honoured Father' and signing off his letter as: 'your Dutiful Son', John Collier's letter, a mere two sentences long, managed to well-wish, gave an update on his own health, requested some books, a speech and some handkerchiefs, showed an interest in his sisters, appropriately distributed the service of friends and reminded his family that he was, indeed, 'dutiful'.

Similarly, John's younger sister, Cordelia, wrote to her mother from school on 1 June 1735 and managed to achieve a similar coverage of dutiful remarks (Figure 6):

Hon[d] Madam
I send this to inquire after your health & my pappas hopeing this will find him safe at Hasting & to let you know I like school very well & will endeavour to improve my self as much as possible pray give my

love to my sister & tell her I Thought I should heard from her before now but expect a long letter from her very soon to make amends, miss Stevens are very obliging to me they joun in service to you & my papa, this with my Duty to him & your self & love to my sisters is all from
>   your Dutifull Daughter
>   Cordelia Collier[8]

Unusually, this letter did not include any requests for clothes or other goods but did show Cordelia Collier's attempts to situate herself in the adult world of correspondence. Despite having scant news to report Cordelia Collier wanted to establish a regular correspondence with her sister who still lived at home. This offer to keep in touch allowed an older sister to take on the role of educator, by engaging in letter-writing with younger siblings and encouraging their development as young people.

Cordelia's younger sister, Mary, maintained this practice, writing to her mother: 'pray tell my sister Jenny I receiv'd her letter & with a great deal of pleasure to see her write so well, & shall be very glad to hear from her often'.[9] Letters home were similarly used to indicate the improving skills of the letter-writer themselves. When Cordelia Collier wrote to her father on 14 October 1735, she had traced herself pencil lines by which to guide her handwriting and to ensure a more polished presentation.[10]

John Collier presumably looked upon his daughter's neat and polite epistle with pride and satisfaction that her education was bearing fruit.

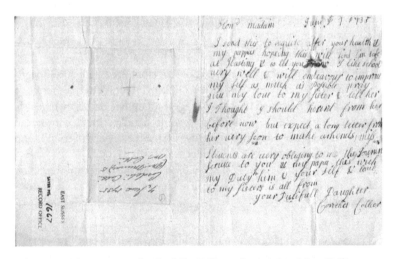

Figure 6: A letter written by Cordelia Collier to her mother, Mary Collier, on 1 June 1735. Courtesy of the Keep Archives, ESRO SAY 1667.

Cordelia was considered to be a precociously able child in the Collier family. However, parents also used letters to urge a higher standard of work from their offspring. When Frances Taylor's daughters, Frances and Dorothy, were staying outside London with their aunts in the spring and summer of 1774, she gave them instructions on the matter of their self-improvement by letter. For example, she wrote on 9 July: 'My Dear Dear Child I have received two little Letters & am sorry to say it, that I think you write worse than you did, but I allow something to hurry & inconveniency but putting a little i where you should put a great I, is entirely giddiness.'[11] In the same letter, Taylor enquired further about her daughter's studies in French, suggesting that she was not applying herself sufficiently:

> how does the French go on
> Your Cousin Betey I believe will get the start of you for she intends to learn when she gets back, if you don't apply to it now, its inexcusable, as you have nothing to do and have got your Books with you, I do assure you if I had known it I would not have sent them down, I cant find by your Cousins that you make any use of them.[12]

[handwritten margin note: anxiety about future – intellectual]

This comment also demonstrated that Frances Taylor expected her daughters to receive an education through the rigours of independent 'book learning' as well as with the guidance of teachers. Despite the apparent criticisms of her daughter's written skills and propensity to study, her letter-writing was whole-heartedly encouraged: 'we desire that you or your sister will write once a week, write every little thing that comes into your head, it will keep your hands in writing & it will give pleasure to your pappa & mamma.'[13] Elizabeth Petty (c. 1636–1708/10) – wife of the natural philosopher and administrator, William Petty – encouraged her children likewise: 'yu must always read yr Letters iust before yu answer ym, & yn you will be able to answer to every particuler.'[14] Writing from the family home in Dublin to her husband's residence in Piccadilly, London, where the children were staying, she hoped to encourage them in this habit by suggesting that 'Mr Banworth take Care to biy yu good Inke Paper, Penns, & wax. & yn yu will take pleasure in writeing, I wld have yu tell me every thing yu hear, & wher yu goe, & who Comes to see yu, & wt Cloths yu have, & wt yr Bro: Harry does'.[15] Later the same month, she chided: 'yr Unkle & Aunt takes it ill yt yu doe not Mention ym in yr Letters, so does yr Brother, don't forget it for ye future.'[16] It seemed that the regular rebukes for not mentioning particular events or people in letters were even imitated by the young Anne Petty, who wrote a neat and polite letter to her aunt, Bridget Cadogan, but complained 'I would know how all my Cousen does, for you never spake of them me thinks if you spake of none elce you should of little Cousen Lopy'.[17] Alongside criticism, the Petty children did receive some positive encouragement about their epistolary style, their mother commenting: 'I Likt yr Last Letter very well becaus it gave me an acco[un]t. of many particulers.'[18]

The fact of writing letters, and gaining practice at doing so, appeared to be paramount. These mothers' statements reveal an emphasis on attaining the habit of writing letters over and above any need to communicate a particular message. An indication of the Taylors' privileged position in society was the implicit understanding that the cost of postage was an affordable and acceptable expense even for practice letters of little communicative value. Likewise, the Petty family encouraged a regular traffic of letters between their homes in Dublin and London, both to keep in touch with their children and also to educate them in this important social practice. These examples show correspondence was used as an explicitly educational exercise for girls and young women, and one that paved the way to adult competence in social life. Similar evidence is detectable in family correspondences across England. A small, stitched exercise book belonging to Henry Shirley of the Manor House at Brailsford in Derbyshire dedicated half its pages to practice letters in Latin, French and English, making clear the link between letter-writing and formative education.[19]

Amongst the extensive manuscript collection associated with vicar's wife Jane Johnson, of Olney in Buckinghamshire, are various letters to her children. Written in the 1750s, Johnson's correspondence with her young son encouraged him to improve his reading and demonstrated her use of the letter as a vehicle for her innovative teaching methods.[20] Most obvious was her strategy of splitting up longer words with hyphens, to help her child sound out the words he was reading: 'Pray give Ben-ny a kiss for me, & tell him I Love him Dear-ly be-cause he is a good Boy. I wish you all a very good jour-ney to Olney. My com-pli-ments wait on M[r] & M[rs] Ansell, & on all their Sons & Daughters'[21] (Figure 7). Johnson told her son that she was 'fearful you neglect your Book, & if you for-get how to read, it will give you a vast deal of trou-ble to learn again' and urged him 'be so good to your self as to read twice a day to pret-ty Miss Pruey.'[22] She also tried to instil a sense of competition and challenged him to exceed his family's expectations: 'Your Brother Wool-sey has read every word of the other side of this Letter very well, every body says they don't think you can read it half so well, but I hope they are mis-ta-ken, for I think Robert will never be such a Fool to let a little Boy out do him, a lit-tle Boy al-most two years & a half younger than your self.'[23] Johnson's letters revealed her calculated efforts to encourage her children to learn.

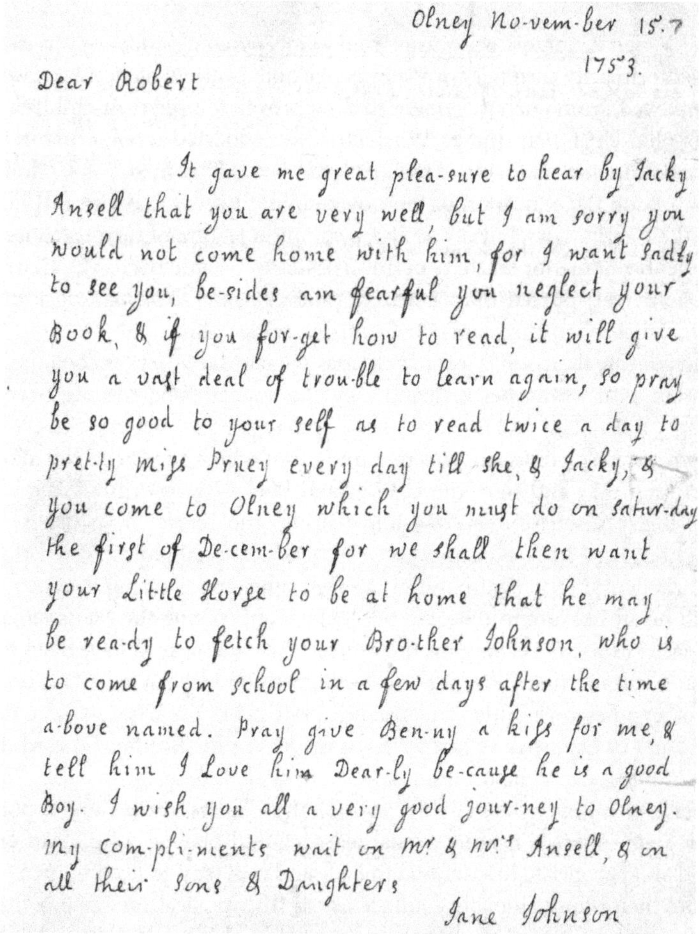

Olney No-vem-ber 15. 7

1753.

Dear Robert

It gave me great plea-sure to hear by Jacky Ansell that you are very well, but I am sorry you would not come home with him, for I want sadly to see you, be-sides am fearful you neglect your Book, & if you for-get how to read, it will give you a vast deal of trou-ble to learn a-gain, so pray be so good to your self as to read twice a day to pret-ty miss Pruey every day till she, & Jacky, & you come to Olney which you must do on Satur-day the first of De-cem-ber for we shall then want your Lit-tle Horse to be at home that he may be rea-dy to fetch your Bro-ther Johnson, who is to come from school in a few days after the time a-bove named. Pray give Ben-ny a kiss for me, & tell him I love him Dear-ly be-cause he is a good Boy. I wish you all a very good jour-ney to Olney. my com-pli-ments wait on mr & mrs Ansell, & on all their sons & Daughters

Jane Johnson

Figure 7: A letter written by Jane Johnson to her son, Robert Johnson, on 15 November 1753, courtesy of The Bodleian Libraries, The University of Oxford, MS Don c190 fo. 7r.

At this time Johnson had four living children,[24] including one daughter, the eldest, and three younger sons.[25] She included passages of verse for them to learn and she wrote, deliberately, in a clear handwriting to aid their comprehension. This level of thought put into the educational pro-cess was unusual but, in effect, Johnson merely elaborated upon parents' widespread and habitual use of the letter as an educational tool.

When daughters were away from home, parental influence was exercised primarily through correspondence and a variety of strategies were employed, from encouragement to disapproval, to urge their children to work harder at their studies. When girls were educated at home, naturally, a more direct monitoring of their progress was maintained. Some parents undertook the education of their own children (boys and girls), at least in their early years, but it was also a common feature of the professional or gentry home for teachers or governesses to be employed. The Clarkes of Somerset spurred John Locke to publish *Some Thoughts Concerning Education* when they consulted him for advice about how to bring up and educate their son.[26] John Locke was in fact Mary Clarke's cousin, and a man with whom her husband also had a strong and lifelong friendship.[27] Both Mary and Edward Clarke exchanged many letters with Locke from the 1680s onwards, several hundred of which survive to this day.[28] Between 1684 and 1691, the Clarkes and Locke engaged in a three-way epistolary discussion about child-rearing, the results of which were immortalised in Locke's famous work of educational philosophy.[29] Mary Clarke wrote to her husband on 22 December 1690, asking 'I hope you will be att Leasure to discorse Mr Locke Concerneing the Management of Jacke as to his Lerning for the future'.[30] There appear to have been two issues at stake, first: 'now hee Growes Bigger I find what a maid Can teach him signifies very Little'; and second: 'he teatches his Little sister to doe all sorts of Dangerouse boy Like trickes Just as his Brother Edward did his other 2 sisters before him, and she will venture as far to breake her neack with him as she is able'.[31] So for the Clarkes, there came a point for their sons when more casual learning and playing were at an end and an appropriate teacher had to be found, not least to keep them away from their impressionable younger sisters. The implication was that their daughters did not require such specialised teaching, but did need to be separated from their male siblings at this stage. The Clarkes already had a teacher in the house, 'Moun^{sr}', teaching their elder son, Edward. However, Mary Clarke's letters to her husband reveal that planning their children's future educations involved a broad range of considerations, from the subjects they might study to how best to develop them as social beings.

Although Clarke's letter outwardly asked her husband and their eminent friend, John Locke, what they thought best, her discussion of the subject shows her own preconceptions about educational scenarios. Initially, she suggested that Jack might join his older brother and learn some discipline and a methodological approach from their in-house French teacher:

If you and Mr Locke thinkes fitt I should think Moun^sr might begin a
Little with him to teatch him his French Letters and to read French and
by that meanes keap him up stayres with him and his Brother that he
might Larne to wolke a Little by rule and method and Grow aLittle in
feare of Moun^sr which I think Absolutely nesesary.[32]

However, she also pointed out the possible benefits of a school education
locally, 'to Larne Einglish or Else he will never Larne I thinke though he
is Capable Enough of that or any thinge Else that he will Give his mind
to'.[33] As Sara Mendelson has shown, whilst Clarke discussed child-rearing
with John Locke, she did not always follow his strictures, relying instead
on her own maternal experience as the best guide.[34] For the Clarke children, letters would feature as a tool in their learning of both French and
English, the former in terms of volumes of literary letters and the latter
in the practice of corresponding with family and friends. Mary Clarke
expressed her own concerns about her children's educations in erratically spelled letters to her husband, betraying the limited nature of her
own childhood education.[35] However, through these communiqués she
explained her determination for her own children to gain high levels of
written literacy and become socialised into the adult world of epistolary
communication.

When tracing the history of female engagement with intellectual life,
these examples of early training in the art of letter-writing are instructive. They point to the centrality of letter-writing as a social and didactic
tool in this period, but they also shed light on the many young women
who were encouraged to read, think and write in sophisticated ways,
often by their own mothers. For all the archival examples of adult women
intellectuals, there are a great number of childhood epistles showing the
seedbed for adult achievement. Of course, many girls must have tired
of their duties to correspondence and ploughed their more concerted
efforts into other activities, but these parent–child letters point towards
the ubiquity of epistolary aptitude amongst the middling sort, gentry and
aristocracy. They are also testimony to the socio-cultural significance of
letter-writing, a skill which was treated seriously by young practition-
ers and their parents anxious for them to meet the world with a flair for
letter-writing.

Address and formality

As we have seen, in order to approach the craft of letter-writing children
were taught appropriate forms of address that reflected the relative status
of the correspondents. These conventions framed letter-writing across

the lifecycle, visually topping and tailing the letter itself. But where did these formulations for address and signature leave women who wished to use correspondence as an outlet for more thoughtful exchange?

The most strictly prescribed aspect of letter-writing was the mode of address and subscription. Indeed, if historians took that evidence at face value, then it would be reasonable to conclude that there was a national obsession with status and appropriate address, especially as expressed in letter-writing. However, in real letters of this period, styles and addresses were used with much greater fluidity, and usage was open to debate. Nevertheless, these letters should be read with the understanding that the modern world's emphasis on individuality as a prerequisite for meaningful self-expression or intimate exchange is anachronistic. Seventeenth- and eighteenth-century understandings of formality stand at odds with those of the twenty-first century and in an era that idealised 'polite' conversation as an edifying activity; the use of pre-planned or learnt phraseology was not necessarily viewed as a barrier to expressive letter-writing.

Some historians, with a socio-linguistic background, have quantitatively tackled the issue of address in early modern letter-writing. Using the *Corpus of Early English Correspondence*, Minna Nevala analysed seventeenth- and eighteenth-century letters and concluded: 'The influence of letter-writing manuals on the actual use of address remains uncertain.'[36] In terms of familiar letters, Nevala comments that 'individual preferences seem to have existed in direct address in letters between mutually close correspondents, like family members and friends'.[37] As has been discussed, if epistolary style could be learnt from books, then it might just as well be learnt from mothers, fathers, governesses and schoolmasters. In reality, letter-writers of this period treated the idea of epistolary best practice with considerable latitude.

To take a contemporary example, an exchange of letters between Yorkshire-based gentlewoman, Ann Worsley, and her brother, Thomas Robinson, written in the 1730s, reveals that, far from adhering to a strict stylistic framework, these correspondents openly discussed use of language in their letters. Ann Worsley regularly took the liberty of critiquing her brother's letters. Their correspondence exhibited lengthy discussion of words and language, as opposed to a slavish conformity to set conventions of expression. In one letter, dated 1737, Worsley decreed a ban on certain words which her brother seemed overfond of using, and revealed that whole letters were devoted to the discussion of the use of language: 'I am disappointed I havnt a Letter from you to day in return to one of mine about y^t Odious word respect, now I find I have a second of the same sort to prohibit which is duty, Oh frightfull formidable sound, ...

let me hear no more such words I beg.'[38] However, Worsley did not stop there; she poked fun at her brother's overblown writing style in general, saying, 'yt Line, I will raise her like a Meteor to ye skies, made me Laugh, was their ever anything more vain'.[39] Aside from the actual language used, Worsley's letters cautioned her brother against a marital match which she felt was unsuitable. The woman in question was often the subject of her brother's more grandiose statements, which redoubled Worsley's criticism of his choice of words. Her brother's use of language reflected his ill-chosen love affair, and as such had to be tempered: 'she that has been yr Aurora Borealis this five years and you only an itenerant Star, y^t has appeared so lately in this Hemisphere, the Curious indeed may with there Telescopes have discovered more than I.'[40] The issue of address and formality, and deviation from prescribed norms, was also discussed in the letters of Jemima Grey and her friends Mary Grey and Catherine Talbot. For example, when Jemima Grey married and moved away from her two friends, Mary Grey requested a return in their correspondence to the informality of their younger days. As Jemima Grey had inherited the title, Marchioness, Mary Grey had felt bound to address her as 'Lady' in their first exchange, but clearly felt uneasy with this formality:

> Will you allow me to lay aside that form in my letters which I will not allow my self out of them & permit me to forget all your Titels [sic] & adres my self to dear Jem: a wonderfull familiar stile surely to use to a Marchioness but the Friend will I hope excuse it to the Peeress. Why then not claim that protection, by invoking Her in the Name; why? because I am very odd perhaps; but it appears to me quite useless where; if the expressions are but tolerably just, every one will sufficiently shew it, without advertising it at the top of the Paper: You are so good you would have excused me perhaps without this long Defence, but I could not have excused my self.[41]

Here Mary Grey distinguished between paying the appropriate respect towards her titled friend and enjoying the familiarity of an informal address. She posed the idea that, whilst the marchioness and 'Jem' were one and the same, they were distinct facets, which could be separated for the sake of the continuation of a relaxed epistolary style. On 14 October 1742, Catherine Talbot echoed these sentiments, writing to Jemima Grey to confess her disappointment at her own reliance on dreary formal phrases:

> When You see Lady Mary tell her how sick I am of all the formal stupid Letters I write her, in answer to Most kind & Agreeable Ones, & let her attribute it to the impossibility of expressing what I most

strongly feel. Tis this impossibility abridges my Conclusion into the dull form of
  Faithfully Yours C. Talbot[42]

Similarly, for the Worsleys, the formalities of address proved a talking point. Ann Worsley wrote on 19 January 1739 to her sister-in-law, Frances Robinson, highlighting that a change in Robinson's status ought to trigger a change in address: 'my dear Sister (I must no longer call you Miss Fanny, or y[e] more familiar plain Fanny, since you are become a Mother)'.[43] In the event, no such change was made and the two women continued addressing one another as they had always done. In 1737, Worsley questioned common epistolary practice more generally when she wrote to her brother, Thomas Robinson. She called into question the ubiquitous practice in letters of sending people your 'respects'. She stated that it was the word 'respect' itself with which she felt most uncomfortable, explaining that when her husband had 'bid me return a great deal of yt respect you always send him, but I never could find a word to sute it, you must know them six Letters put together in yt manner, has always been my Aversion, it Conveys an Idea of Awe & distant regard yt takes off from Affection, friendship & familiarity'.[44] Sending respects to friends and relatives could be said to be the great continuity within the corpus of extant letters – certainly a mainstay of epistolary culture. Worsley's dislike of the word's sense of formality is striking because it suggests that she did see conventional forms as inhibiting the expression of real feeling. Not all correspondents tackled the conventions of letter-writing as directly as did Worsley, Grey or Talbot but there is other evidence of unconventional approaches to address and subversion of typical epistolary forms. For example, when writing to his sister Mary Collier, William Cranston took a whimsical approach to the tradition of giving service (or respects) at the end of letters. In a letter from 1731 describing his recent trip, he concluded:

> and now as I am got to the End of my Journey so likewise am I to that of my Letter excepting to that necessary part of it, Love and Service which I would have distributed in manner and form following that is to say, attempt of some part of the former your self, other part to my Brother Cranston, other to my Cosin Betty other to my Cosin Tarpe att Thorpe and the Remainder to the Children share and share alike as to service after having given a good Lump of it to M[r] Collier I leave it to you to portion out whats left & to give to whom you please provided it be not given to more than 100 people.[45]

So, although conventions were often followed in letter-writing, when correspondents were sufficiently familiar, or so inclined, unconventional forms of address or styles of writing were readily adopted. Traditional forms might even be satirised, increasing the intimacy of the exchange through colluding to abandon redundant convention. Identifying this variation is an obvious point to make, but it is an important one. The study of social codes of behaviour is popular amongst historians and there still exists a problematic juncture between the understanding of prescribed conventions and the much more fluid parameters of lived behaviour. Studies that try to compare, statistically, linguistic usage in advice literature and real correspondence are a helpful demonstration of the indirect mapping of these two spheres. They represent more of a partial overlap than a straightforward correlation. However, it stands to reason that commonly described epistolary rules were followed, bent or entirely disregarded by contemporary letter-writers, much as is the case for parking regulations or any number of other prescribed activities in life today.[46] Women's letters of this period demonstrate that prescribed norms were noted but then adapted freely – allowing highly 'unconventional' correspondences to take place.

Writing and thinking: the importance of correspondence

By providing a reason for women to pick up a pen, letter-writing had a significant role in women's experiences of a life of the mind. Whilst the reader was able to absorb other people's ideas, the process of writing involved a higher level of engagement with a subject. Letter-writing has often been compared with one-to-one conversation, but in reality expectations of the written word rise far above that of the spoken. Whilst letter-writers often emphasised parallels between their exchanged letters and real one-to-one conversation, distinctions were also made. By discussing the similarities and differences between conversing and letter-writing, correspondents were able to carefully negotiate the place of letter-writing in their relationships with others. For example, in October 1745, the poet, Judith Madan, warned her daughter, Maria, that letters did not take the place of good conversation: 'My dear adieu! I love your lett[rs] but dont write so much. I shall soon I hope be with you & then you may talk as much as you please I will insure yr Tongue but give me Leave to be carfull of Eyes.'[47] Likewise, when Elizabeth Denham wrote to her cousin in Hastings, Mary Collier, on 12 November 1739, Denham regretted that she had conversed with her relatives only through letters and not in person. Clearly she felt that the latter outweighed the former in terms of intimacy: 'I have been in expectation of hearing from [you] I sent you a letter from the sessions, and so did bettie but I cant omit this opportunity

because they seldom happen I always shall have a respec for my relations and wish it had been my fortune to have convert with them by
a nearer conversation.'[48] Here Denham demonstrated that she regarded
correspondence as a form of conversation, but one that was necessarily
more 'distant' than socialising in person. Like Elizabeth Denham, many
correspondents had no other choice but to write, as meeting in person
might be a rare event. In these circumstances openness was often encouraged on the page, as the participants attempted to recreate the intimacy
of first-person contact on paper. Alternatively, where letter-writers chose
their mode of communication, written communication was at times
favoured in order to state thoughts in a clear and more orderly way. When
the diarist Sarah Cowper hoped to get an important message across to
her son, she wrote it down. Unfortunately, as she commented below, even
the written word was open to misinterpretation:

> I cou'd not have imagin'd that when I said it was farr from me to insti-
> gate or approve the least undutyfull behaviour to me to y[r] father you
> cou'd wrest my meaning to those harsh terms ... I thought writing less
> liable to mistakes than discourse therefore chose that way to let you
> know my sentim[t] for the expression you seem to dislike I cannot but
> remember [remind] you 'twas your own.[49]

These examples demonstrated that seventeenth- and eighteenth-century
letter-writers gave careful consideration to the advantages and disadvan-
tages of speech versus the written word and, where possible, chose their
communicative medium accordingly. Although the limitations of conversing by pen and paper were recognised, many letter-writers exploited
the dynamics of correspondence to deepen the level of exchange they
could achieve with confidants.

The extent to which letter-writing acted more as catalyst or a forum
for discursive thought was, clearly, individualised. The importance of this
dynamic is exemplified by the fact that letter-writers themselves reflected
in depth on their relationships with correspondence as a written medium.
For example, writing in the 1680s, Oxfordshire gentlewoman Anne
Dormer used the letter as a space to express introspective thought, the
process of putting pen to paper allowed her to explore in detail thoughts
and feelings about her life.[50] Likewise, in a strongly spiritual context,
when Sarah Beck wrote to Ruth Follows on 4 June 1754, she allowed
her thoughts to develop in unexpected directions on the page. Follows
(1718–1808) was a Quaker minister of Castle Donington in Leicestershire
and the Follows family made their living in the rush-basket-making
trade.[51] As a minister, Follows attracted correspondence from a wide

send to Catie?

range of contacts principally on spiritual matters. Having embarked on a disquisition on her current relationship with God and the world at large, Sarah Beck ended her letter in a changed tone as she described how she 'found Satan every where where I have been lead my self ... I find him in ye most secret recesses of my heart'.[52] Beck explained to Follows at the end of her wandering, thoughtful and introspective letter:

> I did not think of writeing these things or had any thing to say when I took pen in hand but have been lead on beyond what I thought as thou may see by my paper I wish it may excite thee to make some return for I know no meaning it has but I want to hear from thee & how thou dost.[53]

The framework of Becks's and Follows's religious outlook was clearly fundamental to their epistolary friendship; however, this correspondence has much in common with others of intellectual intent. The purpose of the women's letter-writing was not merely to keep in touch, but to delve deeper into the details of their spiritual lives. The page was therefore a space in which ideas could be fully explored. For Becks and many other women of this period, the letter was a space for considered thoughts and the process of corresponding was integral to their experiences of intellectual exploration.

The content of letters

This book analyses correspondence for evidence of intellectual motivation and expression amongst women in the seventeenth and eighteenth centuries. However, there is no easy divide between letters of intellectual note and the rest. In many cases, women's letter-writing represented a complex mix of delivering news, requesting goods, discussing matters of household business, sending respects to relations, persuading others of their views and writing about ideas. Moreover, moments of creativity or the assertion of a considered opinion could be prompted by otherwise day-to-day activities. Of course, some letter-writers did engage consciously and concertedly in challenging correspondences with academically minded friends, but there was no dominant format for expressing intellectual activity.

In order to illustrate more clearly the different styles of intellectual letter-writing, a small sample of letters from three letter-writers, featuring prominently in this book, were analysed for their content. For each correspondent a series of topics was devised that encompassed the range exhibited in their letters. The range of categories had to be tailored to the style and scope of the individual letter-writer's correspondence. Then, selected letters were taken for each letter-writer, the contents categorised and the number of words spent on each topic calculated. Five letters written by each writer were chosen to show the distribution of these topics over several missives and over a period of time, in each case about a year.[54]

Mary Grey's letters to her friend Jemima Grey are analysed here, dating from 1740–41 when Jemima Grey had recently moved away to her marital home. Of the three friends, Mary Grey dedicated the smallest portion of her letters to strictly academic discussion, but did maintain a discourse with her friends on her reading and intellectual endeavours. Mary Grey was keen to maintain the intimacy of their friendship by relaying detailed descriptions of her daily life and this emphasis is evidenced in the percentage breakdown of topics in her letters, as shown in Table 1.

On average, across all five letters, she spent 11.24 per cent of her words on discussion of reading or academic exchange. Significantly, comment on friendship and emotional proximity out-stripped purely intellectual matters, averaging at 15.3 per cent which demonstrated Mary Grey's determination to keep her relationship with Jemima Grey alive and emotionally close. By far the largest amount of space was dedicated to descriptions of daily life and health (45.72 per cent), as Grey attempted to keep her friend present in her life despite physical distance. These letters only represent a short period of time in a lifelong friendship and correspondence, but nevertheless demonstrate how commentary on reading was haphazardly combined with other topics concerning daily lived existence.

The second analysis focused on five letters written by Anglo-Saxon scholar, Elizabeth Elstob, to her friend and intellectual companion, George Ballard. At the time these letters were written, Elstob was a village schoolmistress and her time was dominated by the duties of her work. However, it is immediately clear from this breakdown, shown in Table 2, that topics of intellectual note were strongly represented in these letters, dating from 1736–37. Discussion of books and other issues of mutual academic interest takes up 51.32 per cent of Elstob's words. After that, the next largest section was devoted to comment on their intellectual contacts, some of whom, Elstob hoped, might help her improve her life situation with alternative work or income. This primary preoccupation is confirmed in Letter 1, dated 9 May 1736, where Elstob spent 12.5 per cent of her letter commenting on her future prospects. Elstob's financial dependence on her work had rendered her unable to continue meaningfully with her scholarly research and publication and the possibility of effecting change in this arena was an important subject in her correspondence with Ballard.

Despite the strong emphasis on intellectual exchange in this correspondence, the breakdown shows that Elstob's letters also discussed daily life, work and her failing health and spent, on average, 11.64 per cent sending thanks, apologies or general well-wishing to her friend, Ballard. This analysis shows that letters meandered over different topics and cannot easily be denoted as exclusively intellectual or otherwise.

Finally, the letters of seventeenth-century correspondent, Mary Evelyn, were assessed for the distribution of topics (see Table 3). These letters were all written to her friend and son's tutor, Ralph Bohun, in 1667–68 and they represent a section of Evelyn's most consciously intellectual letter-writing. In Evelyn's case, a category had to be included for 'demonstration of epistolary style' because her letters showed the characteristic of using language cleverly to illustrate exceptional epistolary skill and fluency. These flourishes cannot be seen primarily to describe a subject of interest; instead they communicate Evelyn's polished writing style and affinity for the letter as a written form. In Letter 1, sent on 3 April 1667, a substantial 39.21 per cent of the letter was dedicated to prose of this kind. In general, daily life also made an impression on this intellectually motivated correspondence, taking up, on average, 26.69 per cent of the letters.

However, if discussion of ideas, reviews of cultural production, discussion of intellectual personalities and demonstration of exemplary epistolary style are taken together, Evelyn's letters show a narrow majority, in terms of letter inches, in favour of intellectual topics. Looking at Table 3, it is also clear that different letters took a particular focus, for example, a review of a recently published history was the main topic of the letter written on 3 February 1668, and consequently review of cultural production received a weighty 50.94 per cent coverage. Of the three example letter-writers, Evelyn spent the least time on thanks, apology and well-wishing, which occupy a negligible 3.36 per cent of her letters on average. This trend is indicative of the real purpose of Evelyn's correspondence with Bohun, which was concertedly intellectual. This aim was mutually understood and rendered polite niceties largely unnecessary. If other sections of Evelyn's correspondence were to be categorised in this way, then well-wishing would no doubt make a more prominent entry.

A comparative exercise in content analysis could be applied to different periods in these letter-writers' lives or, indeed, to different letter-writers entirely. But the general point emerges sufficiently clearly from these exemplars. The sheer variety of approach taken by three serious-minded women indicates the scope for individualised letter-writing styles used by women of this period. The qualitative analyses of letter-writing in this book indicate just that, and demonstrate why an inclusive attitude to women's intellectual engagement should be taken in order to gain a better understanding of seventeenth- and eighteenth-century women's mental lives as expressed in the diversified form and format of their familiar letters.

Letter-writing offered the chance to create the 'ideal', be that in friendship, love or intellectual exchange, but this goal had to be achieved through highly imperfect means. There has been much research and analysis into the motivations of diary-writers, journal-keepers and annotators of Bibles and sermons,[55] but none of these activities were potentially open to third-party interference in quite the same way as was the letter. Neither diaries nor journals were affected by the enforced gaps in communication that characterised correspondence; and such personal journals denied their authors an immediate and responsive audience. So, despite its potential vulnerability to outside influences, epistolary writing crucially offered the possibility of exchange.

The space offered by a letter to explore thoughts and ideas provided one inducement for individuals to write, but clearly correspondence offered more than that. Indeed, it was the potentially extensive networks of exchange possible through diligent letter-writing that must have provided the inducement for many women to put pen to paper.

Networks and contacts

Letter-writing networks were crucial to cultures of learning in this period and women were key beneficiaries of the broader range of contacts that could be cultivated by correspondence. Most women did not have a great deal of freedom to move independently about the country – treacherous rural roads, long journey times and family responsibilities kept individuals close to home. Schedules of sociable visits tended to be locally based or seasonal; this naturally placed limitations on the degree of face-to-face contact women had with acquaintances outside their immediate vicinity. Moreover, correspondence could open the door to friendships between people who were very unlikely to meet through their usual social circles, and letter-writing offered opportunities to deepen relationships with people who met in person infrequently.

There does remain a question, however, over how much freedom women had to form epistolary relationships with distant others. Letter-writing may have been a legitimate domestic activity, but in this guise it was intended to service the needs of the household and a very particular range of social and familial connections. Aside from the difficulty of recreating the entirety of an individual's correspondence network, the ten key examples of women letter-writers discussed in this book are too few to be able to characterise the demographics of women's contacts in this era.[56] Nonetheless, taken together, they can give a sense of the differences that existed in the way that women cultivated epistolary relationships. For example, Mary Evelyn's central intellectual conversation took place with a man who was not a relation – her son's tutor, Ralph Bohun. This correspondence, as it did not confine itself to the particulars of Jack Evelyn's education, was unconventional by the commonly held standards of propriety in the late seventeenth century. Evelyn also fostered close epistolary relationships with two other men, both distant relations – but, again, the subject matter of these letters ranged far beyond that of correspondence designed to maintain good relations with the extended family. Elizabeth Elstob is the only other example of a woman who primarily wrote to a man outside her family circle, George Ballard in her case. This is an interesting relationship because it sprang purely from shared intellectual interests and it did not fit with contemporary ideas about conversation between the sexes and across barriers of social status. Mary Clarke's letters reveal an important exchange with her husband within a context that allowed for discourse with her distant cousin, John Locke. Clarke may well have sustained intellectually stimulating correspondences with women, but in her surviving corpus, these letters to male relations are her most significant. Ann and Eliza Worsley both wrote their most intense letters to near relations, male and female. Jane Johnson and Anne Dormer also relied on close female relations and the Grey circle, more anomalously, represented a female network of exchange contextualised by broad-ranging, cross-gender epistolary and social networks that facilitated their intellectual interests. Amongst the key correspondences sustained by these women, some were augmented by regular opportunities to meet, some replaced these opportunities and sustained relationships across long periods of separation, and several had to act as a complete substitute for personal contact. Looking in detail at the nature of these relationships suggests that women did not always conform to patterns of acquaintance and exchange that were fully socially sanctioned and, instead, could often find ways of connecting with others to meet more personal needs.[57]

Surviving evidence of the extensive epistolary networks cultivated by individual letter-writers is relatively rare. Even the most avid correspondents leave the historical record more often with isolated pockets of extant letters which can offer only a glimpse of the extensive connections their letter-writing initiated and maintained over their lifetimes. Where they do exist in some substantial quantity, much can be learned about the range of epistolary approaches letter-writers employed, depending on who they wrote to, when and why. In order to explore correspondence networks, Mary Evelyn's diverse surviving letter collection can be examined. Within the bundles of letters that were sent and read by their recipients are two stitched exercise books of copies. Most are in Mary Evelyn's hand and others are written in the handwriting of her grandchild, Mary. The letters Evelyn chose to copy and save in these books are enlightening in terms of the value Evelyn herself placed on certain epistles over others. The copies made by her granddaughter – several of which duplicate copies made first by Evelyn – speak to the extensive epistolary training of young women in this era – a training that referenced family correspondence collections to convey principles of best practice.

The Evelyn Papers as a whole represent a vast family archive including John Evelyn's famous diary,[58] account books, estate inventories and an expansive collection of family correspondence. Within this there are ten volumes of Mary Evelyn's collected correspondence, including letters to and from her correspondents, and her letter books composed of copies of selected letters which she had sent. By sampling this extensive collection through a combination of selection of recipient and type of letter, over 400 examples of Mary Evelyn's letters have been studied. This correspondence is mainly held in three volumes of her collected letters from family members and two volumes containing her letter books.[59] However, further letters have been sourced from the correspondence collections compiled by Mary Evelyn's father, her husband and also her long-term correspondent, Ralph Bohun,[60] in whose collection many of Mary Evelyn's original letters (as opposed to copies) can be found.[61]

Mary Evelyn maintained a wide range of long-term correspondences in her lifetime, requiring a versatile repertoire of letter-writing skills. Some letters display a studied proficiency at writing in the style of contemporary elite civility; others represent the discourse of an intimate friendship through which Mary Evelyn hoped her correspondent would 'learne more of my nature and the secretts of my heart'.[62] Evelyn also wrote short, functional letters to family members in order to keep in regular touch and organise the movement of packages of domestic goods and consumables. Evelyn's daily regime of corresponding was in part a performance of wifely and motherly duties and involved careful cultivation of familial relationships and parental influence. However, other sections of her correspondence reveal more intense epistolary relationships in which Evelyn pursued personal interests. Together this body of correspondence can be seen as a demonstration of the diverse strategies women used within their letter-writing, encouraging entirely different encounters with fellow correspondents depending on the circumstances of the contact.

As has been discussed in Chapter 2, Mary Evelyn conducted an intellectual correspondence with her friend, Ralph Bohun, but she also maintained close epistolary relationships with her relations, William Glanville and Samuel Tuke. All three men emphasised the importance of their friendship with Mary Evelyn in their letters, and made frequent reference to Evelyn's peculiarly diligent approach to making and maintaining her networks. Her particular 'steadiness and stability', or masculine traits, were often cited as reasons for her habit of keeping friends. Ralph Bohun remarked at length upon her particular talent in this direction:

> I must seriously admire your conduct in one circumstance of your life, wch shows a greater constancy then belongs to ye rest of yr sex, ... yt you were never weary of ye friendship you once made; & I have sometimes wonderd, how so many of them, & of so different inclinations could consist together, like ye images in ye phancy or memorie, wch tho they are so various, & contained in ye same subject, remain all distinct without disordering, or ye confusion of each other.[63]

This letter came to Mary Evelyn at a time when she was suffering from self-doubt about her conflicting roles in life and, by way of consolation, Bohun wrote to her reassuring her of the good friend she was to him and many others. However, he did identify Evelyn's especially careful administration of her networks of friends and relatives. Mary Evelyn was seen to be an adaptable person who worked at individual relationships and she used the letter as a key tool in this endeavour.

Details about Mary Evelyn's attitude to friendship are most often found in the written impressions of others but, occasionally, she did comment directly on this subject herself – especially in her letters to Bohun, Glanville and Tuke. She wrote to Samuel Tuke forgiving him for writing infrequently and expressing her strong wish 'for the continuation of soe desirable a friendship'.[64] However, despite her allegedly large network of friends, Mary Evelyn's assessment of her choices certainly suggested a thoughtful selectivity, if it stopped short of rigid criteria. She wrote on this subject to Bohun in 1668:

> Sr
> I allow my selfe as great a sceptic in friendship as you are in philosophy; for after all the search I have made how to place it worthily, I find new

doubts arise and allmost an impossibility to determine where to fix it, but yet I encline to favour some sorts of merit more than others, either for want of true dicernment, or compassion to humane frailty.[65]

Despite these doubts, Evelyn maintained a broad and varied network of social acquaintance, which encompassed carefully composed letters to dignitaries in court circles, swiftly penned pages to immediate family, letters that were copied out in stitched books to be kept and those that were sent in larger packages accompanying the traffic of domestic goods.

The largest component of Mary Evelyn's archive is correspondence with immediate members of the Browne and Evelyn families. At first glance, some interesting disparities emerge. For example, the collection of correspondence from Evelyn's son, Jack, was predominantly presented on large, fine paper and care was clearly taken over layout and handwriting. By contrast, the substantial number of letters from Evelyn's daughter, Susanna, were far more modest offerings, exclusively on small sheets of paper (some bordering on tiny) and with the perfunctory appearance of regular conversational correspondence.

The most consistent members of Mary Evelyn's network of close familiar correspondents were her immediate family; of which her husband, her children, Jack, Susanna and Mary, and her father, Richard Browne, were best represented in the archive. These frequent missives represent the close bond that remained during periods of separation between Evelyn and her family. Her letters to her daughters were frequent and they consistently touched on the subjects of marriage, health, the mending, buying or sending of items of dress, and the forthcoming schedule for visiting friends and family. In particular, her letters to Mary (who died of smallpox as a young woman) were insistent about measures to safeguard good health. It is significant, however, that no examples of Evelyn's letters to her daughters were worthy of inclusion in her letter books. In contrast, several copies were made and kept of particularly pertinent letters to her son, Jack. This pattern was indicative of Evelyn's tendency to save her most erudite comments for her male correspondents. In Evelyn's letter books, there are many more copies of letters written to men than to women, suggesting that Evelyn prized these compositions most highly and exercised her talent as a writer more strenuously in correspondences with men.

Mary Evelyn's extensive surviving correspondence gives an impression of how she cultivated and managed epistolary friendships. Her more intense letter-writing to male confidants provides evidence of where Evelyn derived support and encouragement for her intellectual endeavours. The collection as a whole is rich in examples of the way Mary Evelyn supported others through her dedicated letter-writing. Emotional support, the provision of news and the potential for meaningful exchange were all features of Evelyn's correspondence network but these features can also be traced in other women's letters of this period.

As we have seen, the Grey circle benefited from their place within a generally supportive network of intellectually motivated men and women. Their formative years were influenced by the Reverend Thomas Secker, who had made sure his charge, Catherine Talbot, received an advanced education, one that would mark the aspirations of her adult life. Both Mary Grey and Jemima Campbell made marriages to intellectual men who were sympathetic to their wives' self-development. There is no doubt that being situated within such a network of like-minded people improved the chances of intellectual exploration over the lifecycle. However, the loss of such a supportive context could deal an extremely negative blow.

The unfortunate life events of Elizabeth Elstob's thirty-first year provide ample evidence of the debilitating result of the loss of a supportive network for intellectual endeavour. Elstob was quite literally isolated by her changed circumstances and physically separated from the primary sources and people who might help her regain a footing in the academic world. As she said herself, it was hard to locate relevant reading material for serious study: 'Antiquaries in these parts are so scarce that I cannot hear of one of whom I can borrow it [a key text] unless you have it yourself.'[66] Nevertheless, it was George Ballard's epistolary networks that gave Elstob renewed hope of a change in her circumstances in her fifties. Despite the fact that she did not fully realise this ambition, Elstob's access to like-minded others, such as Ballard and Sarah Chapone, gave her real comfort and an outlet for discussion of intellectual topics if not the opportunity to continue her research. Although Elstob's is a sobering tale of intellectual talent wasted, her example demonstrates the critical importance of contacts and networks in women's pursuit of the life of the mind – networks which provided access to source material for research and contacts that could support the development of intellectual thought.

Conclusion

Through an examination of the ways in which letter-writers learned to correspond and negotiated matters of epistolary convention, it is clear that letter-writing was a highly adaptable tool in the hands of the creative correspondent. More than that, letter-writing was a habitual practice, critical to communication across distance, and as such it conditioned the relationships it facilitated. Looking at letter-writing through the individual missive and the collective network provides an insight into the way correspondence both differentiated and converged an incredible kaleidoscope of purpose. Within one letter-writer's repertoire lay short, perfunctory communiqués, long, complex discussions and systems of preference that saved or copied some letters and not others. Whilst dividing up individual letters by content misses the point of the whole, it does clearly illustrate the way disparate topics and styles collided within the space of one piece of paper. This exercise also suggests the very distinct patterns at work amongst different letter-writers – a matter of style which had ramifications for the expression of thought. Chapter 4 will bring the parlour fireside, closet and bureau into the foreground and examine the role of space and place in the life of the woman thinker.

Notes

1   BL, TP, Add. MS 72516, fo. 201: Anne Dormer to Elizabeth Trumbull, 28 Jan. 1688/89.
2   HALS, CP, D/EP F24: Sarah Cowper to 'Honr^d Mad^m', 23 Sept. 1700.
3   See Clare Brant's discussion of 'Writing as a Parent', in *Eighteenth-Century Letters*, pp. 60–92.
4   See www.gutenberg.org/files/3361/3361-h/3361-h.htm; date accessed: 28 May 2015.
5   BL, PtP, Add. MS 72857, fos 1, 19.
6   SARO, SEP, DD\SF/7/1/31, fo. 13: Mary Clarke to Edward Clarke, 14 Oct. 1690.
7   ESRO, SP, Say/1555: John Collier to John Collier, 5 Feb. 1730.
8   ESRO, SP, Say/1667: Cordelia Collier to Mary Collier, 1 June 1735.
9   ESRO, SP, Say/1761: Mary Collier to Mary Collier, 6 Oct. 1741.
10 ESRO, SP, Say/1674: Cordelia Collier to John Collier, 14 Oct. 1735.
11 Bodl., ColP, MS Eng letter c 142, fo. 32: Frances Taylor to Dorothy Taylor, 9 July 1774.
12 Bodl., ColP, MS Eng letter c 142, fo. 32: Frances Taylor to Dorothy Taylor, 9 July 1774.
13 Bodl., ColP, MS Eng letter c 142, fo. 33: Frances Taylor to Dorothy Taylor, 13 July 1773.
14 BL, PtP, Add. MS 72857, fo. 3: Elizabeth Petty to Harry and Anne Petty, 24 Jan. 1684/5.
15 BL, PtP, Add. MS 72857, fos 3–3v: Elizabeth Petty to Harry and Anne Petty, 24 Jan. 1684/5.
16 BL, PtP, Add. MS 72857, fo. 5v: Elizabeth Petty to Harry and Anne Petty, 31 Jan. 1684/5.
17 BL, PtP, Add. MS 72857, fo. 19: Anne Petty to Bridget Cadogan, c. 1685.
18 BL, PtP, Add. MS 72857, fo. 7: Anne Petty to Bridget Cadogan, 14 Feb. 1684/5.
19 DRO, D5202/10/1, Henry Shirley's exercise book, c. 1705. See Whyman, *Pen and the People* for a more detailed analysis of childhood training through letter-writing.

20 Jane Johnson handmade a series of reading lessons for her children and these materials have since been praised for their 'quality and originality': see Arizpe and Styles, *Reading Lessons*, pp. 69–96, and Whyman, 'Epistolary Literacy', pp. 592–3.

21 Bodl., MS Don c 190, fo. 7: Jane Johnson to Robert Johnson, 15 Nov. 1753.

22 Bodl., MS Don c 190, fo. 7: Jane Johnson to Robert Johnson, 15 Nov. 1753.

23 Bodl., MS Don c 190, fo. 7: Jane Johnson to Robert Johnson, 15 Nov. 1753.

24 One son, Frederick Augustus, born 1743, had died in childhood.

25 Barbara Johnson (1738–1824), George Woolsey Johnson (1740–1814), Robert Augustus Johnson (1745–99) and Charles Woolsey Johnson (1748–1828).

26 J. Locke, *Some Thoughts Concerning Education* (1693; revised edn. Oxford: Clarendon Press, 1989). See also S. F. Pickering, *John Locke and Children's Books in Eighteenth-Century England* (Knoxville: University of Tennessee Press, 1981).

27 J. R. Milton, 'Locke, John (1632–1704)', in *ODNB*; www.oxforddnb.com/view/article/16885; M. Goldie (ed.), *John Locke: Selected correspondence* (Oxford: Oxford University Press, 2002); A. Moseley, *John Locke* (London: Continuum, 2007).

28 See E. S. de Beer (ed.), *The Correspondence of John Locke*, 8 vols (Oxford: Clarendon Press, 1989).

29 S. H. Mendelson, 'Child-Rearing in Theory and Practice: The letters of John Locke and Mary Clarke', *Women's History Review*, 19:2 (2010), pp. 231–43, Locke, *Some Thoughts Concerning Education* and de Beer, *Correspondence of John Locke*. However, despite the fact that the letters themselves discussed the particulars of rearing the Clarkes' children, the published version was stripped of these references and presented Locke's voice alone in its exposition of educational theory.

30 SARO, SEP, DD\SF/7/1/31, fo. 21: Mary Clarke to Edward Clarke, 22 Dec. 1690.

31 SARO, SEP, DD\SF/7/1/31, fo. 21: Mary Clarke to Edward Clarke, 22 Dec. 1690.

32 SARO, SEP, DD\SF/7/1/31, fos 21–21v: Mary Clarke to Edward Clarke, 22 Dec. 1690.

33 SARO, SEP, DD\SF/7/1/31, fo. 21v: Mary Clarke to Edward Clarke, 22 Dec. 1690.

34 See Mendelson, 'Child-Rearing in Theory and Practice'.

35 Although spelling was not regulated in 1690, Mary Clarke's letters display an inconsistency in spelling. Most letter-writers discussed here have their own orthography, or system of spelling, which changes little over time, whereas Clarke's letters, dated only weeks apart, spell the same words differently.

36 M. Nevala, *Address in Early Modern English Correspondence: Its forms and socio-pragmatic functions* (Helsinki: Société Néophilologique, 2004), p. 254.

37 Nevala, *Address in Early Modern English*.

38 WYAS, NH 2822/17, Ann Worsley to Thomas Robinson, c. June 1737.

39 WYAS, NH 2822/17, Ann Worsley to Thomas Robinson, c. June 1737.

40 WYAS, NH 2822/17, Ann Worsley to Thomas Robinson, c. June 1737.

41 BLA, LP, L 30/9/53/2: Mary Grey to Jemima Grey, 11 Aug. 1740.

42 BLA, LP, Letter 447: Catherine Talbot to Jemima Grey, 14 Oct. 1742 [modern transcript].

43 WYAS, NH 2825/3: Ann Worsley to Frances Robinson, 19 Jan. 1739.

44 WYAS, NH 2822/22: Ann Worsley to Thomas Robinson, c. July 1737.

45 ESRO, SP, Say/1569: William Cranston to Mary Collier, c. 1731.

46 For a critique of historians' use of prescriptive literature, see J. Mechling, 'Advice to Historians on Advice to Mothers', *Journal of Social History*, 9 (autumn 1975), pp. 44–63; and P. J. Corfield, 'History and the Challenge of Gender History', *Rethinking History*, 1 (1997), p. 250.

47 Bodl., MP, MSS Eng d 286–7, fo. 4v: Judith Madan to Maria Cowper, 17 Oct. 1745.

48 ESRO, SP, Say/1740: Elizabeth Denham to Mary Collier, 12 Nov. 1739.

49 HALS, CP, D/EP F58: Sarah Cowper to William Cowper, *c.* 1706.

50 See BL, TP Add. MS 72516.

51 See G. Skidmore, 'Follows, Ruth (1718–1808)', in *ODNB*; www.oxforddnb.com/view/article/9797.

52 LSF, FP, Temp MSS 127/1/1: Sarah Beck to Ruth Follows, 4 June 1754.

53 LSF, FP, Temp MSS 127/1/1: Sarah Beck to Ruth Follows, 4 June 1754.

54 Tables 1, 2 and 3 illustrate the percentage breakdown by topic and letter (see Appendix).

55 See E. Findlay, 'Ralph Thoresby the Diarist: The late seventeenth century pious diary and its demise', *The Seventeenth Century*, 17 (2002) pp. 108–30; and S. H. Mendelson, 'Stuart Women's Diaries and Occasional Memoirs', in M. Prior (ed.), *Women in English Society, 1500–1800* (London: Methuen, 1985), pp. 136–57.

56 For mapping of epistolary networks see O'Neill, *The Opened Letter*.

57 Carol Pal, in her study of a seventeenth-century network of female scholars, notes that whilst these women's movement was more restricted than their male counterparts, their use of letter-writing to promote intellectual exchange was not, see *Republic of Women*, p. 16.

58 E. S. de Beer (ed.), *The Diary of John Evelyn*, 6 vols (Oxford: Clarendon Press, 1955).

59 BL, EP, Add. MS 78431, 78432, 78433, and the letter books: Add. MS 78438, 78439.

60 BL, EP, Add. MS 78539; the letters which Bohun received from Evelyn have been incorporated within the Evelyn Papers.

61 BL, EP, Add. MS 78221, 78300, 78539.

62 BL, EP, Add. MS 78438, fo. 15: Mary Evelyn to William Glanville, *c.* 1671. This is a copy of an original letter kept in Evelyn's letter book.

63 BL, EP, Add. MS 78435, fo. 212v: Ralph Bohun to Mary Evelyn, 26 Jan. 1675/6.

64 BL, EP, Add. MS 78439, fo. 5: Mary Evelyn to Samuel Tuke, first half of 1660s [copy].

65 BL, EP, Add. MS 78539: Mary Evelyn to Ralph Bohun, 14 April 1668.

66 Bodl., Ballard 43, fo. 5: Elizabeth Elstob to George Ballard, 29 Aug. 1735.

4

Spaces for writing

I n a period before women had equal educational opportunities, the home was an important arena for self-education. Women worked, in the home, in ways that were not confined to the rigours of household management: they spent time reading, thinking and writing. At the end of the seventeenth century, the philosopher Damaris Masham wrote in a letter to a friend a description of her closet and workspace, in which was scattered a jumble of 'Receits and Account Books with Antoninus's his Meditations, and Des Cartes Principles'.[1] Heavyweight philosophical texts lay next to the ephemera of domestic economy. In this brief comment there is clear evidence of how the domestic and the intellectual, alongside one another, could form a part of everyday life for women in this period. Female letter-writers testified to the importance of their environment in shaping their mental outlook and ability to pursue contemplative activities. Moreover, domestic space was experienced through time and the way that time was allotted mediated letter-writers' experiences of the life of the mind. In other words, a quiet closet with books was no use to a woman without the time to spend in that space. This chapter explores the early modern home as a site of female knowledge production by focusing on the way women won time for quiet study within that space. The discussion also considers the ways in which physical and mental spaces were interconnected.

The home as a site of learning

The early modern home has been overlooked as an important site of intellectual endeavour. Histories of Enlightenment culture, in particular, have focused on the activities that took place in institutions like the Royal Society and social spaces such as coffee houses that operated within the so-called 'public sphere' of eighteenth-century society.[2] A particularly rich contribution from Steven Shapin on the history of science – 'The House of Experiment in Seventeenth-Century England' – was published in 1988 and has not been substantially followed up by subsequent scholarship.[3] In terms of histories of letter-writing, Nichola Deane has usefully highlighted the practice of distinguishing private, familiar letters from 'literary' letter collections and in so doing diminishing the importance of the former.[4] Deane analyses the poet and novelist Charlotte Smith's familiar letters,[5] demonstrating the ways in which the domestic formed part of Smith's literary identity, and she points out that 'previous readers and critics' of Smith's domestic letter-writing 'have tended to overlook the importance of the material, equating domestic and "feminine" preoccupations with the trivial and nonliterary'.[6] By diminishing the importance of categories of writing designated as 'domestic', histories of intellectual life underestimate a vibrant space for early modern scholarship that, crucially, was open to both men and women.

Amongst the letters discussed here, there are hundreds of examples in which correspondents describe the spaces in which they sat and wrote. The home was no static backdrop to the action of domestic life. Instead, bedrooms, nurseries, kitchens, closets, drawing rooms, bustling thoroughfares and quiet firesides all formed a part of the psycho-social space of the household. Domestic space accommodated both public and private moments: social visits, quiet evenings, family gatherings, bouts of sickness, births, marriages and deaths. Letters made it clear that the home was the most important site for knowledge acquisition and production for women of this period, but also that domestic space was imbued with psychological meaning, shaping individuals' experiences of personal privacy, autonomy and well-being.

The home was often visualised within epistolary writing. Imagining a fellow correspondent accurately in the space which they inhabited was perceived as an aid to intimacy, while the absence of this mental image was deemed a sign of true separation. Mary Grey stressed that the more detailed the description which her absent friend could furnish, the greater mental intimacy could be achieved between them. She demanded: 'make me as present by the exactness of your account as I can possibly be at forty miles distance I beg you will tell me how you are disposed of in the House.'[7] Likewise, Eliza Worsley, of Hovingham Hall in North Yorkshire, writing to her sister Frances Robinson two years later in 1742, wrote emotively about her efforts to maintain closeness through physical separation: 'I have a lock of your hair in my hands about ten times in a day, besides your Whole image is wrote in great Capital Letters in my heart.'[8] To help her sister imagine her at home, she wrote a description of herself, writing letters by the fireside (Figure 8).

> Fie Miss Fanny: I do assure you my Dearest Fanny I never mis an opportunity that I have time to write, but I told you in my last how much I set by ye dineing room fire: I am fix't their till one A clock every day sumtimes by chance I get away half an hour sooner ... see I have not so much time as you imagine; so that if Hovingham be like the Town in Tripoly turn'd into stone you may know where to find me when you come over.[9]

This description was in part a defence of her diligence in corresponding – a habit which her sister did not share. However, it represented more than that. Worsley felt the intimacy of first-person contact was disappearing, through an irregular and unreliable correspondence with her absent sister. Without regular letters a conversation was difficult to maintain. Desperate not to lose their emotional proximity entirely, Worsley offered her sister a prospect of her life: personal, visual and quotidian.

As scenes of domestic space were readily illuminated in letters, so too were reading and writing an integral part of the domestic routine. The following lines were written by gentlewoman, Mary Orlebar, of Hinwick Hall in Bedforshire in 1751:

> I always would have breakfasted by nine,
> And thus would spend the time until I dine.
> For works in Church at publick prayr's would bow,
> From thence when ended, on some Friend I'd call,
> Or else for sake of health walk in the Mall.
> My walk or morning visits at an end,
> With books or working some more time would spend.
> [...]
> A chearful Evening t'would with pleasure spend:
> But if at Home from Company I'm free,
> At nine the Supper should on Table be:
> I'd read an hour or two, then go to rest,
> And sleep would banish busy cares my breast.[10]

Orlebar's poem bears the assertive title 'My Choice' and her description of a typical day included time for reading in the morning and in the evening, before bed. Orlebar's experience was typical for women of her class in this period. Similarly, on 8 July 1745 Jemima Grey, wrote to her cousin, Mary Grey, describing the usual structure of her day as punctuated by her chosen reading:

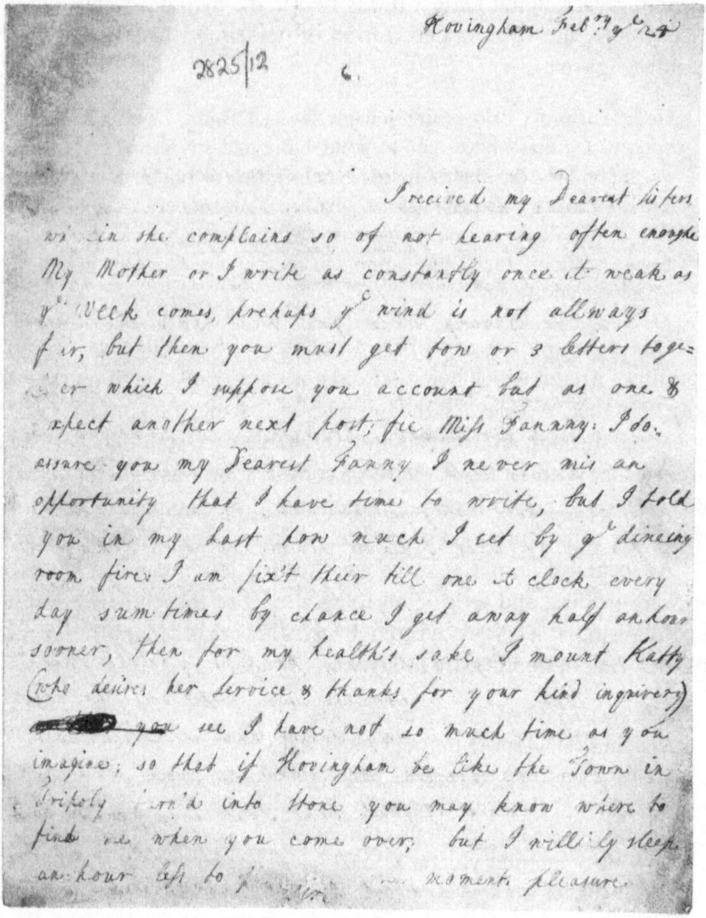

Figure 8: A letter written by Eliza Worsley and addressed to her sister, Frances Robinson, on 24 February 1749, courtesy of West Yorkshire Archive Service, Leeds, WYL5013/2825/12.

The rest of my Morning Occupations besides walking or sitting out if its fine, are writing dull Letters, breaking my Brains over Locke, or relieving them with the Harpsichord, & one or other of these employ me daily. I am reading nothing I think but Locke, for I can afford *that* but part of my Morning which carries it on very slowly; & our Afternoons are all spent as usual together. Billiards perhaps after Dinner, the Harpsichord where Mʳ Wray will only let me play Songs tho' neither he nor I can sing them, (why are you not here to supply that want!) or a bit of Work, Tea, & Walking till Night.[11]

Of all the letter-writers considered here, Jemima Grey was comparatively unhampered in her pursuit of time and space for her studies. When she wrote this letter, Grey was twenty-two years old and had been married to the studious Philip Yorke for five years. Wealthy and wedded to a man who had worked with their mutual friend, Catherine Talbot, on a fictitious work on ancient Greece,[12] Grey's domestic context proved favourable to her pursuit of the life of the mind.[13] But the home as a space of self-education was often contested and the household made demands on women's time that took them away from books and pen. The next section will explore two starkly different examples of female experiences of the life of the mind which make particular reference to the use of domestic space.

Spaces for reading and writing

References in women's letters to spaces within the home for reading and writing appear with striking regularity, but here we will turn to the letters of one Oxfordshire gentlewoman, Anne Dormer. In Dormer's correspondence the closet was described as a space in which it was possible to conduct more contemplative activities, but the importance of this space was amplified by a context of marital conflict. From her closet, Dormer (c. 1648–95) wrote letters to her sister, Elizabeth Trumbull (c. 1652–1704), describing a highly contested domestic environment – the result of Dormer's unhappy marriage to a man she regarded as oppressive. Vivid descriptions of Dormer's feelings about the spaces of the home come through in these letters. This correspondence now consists of forty extant letters from Dormer to her sister, spanning a period of six years (1685–91). Unfortunately none of Elizabeth Trumbull's returning correspondence appears to have survived. Anne and Elizabeth were daughters of Sir Charles Cotterell (1615–1701), a high-ranking courtier of King Charles II. Anne Cotterell married into the Royalist Dormer family, of Rousham House in Oxfordshire, and her sister, Elizabeth Cotterell, married William Trumbull in 1670 and lived abroad with her husband, first in Paris where he was envoy extraordinary to France and later in Constantinople during Trumbull's tenure as ambassador.[14] It was this circumstance of separation that led to a regular correspondence between the sisters during the late 1680s.

Anne Dormer's approach to her correspondence was, in large part, predicated by her unhappy marriage. Her frustration with her domestic

existence and the unfulfilling nature of her marital relationship both propelled her to write and provided the subject matter for her letters. On
marriage, in December 1668, Anne Dormer had become stepmother to a
ten-year-old stepson, Robert, and had subsequently given birth to eleven
children, eight of whom survived into adulthood. The letters describe
in detail her frustrations at sharing the home with her husband but also
delve into the invasive control that he exerted over her movement about
that space.

Through Dormer's epistolary narrative of domestic ill-harmony, the
space of refuge and privacy offered by the closet was illuminated for all
its psychological, as well as cerebral, significance.[15] In September *c.* 1687,
she described the solace she found in retreating to her books: 'I bless God
I find every day more pleasure, and more and more comfort in reading,
and see less and less pleasure in anything in this world.'[16] Over a year
later, books remained an important refuge for Dormer as her marriage
became increasingly embattled:

> then I gett a little release and run to my deare Book to put some
> thoughts in my mind that looks reasonable to me, for I can hear noth-
> ing from my Ld that either entertaines or satisfies my mind nor speake
> nothing that he doth not object against or find fault with, I have lived
> this winter I may almost say quite alone.[17]

For Dormer, intellectual fulfilment was a remote prospect, but books provided her with an escape and a salve for her peculiarly miserable home
life: 'when my soul is sad to death I run and play with the children after
I have prayed and almost read my eyes out.'[18] These surviving letters from
Dormer's correspondence centred on a period in her marriage when her
husband was spending most of his time at home. She noted the domestic
routines which her husband preferred, criticising what she viewed as his
idle behaviour: 'he spends his time as he used to do, loiters aboute, sometimes stues some prunes, sometimes makes chocolate, and this sumer
he is much taken with preserving.'[19] She described her closet as a 'safe
shelter', where she read and wrote in privacy, but complained that 'out of
it is little quiett because he whose life is idleness is seldom from home'.[20]

Anne Dormer's closet at Rousham House was probably a small ante-
chamber adjacent to the bedroom. Although the size and layout were
never described, Dormer mentioned more than once the lack of a fire
as a drawback: 'I had my choice either of my clossett which was too
cold in winter, or a fire [in another room] where I must loose my time,
I might warm myself but then I should neither heare speak or do anything to the purpose.'[21] The closet has often been described by historians

as a 'gendered' space available to women.[22] In this period, country house design routinely incorporated the use of smaller rooms, away from the noise of larger social spaces, specifically aimed at women who wished to retire to quieter or more private rooms.[23] During the seventeenth century, commemorative literature accompanying the funeral of an important woman routinely set the life story of the deceased against the backdrop of the domestic interior.[24] Within these commemorative texts, there were many references to closets, and, in the case of godly women, they were consistently described as places 'in which women read, prayed, meditated and conducted their devotions in private'.[25] Some closets were furnished, but others were 'little more than spaces through which there was no household traffic'.[26] As John Spurr has emphasised, living a devout existence was 'a widespread ideal' in this period and one that, if conducted properly, involved private and communal prayer, reading of the Bible and other religious works, careful scrutiny of personal conduct and the recording of spiritual development.[27] The closet occupied an important place within a culture that prioritised religious reading and private meditation. Anne Dormer's retreat to her closet for privacy, therefore, was in keeping with other accounts of women's use of this domestic space.

Other historical studies of Dormer's letters have dwelt on the themes of sisterly love and marital conflict in their analysis and Dormer's attachment to reading has not been emphasised.[28] This might be explained by the relative lack of detail provided by Dormer on the kinds of books that she read. The genre that Dormer names in her letters is exclusively religious (although, of course, she may have read other kinds of literature), but her frame of cultural reference was much more encompassing. Dormer mentioned reading religious writers such as Isaac Barrow:[29] 'oh the Divine Dr Barrow how much do I owe of my happyness to his most admirable sermons especiall those all her wayes are pleasantness and all her paths are peace and another he that walketh uprightly walketh truly.'[30] Moreover, she viewed this reading as a way of connecting with her absent sister who, she assumed, would also have a copy of Barrow's work close at hand: 'you have them I suppose, when you read them my deare heart think of me as I do of thee with more tenderness then is good for either of us at this distance to taulk of.'[31] Isaac Barrow's works were mainly published posthumously and it was John Tillotson, another religious writer and scholar read by Dormer, who was largely responsible for the publication of three volumes of his sermons between 1678 and 1680.[32] Barrow's intellectual energies had not been entirely focused on the theological; holding multiple university professorships, he had specialised in mathematics and astronomy amongst many other subjects.

John Tillotson was also a fellow of the Royal Society and close friend of the theologian and natural philosopher, John Wilkins. Dormer's reading on religious subjects, then, focused to some extent on a particular milieu of seventeenth-century clerics, theologians and Royal Society scholars – men who were engaged not only with religion, but also with the other great intellectual questions of their day.

Another writer who gained a mention in Dormer's letters was Bishop Jeremy Taylor.[33] In fact, Dormer reported her father's negative response to her reading his work: 'my fa:[ther] reproaches me for my scruples and cryes I am righteous over much and then wishes I had never read B[P] Taylor.'[34] Taylor, an Episcopalian who earned a reputation both for his early writing on religious toleration and for his large work of English casuistry, also wrote devotional works, which were the most popularly read of his works. In particular, his works *Holy Living* (1650) and *Holy Dying* (1651) offered the reader practical guidelines for living a Christian life.[35] Taylor's elegant use of language secured him a loyal readership, but his works also demanded a lot of the reader in terms of their personal commitment to pious life. Unsurprisingly, Taylor's works appealed to devout Anglicans but they also enjoyed longevity, being reprinted well into the nineteenth century.[36] In this case, it seems that Anne Dormer's will had been steeled by the exacting principles of Taylor's writings, much to the disappointment of her father.

Dormer expressed herself eloquently on the emotional, religious and educational importance of reading. On the one occasion she commented on her husband's reading, in a passage describing his last illness, her focus was again spiritual:

> two dayes before he was taken ill he read a sermon of D[r] Tillotsons[37] upon this Text while we are present in the body we are absent from the Lord, and when I came into the roome my deare said here methinks here is a pritty passage and so discoursed to me of what he had read, which I scarce ever knew him to before in his life; or so much as owne he had read when he did read, and methought since he died it was a little remarckable that he should read that sermon and fix upon the passage in it where it sayes that God Almighty concealed from Men the happyness of dying to make them contented to live.[38]

Dormer's reading of Jeremy Taylor's exacting guidelines for the pious Christian might have suggested to her that a death-bed repentance was inadequate, but John Tillotson's plainly worded sermons, no doubt, provided greater comfort.[39] Although these last two examples name texts with which Dormer was familiar, they also evidence the lack of encouragement she received from her family in relation to her bookish interests. Whilst her husband had never before his last moments discussed a book with Dormer, her father had concretely disapproved of her reading. In this unfavourable environment, it was no surprise that Anne Dormer viewed her engagement with reading, thinking and expressing her opinions as oppositional and unvalued.

Anne Dormer sought self-betterment through the reading of religious and devotional texts; she absorbed their meaning and applied their precepts to her daily life. In argument, she incorporated her understanding of Barrow, Taylor and Tillotson to bolster her defence – even to the annoyance of other family members.[40] However, she could not pursue a life of the mind unhampered, and reading ultimately became more of a refuge than a recreation. Although she expressed thoughtful and thought-provoking ideas in her letters to her sister, she lacked the meaningful exchange that would have brought more satisfying results for her mental life. Nevertheless, Dormer's relationship with the life of the mind is evident in these letters, however obstructed by her domestic and social environment, and she provides an important example of the seventeenth-century thinking woman.

Sixty years after Anne Dormer put pen to paper on the trials of her troubled domestic existence, the more fortunate Grey circle were in the full throes of intellectual exploration. They conducted this expansive self-education from the comfort of home. On marriage, Jemima Grey moved back to her childhood home, Wrest Park in Bedfordshire. As a married woman, she inhabited a different wing on the south side of this French-style mansion. Wrest Park was a grand manor house situated amongst early eighteenth-century style formal wooded walks, canals and gardens. Grey's first comments on returning to Wrest referred to her new closet:

> I am writing in the prettiest Closet in the World, ornamented so elegantly, looking so neat & cheerful, – so, – in short that I am fonder of it than I ever was of my old Friend on t'other side of the House: not to mention my Dressing room, which though the Closet is my greatest Attraction has its Merits too, & while your Two Pictures are there you can't doubt but I love it.[41]

This comparison of closets reveals that, as a child, Jemima Grey was given her own closet, indicative both of her elite upbringing and the size of the property. Grey went on to discuss the benefits of being on the sunnier side of the house, joking that the almost tropical temperatures might be sufficient to grow a pineapple:

Another Perfection they [the rooms] have which I don't know but some time or other may be very useful, & that is, – that I really am in doubt whether they would not raise a Pineapple. To be serious, this is their only Fault but it has not disturb'd me, & I am still glad I have chang'd though to get into the Heat, for some Things do not trouble One in some Places as they do in others, & the Sun is much more welcome at Rest than any where else.[42]

Whilst this personal room within the household was important on a day-to-day basis, quiet spaces for writing were also sought out when women were further from home. On a trip to London in 1741, Jemima Grey again detailed her reaction to the closet above other rooms in the residence in a letter to Catherine Talbot. In this case she had been faced with sharing the workspace with her friend:

I have taken Possession of the Lady's Closet, (which I may now again call Mine) & all her Papers & Books which strew the Floor, cover the Tea-Table & fill every other Table & Chair in the Room. So that after having committed great Devestations, displacing Drawers & laying out of the way many Curious Miscellanies, I have with some Difficulty found the Corner of a Table (which is at present cover'd with no less a Book than D[r] Middleton)[43] to write upon.[44]

Grey's description reinforces the concept of the closet as a functional space for intellectual and devotional activities. Far from being just a femininely decorated little room, the closet was packed with books, papers and miscellanies, partially housed in drawers or on the table, indicative of a room being daily used for reading, writing and thinking.

In the letters exchanged by the Grey circle during the 1740s, the surroundings which they inhabited, and the moods which those spaces encouraged, were regularly described. Large sections of the correspondence between these women survives today, spanning from their childhood and young womanhood until their deaths.[45] Throughout these years, the three women commented on the importance of their surroundings for the satisfactory accomplishment of scholarly activities. For example, Jemima Grey wrote gleefully to Mary Grey on 25 September 1745 about the beauty she found in her environment and the changes the seasons brought to her lifestyle: 'The Moon too us come again to make the Evenings more beautiful, but I have been a little disappointed lately to feel them too cold for staying out as late as I should like to do.'[46] As the nights drew in, Jemima Grey took overt pleasure in her reading, not only for the intellectual stimulus but also for the material and spatial comforts she enjoyed in so doing: 'However I have left the Garden more willingly that I might find the Library ready with Tea, Books, a Fire & Candles, & you can't imagine anything more cheerful than that Room, nor more comfortable than reading there the rest of the Evening.'[47] In seventeenth- and eighteenth-century England, extensive private libraries were becom- ing an increasingly common feature of the homes of the elite. Large numbers of books were also frequently to be found in the private col- lections of the middling sort, in particular clergymen. A study of private libraries in Surrey in this period highlighted the prevalence and diversity of these holdings.[48] Some of the larger libraries in the county included the impressive antiquarian collection amassed by John Maitland, first Duke of Lauderdale (1616–82), at Ham House in the 1670s, the Evelyn library at Wotton, near Guildford, which stood at nearly 5,500 volumes in the early 1680s, and the library of Speaker of the House of Commons, Arthur Onslow (1691–1763), who housed his collection of largely seventeenth- and eighteenth-century volumes at Clandon Park in Surrey.[49] Sometimes these libraries represented collections of the rare and wonderful, but more usually they provided a good range of contemporary literature, which was expected to be read by members of the household and their visitors.[50] Even amongst the more modest households of clerical families an ample supply of home reading could be found.[51] Jemima Grey, and her circle, certainly had access to the content of libraries of the more elite kind and, where necessary, books were passed between friends.

Whilst Jemima Grey revelled in her new-found space on a large coun- try estate, Mary Grey and Catherine Talbot continued to share accom- modation at Thomas Secker's residence at Cuddesden in Oxfordshire.[52] At times their proximity caused irritation, upon which Mary Grey pro- vided a running commentary. In a letter, dated 29 September 1740, she complained of Talbot's carelessness:

> Indeed I am very angry at Kate for she is rode out with the key of Her Bureau & so I cannot possibly get at a letter I began to my Dear Jem Yesterday & I have saunter'd away this morning in expectation of Her return rather than begin a new one w[ch] however I find my self reduced to after One OClock or else dissapoint you on Wednesday, in this poor impison'd letter I gave you an account of a journey my L[d] M[rs] Secker M[rs] Talbot & my self took on Friday to Oxford.[53]

Grey concluded her letter more abruptly than usual, with the excuse: 'I am so out of humour at having lost my first letter that I cannot make this a long one.'[54] The letter ended with a note from Talbot to say:

> After a ride of three hours & a half I am returned Dear Lady Grey just time enough to beg your pardon for having hinder'd You of a Longer

letter, tho' I assure You that that is locked up in my Bureau is not above half a page & You see I am making You what amends I can by adding this Postscript which at least will save You the disappointment on Opening Your letter of finding one Side blank paper.[55]

This anecdote shows that where a private closet was not available, writing desks were shared between women within the household, but that the contents could be kept under lock and key. Mary Grey and Catherine Talbot operated a jovial communality in regard to their correspondence with Jemima Grey in these first years of separation, their lives constituting a concert of shared experiences. However, the accident reported in this letter reveals that, whilst they read and wrote together, there was room for personal privacy in the drawers of a locked bureau. Although Mary Grey and Catherine Talbot enjoyed intellectual proximity through the exchange of ideas, personal privacy was still important for activities requiring deeper thought and concentration.[56]

Time and the domestic space

The regularity of the post, or access to a dependable carrier, alongside the demands of keeping a household, predicated the best times of the day for letter-writing. Women correspondents were highly knowledgeable about the times of the post and the likelihood of their addressees receiving a letter and having time to reply by the next post. However, the level and reliability of service varied widely, depending on where correspondents lived. As Susan Whyman has described, the British postal system was shaped by the twin forces of 'an evolving bureaucracy in a commercial society' and the demands placed on the service by 'a growing number of people who possessed epistolary literacy'.[57] By the late 1670s the General Letter Office, based in London, employed forty-three staff and 'Clerks of the Road' oversaw the carriage of post three times a week along six post roads.[58] Less frequent deliveries were made to other English destinations and across the channel to Europe. By 1711 the Post Office's service encompassed Scotland and the proliferation of cross roads in the eighteenth century sped up delivery times across the country, principally by avoiding detours through London.[59] Still, significant differences existed in the waiting time that could be expected between sending and receiving letters.

Letter-writers within London might expect an incredibly swift turn-around and many posts a day allowing for conversational correspondence. Those letter-writers living more remotely, however, might experience difficulties as post made its way slowly along post road, cross road and through the premises of various postmasters before reaching their hands. In 1737, Frances Robinson, who hailed from an important gentry family, based at Hovingham Hall near York, complained of just this problem in a letter to her husband: 'You will think me a strange creature for not writeing to you all this time but now that I am with my sister I cant get your letters tell the post after thay come to Hovingham wich is one reason that I wish myself att home.'[60] Fifteen years earlier, two young women were able to send and receive letters with much greater ease, owing to their location in or near to London. Sarah Cowper[61] and Anna Maria Mordaunt[62] saw each other regularly at social gatherings, plays and concerts but still wrote frequently, in intimate terms, and in letters that often included lines of verse. At this time Anna Maria Mordaunt was in the household of Princess Caroline (later Queen Caroline) as a maid of honour from 1724 to 1732 and would have spent her time variously at St James's Palace, Leicester House (on the location of Leicester Square, London), Richmond Lodge and Kensington Palace. Other royal palaces are mentioned in the letters, often in a loose code, such as, 'Versailles' for Hampton Court. Sarah Cowper's movements are less clear, but from the letters it seems she spent a significant portion of the year in London in easy reach of her friend Mordaunt. Cowper wrote often and valued Mordaunt's friendship very highly. Thus, when she was disappointed by the lack of a letter, she said so: 'Sunday July 11th: you don't deserve I shou'd write to you at all since y° have disapointed me this morning of a Letter I have heard of y° but twice ys week & would scold but that I shall be so happy as to have it in my power soon to do it in person.'[63] For these women, long waits between posts was not an issue and, instead, frequent contact could be expected. Thus, their letters represented just one facet of their shared social lives, but nevertheless an important one which heightened and confirmed their friendship.[64]

Whilst some of the key developments in postal history, such as the introduction of coaches or the penny post, would not take place for many decades, by the mid-eighteenth century letter-writers of all classes were able to communicate with friends and relatives across the country and many conducted long-term correspondences with loved ones abroad. However, the system itself shaped correspondents' relationships with others, determining times of writing and expectations of response. A good example of this can be found in the letters of Anne Conway (1631–79), a philosopher associated with the Cambridge Platonists and

in particular contact with Henry More.[65] Conway wrote letters to her
husband when they were apart, and in the opening lines of a missive
dated 22 October 1665, she demonstrated that the lazy correspondent was
easily discovered: 'I was disappointed in my expectation of hearing from
you by the carrier upon fryday, but I hope by the returne of this mes-
senger to be assured of yor health, & y^t nothing but urgency of businesse
made you loose y^t oppertunity of sending.'[66] Conway used information
gleaned from other friends and relatives to determine both her husband's
whereabouts and, consequently, the likelihood he would have the time to
write her a letter:

> My Dearest Deare,
> It was some dissatisfaction to me to hear nothing of you the last post
> but what I had from my Sister Rawdon & Miss Hill (who dined here yt
> day) especially, they both assuring me you were in Dublin, & not gone
> to the race wch before I supposed when I missed yor letter, however the
> knowledge of yor being well, though from other hands, was extreamly
> acceptable to me.[67]

Letter-writers like Anne Conway were highly attuned to the system and,
as these examples show, correspondents demonstrated both a firm grasp
of the limits and potentialities of the post and a strong emotional need
for epistolary contact.[68]

Free time as well as space was crucial to engaging with the life of
the mind. In the correspondence exchanged between Mary Grey, Jemima
Grey and Catherine Talbot, the rhythms of their daily existence were
often described in relation to the progress of their studies. In a letter dated 30 October 1744, Jemima Grey identified the times of the day
which were hers alone, in contrast to those that were necessarily of a
more public nature. 'In this last Week which we have passed very qui-
etly alone & sat every Evening mighty comfortably by the Library Fire,
I have dispatched Machiavel's – History[69] you may suppose not Politics;
& am going on to Guichardin's[70] which I find I must *devour* fast, being
a pretty thick fat Volume & a small Print or I shall not get through it.'[71]
Sometimes company intruded on her solitary studies, but since reading aloud to others was an established custom at this time, this could
become a shared activity: 'In the Summer I seem to myself to read nothing, our afternoons have been spent just as last Year, which you know
were all in Public. The Mornings I had partly alone but when Miss Yorke
was here, when they were employed in reading with her, Lucan,[72] some
Athenians again, & various other Books.'[73] Grey told her friend that 'my
Time of *devouring* (as you call it) is the long Evenings,'[74] in which she

'read the latter part of Echard's Roman History from the Cesars to the Destruction of the Byzantine Empire,[75] dull enough perhaps you may think, but I can't say so; it was better than I expected & new to me which is always a Pleasure'.[76] In August 1740, Mary Grey wrote describing the quieter days at Cuddesden, and the time which they allowed for contemplation: 'now I suppose your curiosity will be alittle [sic] raised to know how we employ our selves. ... thus we pass our Days in spite of solitude in no uncomfortable manner, & in such a one as affords some pleasure in reflection as well as in its practice'.[77] The Grey circle was engaging with a programme of reading that would have been considered learned by male standards of the day. Classics, such as Roman poet Lucan, featured alongside 'modern' classics of the likes of Machiavelli. Extensive histories, spiritual literature, philosophical works and contemporary fiction were all included in their schedule. The women of the Grey circle were, in the 1740s, comparatively privileged in terms of time and domestic responsibility. However, as we have seen, such relative freedom did not entirely remain the case throughout their life stages.

This mid-life picture of competing responsibilities and the ascendancy of the domestic routine strikingly matched the experiences of other letter-writers who have been discussed here. As we have seen, domestic responsibility was a key reason for Mary Evelyn's final retirement from intellectual exchange. This dramatic reversal of policy for the intellectually motivated Evelyn was particularly sudden, but the pressures of children and the upkeep of the home commonly distracted would-be learned women from quieter pursuits. For example, on 23 March 1699, gentlewoman Lady Elizabeth Isham wrote to her husband, Sir Justinian Isham, complaining of her inability to concentrate on her letter-writing: 'If I think of any thing else my next shall acquaint you for I am weary with writing as you may well be with reading and they [children] make such a Noise that I write my words twice over'.[78] Similarly, in the correspondence of Ann and Eliza Worsley with their sister-in-law/sister, Frances Robinson, the absent young woman's motherhood was used to explain her lack of time for writing letters. As Ann Worsley cattily remarked in a letter to her brother, Fanny's husband: 'you often complain of our not writeing but I wonder who has reason now, I have at least writ three for one, I wish my Dear fannys head was as fruitfull as her other parts, & she would never want something to say'.[79] Although, it should be noted, the Worsleys were not prepared to give up entirely their hopes of hearing from Frances Robinson, despite her new status as a mother.

Women letter-writers of this period described the conflict produced by different activities competing for their limited time. In the first half of the eighteenth century, Jane Johnson channelled her creative talents into the education of her children, but her role as teacher was not the only focus of her energies. Her letters to her aunt Rebecca Garth reveal a highly creative and thoughtful woman.[80] Johnson was also deeply religious and wrote to her aunt long, detailed epistles on subjects, such as God as father. She confessed 'Ever since I was a Girl, Reading the Scriptures has always been my favourite study'.[81] In a letter, dated 8 July 1742, Johnson wrote to Garth:

> What I propose then to be the subject of the following Letter is to consider God as set forth in scripture to be *our Father* not only by having created us out of Nothing, but also in the Natural, & mortal meaning of the Word that he even pitieth us as an Earthly Parent pitieth his own Children, because he knoweth whereof we are made, & remembers that we are but Dust.[82]

Johnson found that her drive to spend time reading and considering the scriptures was compromised by the pleasure she took in making things and indulging her creativity. She identified a conflict between the enjoyable tasks associated with motherhood and the weightier concerns of religious piety. In a letter to her aunt, Johnson wrote a story featuring a protagonist, 'Clarissa', who struggled to achieve the correct balance between moral existence and the joys of the material world.[83] 'Clarissa' represented Johnson herself, and the story was the medium she chose to confide her concerns to her friend. In her story, Clarissa is first described taking 'intoxicating pleasure ... in making Prizes, Flowers, Stomachers, needle books, cutting watch papers, & many other pretty things'.[84] However, when Clarissa became life-threateningly ill, she realised 'that all the remainder of her days shou'd be spent in his Glory' reading scripture and engaging in good works.[85]

Jane Johnson's tale did not have a firm resolution as she slalomed between seeing arts and crafts as a distraction for Clarissa from more pious duties and arguing that her natural skill in this field should be used to make clothes for the poor and relieve society's ills. The inconclusive nature of Jane Johnson's exploration of the conflict between the competing responsibilities of a good wife, mother and Christian was significant. Time was of the essence. In earlier days, Mary Evelyn had dreamed of living in a cloistered, scholarly community – the antithesis of the family environment in which she ultimately conducted her intellectual activities.[86] Whether the ideal focus of a woman's life was her reading, her religion, her children or her household, there was a wide range of responsibilities that jostled for pre-eminence in a busy weekly schedule. The decision over how time should be apportioned was, for some, a matter of philosophical importance and, potentially, a source of great personal distress.

The concerns described above over the acquisition of uninterrupted time within a secluded space in which to read and write were issues that related centrally to the question of personal autonomy. The thwarted life history of the eminent scholar, Elizabeth Elstob, was a famed case in point. For Elstob, her diminishing time and space for study were the direct result of her financial impoverishment. Elstob complained of her 'unhappy Circumstances ... which depriv'd me of Leisure to follow those Studies, which were my only delight and employment when I had nothing else to do'.[87] However, she also recognised her dependence on the income from teaching and was wary of abandoning too lightly the respected position which she had won in her local community through years of hard work. When offered the prospect of a more prestigious teaching position, she was cautious:

> Had your Proposal come some time ago, I had been at Liberty to accept it. But at present, after seven years patience, and endeavours for a school, I have obtain'd such a one as I desir'd; ... and having met with a great deal of Friendship and Generosity from the Good Ladies in this Place. I shou'd think it the Greatest peice of ingratitude, to neglect the Dear little ones committed to my Care.[88]

Elstob's letters reveal her very real difficulties in finding time, energy and access to reading materials in order to answer Ballard's frequent questions, writing 'But you being sensible I have but little time to think or do any thing else, will I hope excuse me, if it is not done as soon as you or I cou'd wish'.[89] However, space (both mental and physical) in which to read and write only got one so far. Domestically situated as they were, women's lives could be subject to significant intrusion by members of the household and personal privacy was not always guaranteed.

Privacy and the psychology of space

Understandings of, and attitudes towards, the concept of privacy have, naturally, altered greatly over time and the period under discussion here has been positioned by historians as a time of significant change in terms of the organisation of domestic space to meet an emerging social demand amongst the privileged for personal privacy.[90] However, a linear historical narrative which traces society's evolution from medieval communality to the modern, private self has been called into question, with scholars such as Tim Meldrum, amongst many others, complicating this oversimplified view.[91] Nevertheless, reading and writing letters often demanded a quiet place, free of distractions, and scholars such as Naomi Tadmor have illuminated the ways in which early modern readers fitted time with their books into their lives and homes.[92] But finding physical space to read and write was only part of the issue. As Patricia Spacks has explored in depth, concerns about psychological privacy – more than physical privacy – recurred frequently in the literature of the eighteenth century. Privacy in this sense was a 'privacy of the mind and heart' and 'a breathing space' from the rest of life's demands.[93] Spacks examines in particular 'the strategies writers devise or describe for being let alone, and the anxieties that develop about what it might mean to let one another alone'.[94] Of course, the positive connotations of private devotional reading ran alongside societal fears about the dangerous potentialities of concealment. Nevertheless, private space was certainly sought out and enjoyed by women who wished to maintain a thought-provoking correspondence.

Letters of this period, as we have seen, trace the dynamic social, functional and familial environment of the home, providing qualitative detail about early modern experiences of company and solitude and the degree to which quiet, personal space could be valued. But analyses of physical space can only get us so far. Individuals who lived leisured lives within vast, rambling edifices could feel trapped by the walls around them rather than liberated by the many rooms there contained. Domestic inhabitants might feel harried by the bustle of household bodies despite the luxury of a private room, or deathly lonely for lack of company despite a nursery full of children. Ultimately, domestic space had a psychological dimension and feelings of upset or well-being related not simply to the dimensions of a room, but to the personalised relationships developed between the individual and their home.

Comments in letters about attitudes towards solitude often act as a marker for evidence of engagement with the life of the mind. Amongst the letter-writers studied here, where mention is made of the pros and cons of being alone, there is invariably comment on time for contemplative activities. On occasion, this relationship with privacy was not straightforward. Correspondents veered between complaints of loneliness, on the one hand, and declarations of need for the peace of a solitary existence, on the other.

For women of this period (and perhaps any other), privacy and solitude had challenging connotations. These requirements not only were bound with the functionality of their everyday lives and homes, but also influenced their emotional well-being and sense of self. For those women who wished to carve out space for the development of their mental lives, the domestic environment took on a particular character: the everyday and the intellectual were entirely interrelated.

The case of Dorothy Osborne's letters to William Temple illustrates some of the problems which women could encounter in terms of lack of privacy. Osborne was the youngest daughter of the Royalist Sir Peter Osborne, and lived her young life at Chicksands Priory in Bedfordshire. In particular, it was Dorothy's exchange with William Temple that provoked her brother Henry Osborne's mistrust. The pair eventually married, but only after a lengthy epistolary friendship and secret engagement.[95] Living with her father and overbearing brother, Dorothy Osborne had to go to some lengths to secure the privacy of her correspondence with Temple. On 23 July 1653 she reported: 'Nan tells mee hee [her brother] had the curiosity to ask your Boy questions ... My B[rother]. comeing from London, mett him goeing up & cald to him, & asked what letters hee had of mine, the fellow sayed none.'[96] Determined and suspicious, Henry Osborne persevered with his request.

> My B. sayed I tolde him hee had and bid him call for them, hee sayed there was some mistake int for hee had none, and soe they Parted for a while. But my B. not sattisfied with this rides after him, and in some anger threatned the Poor fellow, whoe whould not bee frighted out of his letter. ... My B. smiled at his innocence and left him, and I was hugely pleased to heare, how hee had bin defeated.[97]

Despite this victory, Osborne hastily made arrangements with Temple to secure their future correspondence, saying:

> You will have time Enough to think of a new addresse, hee goes no more [to London] till after harvest, and you will receive this by your, old friend Collins. But because my B. is with him [the carrier] every week as soone as hee com's and takes up all the letters, if you please lett yours bee made up in some other forme then usuall, and directed to Mr Gibson at Ch: in some od hande.[98]

However, the surveillance continued in the home and, in the following letter, Osborne discussed her brother's increasingly invasive tactics: 'I cannot imagin what should tempt to soe severe a search for them [the letters], unless it bee that hee is not yet fully sattisfyed to what degrees our friendship is growne and thinks hee may best informe himself from them.'[99] Dorothy Osborne's home life was dominated by a suspicious brother and by caring for her dying father. A clever, outspoken woman,

Osborne reported articulately challenging her brother's behaviour on many occasions. Nevertheless, there was a sense of claustrophobia in her letters, tainted by the atmosphere and conflicts of her immediate surroundings.

The surveillance reported by Dorothy Osborne would not have sounded unfamiliar to Anne Dormer, writing three decades later in the 1680s. As we have seen, Dormer's case indicates the importance of separate physical space within the home for independent study. Her attachment to the quiet privacy of her closet was essential for her engagement with reading and writing. However, this safe haven became, at times, more a place of hiding. Dormer reported that her movements about the house were monitored by her controlling husband, Robert Dormer, who was capable of violence if she slipped out of his sight. Without a peaceful and habitable space in which to read, Dormer found herself all the more agitated and focused on the disruptive influence of her husband on her intellectual self-betterment and physical well-being: 'if I can sleepe in the night well, but in the day I have no resting place my clossett in the winter is too cold, and in the somer too hott and in my chamber when once he is up he is always passing too and fro and in the Nursery if I stay half an houre he is in a fury'.[100] However, this familiar narrative, describing the catalogue of daily irritations involved in their married life, became more dramatic in Dormer's next few sentences: 'once this winter [he] broke the doore and made it flie cross the roome when he fancied I was there but I was not nor no creature but Clem [their son] and his maid'.[101] From a modern perspective, this anecdote of domestic violence appears too casually related. The more sinister aspects to her husband's supervision become apparent as Anne Dormer described him as 'a constant spie he is over me'.[102] At times her movements were virtually tracked around the house, as Robert Dormer demanded a high level of control over her whereabouts: 'my Ld has as constant a watch over my steps as ever and can tell exactly how many will carry me from my chamber to the garden and if I happen to stopp one minute I am sure to be askt the reason'.[103] She ridiculed his concerns about her safety as excessive bouts of unwarranted jealous anger: 'his jealousy is a sort of madness I think for now I am growne so gray so leane and so hagged that I might justly hope I might now be trusted in the garden without the fear of any bodyes running away with me'.[104] Anne Dormer recognised her husband's behaviour as out of the ordinary, or even a form of 'madness'. But she treated these features as part and parcel of his peculiar temperament and placed no greater emphasis on them than on his other antisocial characteristics. The lack of freedom of movement in her own home must have contributed to Dormer's many references to attaining seemingly elusive time alone.

Although Robert Dormer's influence over his wife became a focus in Anne Dormer's letters to her sister, the house itself assumed a significant presence in the correspondence. For Dormer, the spaces of the home affected her psychological well-being. In the immediate aftermath of her husband's death, Dormer gave a poignant description of her movements around a home previously dominated by the personality of Robert Dormer. She described the trepidation she felt in disturbing her husband's things: 'a heart less sensible then mine sure must feele some remorse to be looking in his boxes and Trunks which he kept so closs and locked.'[105] Dormer described, in a letter to her sister, her feeling of intruding on her husband's privacy and the house itself took on an air of prohibition: 'when I am going up and downe his house and using such things as he would scarce suffer me to look upon, I am I think like one haunted with an evill spirit or who has committed some crime.'[106] The indignation, which Dormer had expressed in earlier letters about the level of influence exerted over her by her husband, and her unfaltering criticism of his approach to their marriage, was suddenly undermined by the anxiety which she felt in the absence of his control. Instead, she mapped her mourning for him onto the physical landscape of the home they had shared. To explain her personal unhappiness to her sister, she not only had to place herself in the context of the home, but also to demonstrate the home's effect upon her.

Imagined spaces

Letters of this period give an insight into the spaces of the home and the ways in which these influenced women's thinking and working lives. For these women, correspondence also provided a forum for creating different, imagined spaces. As a form of escapism, letter-writing did not root its participants exclusively in their daily reality, but offered the possibility of breaking free. Mary Clarke's letters to her husband often concerned the practical sides of life. As Edward Clarke was frequently away from home attending to his duties as MP for Taunton,[107] Clarke was left with the management of the farm and estate. However, Mary Clarke had a playful imagination and a clear sense of humour, and her letters make for lively reading as she swerved from business to news about the children and on to musing about a plot against King William III. In a letter dated 22 October 1694, Clarke told her husband about her recent bout of ill-health. At first she described herself at home trying to manage the pain in her kidney and documented the measures she had employed to treat herself, chiefly drinking water from therapeutic springs: 'I have my bottle and Glass brought and gett in the Gallery window by my Chamber wheare I walke and drinke them with a Great deale of plesure though all heare will have it they have a nasty tast and doe stinke.'[108] Talk of this treatment provoked Clarke to imagine that she had left her chamber and 'phancey I am att the bath Gallary that lookes in-to the hall which I phancey to be the Cross bath'.[109] Clarke informed her husband that her sons Jepp and Sam, along with the other children, 'are my bead Fellowes', spending time with her during her sickness.[110] As if to give Edward Clarke a more intimate view into their home life, Clarke described her incorporation of the children into her fantasy of taking the waters at Bath, writing that 'I take as much pleasure in teaching summy to Goe as the fine ladyes doe in the hopes of having such by drinking the waters'.[111] The companionship of her children may have elicited Clarke's whimsical mood, but the letter was at once designed to entertain (her husband and herself) and to provide a portrait of the family life which he was missing in his absence. Despite the subject of Clarke's letter being a routine bout of family sickness, she used her correspondence to indulge in an entertaining style of writing. For Mary Clarke, both the real and the imagined spaces of the home were valid subjects for the letters which she wrote to her husband, and the correspondence evoked her humour, creativity and sense of intimacy.

In the 1660s, the diarist and poet, Katherine Austen,[112] committed to paper a book of miscellanies, otherwise known as 'Book M'.[113] In this volume, she wrote essays and meditations, including several descriptions of her dreams. Believing in her ability to predict future events via an analysis of the meaning of dreams, she declared: 'Certainly I may have an expectation, a dependance of something extraordinary, to befal me at the period of that time when I find stories from Monitions and notices given to some persons, yeares before it coud so pas.'[114] The recording of dreams did not make Katherine Austen unique. Mary Evelyn had also been encouraged by her husband, John Evelyn, to write down her more intriguing dreams, in order that they might be analysed for meaning.[115] Unfortunately these documents have not survived. This interest in the subconscious was echoed in the letters of Jane Johnson to her aunt, Rebecca Brompton (née Garth), written in the 1750s. For Johnson, the realm of the imagination held a strong allure.[116] She used a report of a dream to open a lengthy letter, writing on 28 February 1756: 'I Dream'd last night that (Arachne like)[117] I was Metamorphosed into a spider as big as the full moon, & sat upon a Throne in the Center of a Web of my own spinning as Large as Lincolns-Inn-Fields.'[118] She interpreted this dream as a sign: 'As soon as I awaked, I wonder'd what this extraordinary Dream should portend, & not having any Magician, Astrologer, Soothsayer, or Children to resort to, explain'd it my self, to signifie, that I must this day spin out of my Brains a Long Letter to Dear Mrs Brompton.'[119] The letter was partly a work of fantasy and partly testimony to her own impulse to take up the pen. However, after a startling beginning to the letter, Johnson retreated into self-effacing apology, claiming of her writing that once 'wrote & Read will be no more worth than a monstrous Spider's Web',[120] and imagining instead that 'had I Dream'd of a Silk-Worm should have thought it a far more fortunate Prognostick, & not have doubled making this sheet of paper the better instead of the worse by covering it with my ink'.[121] In the context of Johnson's confident written style, however, this apology appears more as a nod to polite modesty than as a genuine denial of her talents. By beginning her letter with the content of a dream, Johnson immediately placed her writing in an alternative sphere. Letters written by women of this period were often prosaic and practical in their communications, but examples such as this demonstrate that, where wished, the epistolary form was transformed into a much more imaginative medium. As Patricia Spacks has discussed, the 'privacy of the mind and heart, depends more obviously on particular modes of self-imagining and of imagining the other'.[122] Johnson used her letters to experience a separate space for creative thought, a 'privacy' of a kind. Like Mary Clarke, writing sixty years earlier, Johnson used letters to create alternative, imagined spaces. Johnson also used everyday occurrences as a starting point for telling stories – stories that actively discussed ideas and entertained the reader in the process.[123]

The home shaped women's experiences of the life of the mind in seventeenth- and eighteenth-century England, but it also delivered corners and rooms in which serious intellectual work could be undertaken. Homes were also sociable sites of intellectual exchange and places where letters and other textual production were written, read aloud, discussed and digested. Domestic space was also intricately involved with the important freedoms brought by free time, privacy and personal autonomy and different household environments acted to constrain and empower individuals in their pursuit of a life of the mind. Ultimately, space was psychological and the home occupied a central position within women's mental worlds – a position that should not be underestimated in our histories of intellectual life.

Notes

1   Damaris Masham, as quoted in S. Hutton, 'Damaris Cudworth, Lady Masham: Between Platonism and Enlightenment', *British Journal for the History of Philosophy*, 1 (1993), pp. 29–54.

2   See, for example, M. Ellis, 'Coffee-House Libraries in Mid-Eighteenth-Century London', *The Library: Transactions of the Bibliographical Society*, 10:1 (2009), pp. 3–40 and for the definitive text on the formation of the public sphere, see sociologist and philosopher, Habermas's *The Structural Transformation of the Public Sphere*.

3   S. Shapin, 'The House of Experiment in Seventeenth-Century England', *Isis*, 79:3 (1988), pp. 373–404.

4   N. Deane, 'Reading Romantic Letters: Charlotte Smith at the Huntington', *Huntington Library Quarterly*, 66:3/4 (2003), pp. 393–410.

5   See S. M. Zimmerman, 'Smith, Charlotte (1749–1806)', in *ODNB*; www.oxforddnb.com/view/article/25790.

6   Deane, 'Reading Romantic Letters', p. 403.

7   BLA, LP, L 30/9/53/3: Mary Grey to Jemima Grey, 17 Aug. 1740.

8   WYA, NH 2828/34: Eliza Worsley to Frances Robinson, 1 Oct. 1742.

9   WYA, NH 2825/12: Eliza Worsley to Frances Robinson, 24 Feb. 1749.

10 J. Collett-White, '*My Choice*: A Poem Written in 1751 by Mary Orlebar', *Bedfordshire Historical Miscellany*, 72 (1993), pp. 129–41.

11 BLA, LP, L 30/9a/1, fos 50–1: Jemima Grey to Mary Grey, 1745 [copy].

12 P. Yorke, *Athenian Letters* (London, 1741).

13 See Godber, *The Marchioness*, p. 18.

14 See R. Clark, *Sir William Trumbull in Paris, 1685–86* (Cambridge: Cambridge University Press, 1938) and A. A. Hanham, 'Trumbull, Sir William (1639–1716)', in *ODNB*; www.oxforddnb.com/view/article/27776.

15 For the significance of the closet in early modern discourse, see A. Stewart, 'The Early Modern Closet Discovered', *Representations*, 50 (1995), pp. 76–100; for women's emotional and psychological reading practices, see F. Molekamp, 'Early Modern Women and Affective Devotional Reading', *European Review of History*, 17:1 (2010), pp. 53–74.

16 BL, TP, Add. MS 72516, fo. 168: Anne Dormer to Elizabeth Trumbull, 10 Sept. *c.* 1687.

17 BL, TP, Add. MS 72516, fo. 201: Anne Dormer to Elizabeth Trumbull, 28 Jan. 1688/89.

18 BL, TP, Add. MS 72516, fos 163–4: Anne Dormer to Elizabeth Trumbull, 24 Aug. C.1687.

19 BL, TP, Add. MS 72516, fo. 166: Anne Dormer to Elizabeth Trumbull, 22 June *c.* 1687.

20 BL, TP, Add. MS 72516, fo. 159: Anne Dormer to Elizabeth Trumbull, 8 Aug. *c.* 1686.

21 BL, TP, Add. MS 72516, fo. 192: Anne Dormer to Elizabeth Trumbull, 3 Nov. *c.* 1688.

22 Lipsedge, ' "Enter into thy Closet" '.

23 See Christie, *The British Country House*, pp. 71–3.

24 Laurence, 'Women Using Building', pp. 298–9.

25 Laurence, 'Women Using Building', p. 299.

26 Laurence, 'Women Using Building', p. 299.

27 J. Spurr, *The Post-Reformation: Religion, politics and society in Britain, 1603–1714* (Harlow: Pearson Education Limited, 2006) pp. 306–7.

28 See Mendelson and O'Connor, '"Thy Passionately Loving Sister"'; O'Connor, 'Representations of Intimacy'; M. O'Connor, 'Interpreting Early Modern Woman Abuse: The case of Anne Dormer', *Quidditas*, 23 (2002), pp. 49–66; and Mendelson, 'Neighbourhood as Female Community'.

29 'Dr Barrow' refers to Isaac Barrow (1630–77), fellow of Trinity College, Cambridge, who was the celebrated author of theological works.

30 BL, TP, Add. MS 72516, fos 192–192v: Anne Dormer to Elizabeth Trumbull, 3 Nov. *c.* 1688.

31 BL, TP, Add. MS 72516, fo. 192v: Anne Dormer to Elizabeth Trumbull, 3 Nov. *c.* 1688.

32 M. Feingold, 'Barrow, Isaac (1630–1677)', in *ODNB*; www.oxforddnb.com/view/article/1541.

33 Bishop Jeremy Taylor (1613–67), preacher, scholar and man of letters.

34 BL, TP, Add. MS 72516, fo. 213v: Anne Dormer to Elizabeth Trumbull, 10 Dec. *c.* 1689.

35 J. Spurr, 'Taylor, Jeremy (*bap.* 1613, *d.* 1667)', in *ODNB*; www.oxforddnb.com/view/article/27041.

36 For instance, both the diarist John Evelyn and the letter-writer Dorothy Osborne (discussed below) are known to have read Jeremy Taylor's works, see Spurr 'Taylor, Jeremy'.

37 Archbishop John Tillotson (1630–94) published a sermon on 'The Wisdom of being Religious', in 1663 and a pamphlet entitled 'The Rule of Faith', in 1666.

38 BL, TP, Add. MS 72516, fo. 203: Anne Dormer to Elizabeth Trumbull, St James's Day (25 July *c.* 1689).

39 I. Rivers, 'Tillotson, John (1630–1694)', in *ODNB*; www.oxforddnb.com/view/article/27449.

40 See E. Longfellow, *Women and Religious Writing in Early Modern England* (Cambridge: Cambridge University Press, 2004) for a detailed discussion of the way women assumed religious authority through their reading and writing, especially pp. 11–17.

41 BLA, LP, L 30/9a/1, fo. 6: Jemima Grey to Mary Grey, 12 May 1743 [copy].

42 BLA, LP, L 30/9a/1, fos 6–7: Jemima Grey to Mary Grey, 12 May 1743 [copy].

43 The clergyman and author, Conyers Middleton; see J. A. Dussinger, 'Middleton, Conyers (1683–1750)', in *ODNB*; www.oxforddnb.com/view/article/18669.

44 BLA, LP, L 30/9a/3, fo. 64: Jemima Grey to Catherine Talbot, 6 June 1741 [copy].

45 Mary Gregory (née Grey) died in 1761; Catherine Talbot died of cancer in 1770; and Jemima, Marchioness Grey (née Campbell) outlived both friends by several decades, dying in 1797.

46 BLA, LP, L 30/9a/1, fo. 66: Jemima Grey to Mary Grey, 25 Sept. 1745 [copy].

47 BLA, LP, L 30/9a/1, fo. 66: Jemima Grey to Mary Grey, 25 Sept. 1745.

48 See M. Purcell, 'The Private Library in Seventeenth- and Eighteenth-Century Surrey', *Library History*, 19 (2003), pp. 119–28.

49 Purcell, 'The Private Library', pp. 119–28.

50 Purcell, 'The Private Library', p. 125.

51 See Eales's analysis of 164 wills made by clerics in the dioceses of Rochester and Canterbury in 'Female Literacy', pp. 67–81.

52 From 1737 onwards, Thomas Secker (in his role as Bishop of Oxford) spent summers at the palace in Cuddesden and during the winter he resided at the deanery of St Paul's; the Talbots remained members of his household during this period.

53 BLA, LP, L 30/9/53/9: Mary Grey to Jemima Grey, 29 Sept. 1740.

54 BLA, LP, L 30/9/53/9: Mary Grey to Jemima Grey, 29 Sept. 1740.

55 BLA, LP, L 30/9/53/9: Mary Grey to Jemima Grey, 29 Sept. 1740.

56 On this theme more generally, consult Spacks, *Privacy*.

57 Whyman, *Pen and the People*, p. 48.

58 Whyman, *Pen and the People*, p. 50. The post roads led to Kent, Yarmouth, Chester, Bristol, Plymouth and the north, although regular posts were also destined for routes to Dublin and Edinburgh.

59 See Whyman, *Pen and the People*, pp. 53–8.

60 WYAS, NH 2822/16: Frances Robinson to Thomas Robinson, 21 June 1737.

61 Sarah Cowper was the daughter of the politician and Lord Chancellor, William Cowper, first Earl Cowper (1665–1723) and his wife Mary Cowper (neé Clavering). William Cowper was the first-born son of the diary-writer, Sarah Cowper, discussed briefly in the Introduction and in Chapter 3.

62 Anna Maria Mordaunt (d. 1771) married Stephen Poyntz in 1733 and then moved to live on her husband's estate at Thatcham in Berkshire.

63 BL, AP, Add. MS 75460: Sarah Cowper to Anna Maria Mordaunt, 11 July 1725.

64 For a more detailed discussion on the Cowper–Mordaunt friendship through letters, see Chapter 5, pp. 171–2.

65 The celebrated theologian and philosopher, Henry More (1614–87), exchanged ideas via correspondence with Anne Conway. For an exploration of Conway's intellectual contribution to theological and philosophical thought, see Hutton, *Anne Conway*.

66 BL, CP, Add. MS 23214, fo. 34: Anne Conway to Edward Conway, 22 Oct. 1665.

67 BL, CP, Add. MS 23214, fo. 23: Anne Conway to Edward Conway, 21 March 1662/63.

68 This subject will be discussed more fully in Chapter 5.

69 N. Machiavelli, *Discorsi* (Venice, 1531).

70 Francesco Guicciardini (1483–1540), friend and critic of Niccolò Machiavelli, and a celebrated political writer of the Italian Renaissance in his own right.

71 BLA, LP, L 30/9a/1, fo. 40: Jemima Grey to Mary Grey, 30 Oct. 1744 [copy].

72 Marcus Annaeus Lucanus (AD 39–65), the Roman poet.

73 BLA, LP, L 30/9a/1, fo. 40: Jemima Grey to Mary Grey, 30 Oct. 1744 [copy].

74 BLA, LP, L 30/9a/1, fo. 40: Jemima Grey to Mary Grey, 30 Oct. 1744.

75 This referred to the two-volume history by the British historian, Laurence Echard (*c.* 1670–1730), *The Roman History from the Building of the City to the Perfect Settlement of the Empire by Augustus Caesar*, vol. 1 (1724); and *The Roman History from the Settlement of the Empire by Augustus Caesar*, vol. 2 (1724).

76 BLA, LP, L 30/9a/1, fos 40–1. Jemima Grey to Mary Grey, 30 Oct. 1744 [copy].

77 BLA, LP, L 30/9/53/3: Mary Grey to Jemima Grey, 17 Aug. 1740.

78 NRO, IP, I.C. 4214: Elizabeth Isham to Justinian Isham, 23 March 1700.

79 WYAS, NH, 2828/7: Ann Worsley to Thomas Robinson, 18 March c. 1743.

80 See examples of her teaching methods at: http://webapp1.dlib.indiana.edu/
findingaids/view?brand=general&docId=InU-Li-VAA1275.xml&chunk.
id=d1e142&text1=jane%20johnson&startDoc=1#1 (accessed 5 Nov. 2015).

81 Bodl., MS Don c190, fo. 21: Jane Johnson to Rebecca Garth, 8 July 1742.

82 Bodl., MS Don c190, fo. 21: Jane Johnson to Rebecca Garth, 8 July 1742.

83 Johnson's choice of the name 'Clarissa' deliberately invoked Richardson's protagonist
of the same name and shows Johnson's incorporation of literary influences in her own
creative expression: see Whyman, 'Epistolary Literacy', pp. 597–601.

84 Bodl., MS Don c190, fo. 11: Jane Johnson to Rebecca Brompton, 1749.

85 Bodl., MS Don c190, fo. 11: Jane Johnson to Rebecca Brompton, 1749.

86 Harris, Transformations of Love, pp. 66–7.

87 Bodl., Ballard 43, fo. 3: Elizabeth Elstob to George Ballard, 17 Aug. 1735.

88 Bodl., Ballard 43, fo. 3: Elizabeth Elstob to George Ballard, 17 Aug. 1735.

89 Bodl., Ballard 43, fo. 9: Elizabeth Elstob to George Ballard, 16 Nov. 1735.

90 Most famously and influentially by Lawrence Stone in his classic work The Family, Sex
and Marriage in England, 1500–1800 (London: Weidenfeld and Nicolson, 1977), pp. 27,
254. This theme has been taken up by Mark Girouard in Life in the English Country
House: A social and architectural history (Harmondsworth: Penguin, 1980) and more
recently by Christopher Christie, in The British Country House, who has discussed the
changing fashions in country house architecture over the eighteenth century, which
both prioritised the lavish and public and made room for small, private spaces for
withdrawal.

91 T. Meldrum, 'Domestic Service, Privacy and the Eighteenth-Century Metropolitan
Household', Urban History, 26:1 (1999), pp. 27–39; in particular, Meldrum has questioned an overly simplistic model of the 'growth of privacy' in the eighteenth century and argued that the use of architectural and inventory evidence must be married
with other sources, such as servant testimonies in London's church courts, to reach a
clearer picture of continuity and change in the domestic enactment and experience of
'privacy'.

92 See Tadmor, ' "In the even my wife read to me" '.

93 Spacks, Privacy, p. 8.

94 Spacks, Privacy, p. 24.

95 See Parker, Dorothy Osborne.

96 Parker, Dorothy Osborne, p. 117; the letter reproduced in this edited volume does not
survive in the original manuscript collection, but has been sourced from earlier edited
volumes of the Osborne letters.

97 Parker, Dorothy Osborne, p. 117.

98 Parker, Dorothy Osborne, p. 117.

99 BL, Add. MS 33975, fo. 43: Dorothy Osborne to William Temple, 30/31 July 1653.

100 BL, TP, Add. MS 72516, fo. 193: Anne Dormer to Elizabeth Trumbull, 3 Nov. c. 1688.

101 BL, TP, Add. MS 72516, fo. 193: Anne Dormer to Elizabeth Trumbull, 3 Nov. c. 1688.

102 BL, TP, Add. MS 72516, fo. 195: Anne Dormer to Elizabeth Trumbull, 29 Nov. *c.* 1688.

103 BL, TP, Add. MS 72516, fo. 193: Anne Dormer to Elizabeth Trumbull, 3 Nov. *c.* 1688.

104 BL, TP, Add. MS 72516, fo. 193: Anne Dormer to Elizabeth Trumbull, 3 Nov. *c.* 1688.

105 BL, TP, Add. MS 72516, fo. 202: Anne Dormer to Elizabeth Trumbull, St James's Day (25 July) *c.* 1689.

106 BL, TP, Add. MS 72516, fo. 202: Anne Dormer to Elizabeth Trumbull, St James's Day (25 July) *c.* 1689.

107 Edward Clarke (1649/51–1710), Whig politician and agricultural innovator; see B. Rand (ed.), *The Correspondence of John Locke and Edward Clarke* (London: Humphrey Milford, 1927) and Milton, 'Locke, John'.

108 SARO, SEP, DD\SF/7/1/31, fo. 29: Mary Clarke to Edward Clarke, 22 Oct. 1694.

109 SARO, SEP, DD\SF/7/1/31, fo. 29: Mary Clarke to Edward Clarke, 22 Oct. 1694.

110 SARO, SEP, DD\SF/7/1/31, fo. 29: Mary Clarke to Edward Clarke, 22 Oct. 1694.

111 SARO, SEP, DD\SF/7/1/31, fo. 29: Mary Clarke to Edward Clarke, 22 Oct. 1694.

112 Katherine Austen (1629–83) married barrister Thomas Austen, but was left a widow with three young children at the age of twenty-nine; see S. Ross, 'Austen, Katherine (*b.* 1629, *d.* in or before 1683)', in *ODNB*; www.oxforddnb.com/view/article/68248.

113 BL, BC, Add. MS 4454, 1664–8.

114 BL, BC, Add MS 4454, fo. 21.

115 See P. Crawford, 'Women's Dreams in Early Modern England', in D. Pick and L. Roper (eds), *Dreams and History: The interpretation of dreams from Ancient Greece to modern psychoanalysis* (Hove: Brunner Routledge, 2004), pp. 91–104.

116 See Arizpe and Styles, *Reading Lessons*, pp. 97–116.

117 Johnson's reference to the mythical figure of Arachne acknowledged that too much pride in her work will lead to a fall: see Whyman, 'Epistolary Literacy', p. 594.

118 Bodl., MS Don c190, fo. 13: Jane Johnson to Rebecca Brompton, 28 Feb. 1756; 'Lincoln's-Inn-Fields' refers to the large square in central London that still exists today.

119 Bodl., MS Don c190, fo. 13: Jane Johnson to Rebecca Brompton, 28 Feb. 1756.

120 Bodl., MS Don c190, fo. 13: Jane Johnson to Rebecca Brompton, 28 Feb. 1756.

121 Bodl., MS Don c190, fo. 13: Jane Johnson to Rebecca Brompton, 28 Feb. 1756.

122 Spacks, *Privacy*, p. 8.

123 See Whyman, 'Epistolary Literacy', p. 589.

PART III

Hearts and minds

5

Connecting reason and emotion

Writing, like reading, was an activity that held a magnetic draw for some women of this period. Writing could be a strong impulse, a necessity that kept the mind free, the thoughts flowing and the writer psychologically stable. Eighteenth-century correspondents commonly spent many lines of ink on the very subject of how writing letters to their friends acted as an emotional salve. As Femke Molekamp has argued, 'the lived approach to emotional life as expressed, and indeed negotiated, within a given relationship in correspondence' has been under-explored by scholarship.[1] In letters, emotional responses to life were articulated and both the expression of those feelings and the manner in which they were expressed provide important insights into the history of emotions. Relationships were forged and fostered through letter-writing and, thus, correspondence played a critical role in the continuation of significant friendships. The reciprocal nature of letter-writing prompted some correspondents to cover pages in ink at a staggering pace and regularity, using the expanding postal network to their advantage. Some wrote to ease the pain of separation, but others used their correspondence as a means to explore new avenues of exchange alongside a friendship conducted in person.[2] When this practice of daily writing became a task of intellectual note, in general, the intensity of the connection increased as the correspondence moved from cheerful conversation to contemplative exchange.

Before discussing the emotional world of the early modern letter-writer, we must acknowledge the emotional significance of the letter itself. As we have seen, the physical process of writing and the patterns of the postal system influenced the way individuals engaged with the world of ideas. But whilst the process of writing and sending a letter was important, so was the material artefact of the epistle itself. As Elizabeth Poley confessed to her sister Anne D'Ewes: 'I take much comfort in your lines which want not often reading.'[3] In this case, the letter itself acted as a physical memento of the sender and, as such, played a role in the intimacy of the sisters' relationship.

In the first instance, correspondence was appreciated for the message it contained but, as time passed, letters could be kept, reread and treasured for their sentimental value. Where a relationship was emotionally engaged, the material significance of the letter was heightened. Letters were also prized for the sense of physical proximity they engendered in the recipient, the feel of the letter in the hand making the author all the more present in her absence. The letter engaged not only the reader's literate faculties, but also their senses which read the material evidence of their fellow correspondent's condition. As such, letter-writing – both in its dexterous practice and through its circulation of thousands of paper tokens – co-opted correspondents into a sensory engagement with writing, reading and thinking which fused the emotional and the cerebral.

Mind and body

The relationship between thought and feeling had important implications for how gender was constructed in this period and how individuals could operate within established cultural frameworks. In contemporary literature, thought and feeling were often conceptually juxtaposed and, frequently, gendered as masculine and feminine.[4] Thinking women of this period were subject to prevailing assumptions about the weaknesses of the female mind – a mind that was considered expertly adapted to the realm of polite sociable conversation but was desperately ill-equipped to deal with serious scholarly endeavour. As the author of a 1743 prescriptive volume *The Lady's Preceptor* put it: 'There are as great a Variety of Rules for Writing well, as for Talking well; the Ignorance of most of your Sex, therefore, in this Science, who generally are guilty of as many Faults as they pen Words, arises from their not caring to be at the pains required to excel in it.'[5] So women were expected to excel in drawing-room conversations but were deemed deficient when it came to the accuracy required for skilled writing. Women may have had the urge to write, and even a passion for letter-writing in particular, but according to much contemporary comment they were inexpert in this endeavour, relying on superficial flourishes over thorough-going substance. Women were characterised as relying on instinct and retaining a natural softness in their communicative style, but were considered ultimately lacking in rigour in their mental processes. The descriptions contemporary correspondents made of their mental worlds, emotional and thoughtful, indicate complex negotiations over mind and body, and reveal that far from being conceptually separate, the head and the heart were very much entangled.

This opposition between mind and body, male and female, had important consequences for the way female intellectuals were perceived or, indeed, how they perceived themselves. In the late seventeenth century, Mary Evelyn conducted a series of intellectually motivated correspondences with male friends. In these letters her ability to 'reason' in a masculine way was commented upon with surprise and awe. Even Mary Evelyn herself juxtaposed her intellectual strengths and calmness of spirit against more typically feminine traits, such as appearing emotional or speaking rashly and without considered thought. The relationship between 'reason' and 'emotion' certainly had important implications for the way Evelyn presented herself in her letters. The necessity for Evelyn to defend her character and abilities on this basis becomes clear when reading letters written by her male confidants. For example, in 1667 her son's tutor, Ralph Bohun, openly designated 'false' writing as a female trait and felt assured in doing so because it was well established that Evelyn displayed unusually 'masculine' sense:

> I am so much let loose to my old improprieties of speech yt I now boldly give it under my hand yt I can both write & speak bad English, & I know no reason but that I may as well make use of ye priviledge of women to write false; as you have so constantly invaded ye right of men & renounced your sex both to write true & masculine sense.[6]

Later in the same letter Bohun makes typically flattering comments about Evelyn's particular talents and, again, the attribute of steady thoughtfulness was described as masculine and implicitly contrasted with the giddy, female mind. 'But though I have so often been witnes of yr Even Style, & masculine notions, yet I thinke it more reas'nable to distrust ye very perceptions of sense then believe a woman to write so well: Certainly yr witt is greater then any thing but yr modesty wch regulates it.'[7] Bohun may have registered flattering surprise over Evelyn's talents, but he was fully aware of her abilities – introducing her letters as elevated reading for his circles of acquaintance at the University of Oxford. But, for Evelyn, it is likely that reference to these truisms of their day reinforced her chosen position of measured, critical distance. She rarely broke into more emotional terms, no doubt for fear of conforming to an inferior, 'feminine' character. Despite Bohun's penchant for such gendered commentary it was another of Evelyn's male confidants – William Glanville – who would place feminine emotion in contrast with masculine reason most defiantly. And whereas Bohun's descriptions of Evelyn's gender-atypical qualities were born out of intellectual admiration, Glanville's approach would test the very boundaries of epistolary friendship.

Epistolary relationships

Letters were used to maintain relationships during separation, but they also provided an arena for the deepening of intimacy between two people. As such, letters carried the heavy emotional investments of the people who penned them. The process of sitting down and writing encouraged the necessary reflection and introspection to speak openly about important topics such as religion, philosophy, love or friendship. For the letter-writers discussed in this book, intellectual fulfilment could be reached through epistolary relationships with like-minded friends. The personal well-being of committed and thoughtful letter-writers therefore depended on maintaining good relations with fellow correspondents, connecting the exercise of the rational mind with the cultivation of personal relationships. Through examples of women's epistolary relationships with intellectual companions, it will be possible to see the highly interrelated dynamics of reason and emotion in the lives of early modern women.

Mary Evelyn wrote considered letters not only to Ralph Bohun, but also to other men outside of her immediate family circle. A regular correspondent over a period of more than thirty years was William Glanville (1618–1702). Glanville was John Evelyn's brother-in-law, a firm friend of Mary Evelyn and seventeen years Mary Evelyn's junior. Another major correspondent and supportive friend was Samuel Tuke (c. 1615–74), a distant relative of John Evelyn, a Royalist playwright and twenty years Mary Evelyn's senior. By treating Bohun, Glanville and Tuke as a category of correspondents within Evelyn's broader network of letter-writing, interesting dynamics in cross-gender intellectual exchange and personal and social relationships can be revealed. On the one hand, Bohun encouraged Evelyn's letter-writing for the notice of a learned circle, but likewise Evelyn encouraged Bohun in his intellectual endeavours. The Glanville and Tuke correspondences were less clearly intellectual in tone, but were intense and thoughtful and contributed to the social and emotional framework within which Evelyn exercised her intellectual abilities.

As we have seen, through convention, politeness or genuine surprise, Ralph Bohun repeatedly remarked upon Evelyn as 'extraordinary' for her sex. However, this theme was also taken up in the letters of William Glanville. On 4 March 1664, he wrote: 'Could yore perfections bee found in any considerable number of women, I am Confident the Vertue of yore Sexe would leave as many Captives as even did the Beauty; I will say no more least my friendship run the hazard of passing for (that wch I know you hate) Flattery.'[8] Indeed, Glanville felt the need to qualify all his praise for Mary Evelyn with statements to assure her his sentiments were not idle flattery, but genuine admiration: 'But since there are very few of yor Sexe that come neere you, there cannot bee too many Coppyes of so unparalel'd an Originall, ... This at this time I am sure you cannot call Compliment, for tis a very improper Season, to make Court to a Lady with so bigg a belly as yo^rs.'[9] Mary Evelyn informed each of her correspondents frequently that they must curb this tendency, as 'praise, and flattery shall never long prevail with me'.[10] Behind the references to female modesty, expected of a woman of her time, and the somewhat patronising nature of Bohun's praise for a female writer who possessed 'thousands of reall vertues & perfections combin'd, wch singly would make ye happiest of yr Sex' was a genuinely responsive dialogue between the correspondents.[11] Of the three, Samuel Tuke was something of an exception. Although he often praised Mary Evelyn's gift, he did not usually reference gender. Moreover, by comparison with Glanville and Bohun, Samuel Tuke proved an undemanding correspondent and the overriding sense is one of a warm and supportive friendship. Tuke wrote in a calligraphic hand and began most of his letters with the address: 'My Best Cosin',[12] writing instructions for delivery to 'The faire hands of Mrs Evelyn'.[13] Among all the copies in Mary Evelyn's letter books, her correspondence with Samuel Tuke featured heavily. To take one example of a letter book: out of the twenty-six copies (not all autograph), seven were verifiably addressed to Samuel Tuke, two letters went to William Glanville and the rest to a broad range of extended family and acquaintances.

Letters between Samuel Tuke and Mary Evelyn were just as punctuated with expressions of mutual appreciation as were the Evelyn–Glanville and Evelyn–Bohun correspondence. As Tuke wrote:

> But Madam I am soe conscious of my owne unworthines, that all the merit wch I dare assume is only a just esteeme of those qualities wch yor Ladiship has soe civilly misaply'd ... Therefore Mada- least yor Civillitie should invade yor judgment I humblie advise yo^u to reforme my character until I am able soe to coppie yor perfections.[14]

Tuke's stay in Norwich during the 1660s made a necessity of correspondence with his Deptford-based relative, Evelyn. In his letters, Tuke made a claim at once to his inferiority as a correspondent and to his determination to keep in contact by both visits and 'paper visitations'.[15] In characteristically modest terms, he made his request to Evelyn for their continued epistolary friendship in the 1660s: 'My best Cosin I cannot bee so unkinde to my self as not to covett yor conversation, & therefore I pray forgive mee if I provoke yor good nature to neglect yor business, ... to entertaine an impertinent kinsman.'[16] However, these familiar and flattering phrases were not empty of real sentiment. With no obvious ulterior motive, Tuke maintained a supportive stance towards his female friend and her written endeavours. Evelyn certainly appreciated this attitude, as she explained:

> The encouragment you give me that my letters may be suffered is very agreeable to me, and I assure you that besides the esteeme and friendship time only allowed me in yr thoughts, I will add that merit and Inclination fortifies you in mine, by which yet I pretend to receive noe other advantage then the continuance of yr good opinion, which I infintly value.[17]

This long-term correspondence between Evelyn and Tuke, whilst valued as written compositions, copied and kept in personal letter books, also dealt with the victories and defeats, trivial and terrible, of everyday life. On 22 April 1665, sickness did not keep Tuke from maintaining his exchange with Evelyn via his wife, who wrote: 'Dearest Cosen Though I am hartyly sory for the cause yet there is no office which I can render my husband more willingly then in writing to you; hee not being in a condition to serve himselfe of his owne hand.'[18] Only a year later more serious calamity struck, in the form of plague, taking with it Samuel Tuke's wife and child. He wrote to Evelyn from Paris, in the midst of his grief but full of concern for the Evelyns' endangered position in England, surrounded by outbreaks of the disease. Tuke's subsequent transition to holy orders in France was also documented in his letters to Evelyn, which at this stage were often written in a scribe's elaborate hand.[19] He told her that he had 'entred into the society of Men', finding himself 'never in so serene a Calme as present'.[20] Tuke and Evelyn thus supported one another in times of crisis and in the paths that their lives took.

Mary Evelyn's letters to her three male correspondents are the most skilfully and carefully constructed of her surviving epistles. The encouragement Evelyn received from Tuke, alongside Glanville and Bohun, galvanised her determination to write. In some respects, this correspondence could be understood as evidence of the importance of male mentors for a female intellectual, but this places the wrong emphasis on the relationship. As Bohun wrote, in January 1676, 'those who have observd your Brother Glanvil & my self, sitting at your L[adyshi]^{ps} table amidst all our disputes, wch I hope are now forgotten, must conclude yt Mrs Evelyn had no less an influence in governing ye passions of others then her own'.[21] Mary Evelyn had placed herself at the centre of this group of men, each linked with one another via their relationship with her. They often deferred to her authority on matters of literature or advice on life. Her 'wooden parlour' at Sayes Court in Deptford provided them with a space for discussion, at times antagonistic argument, over which Mary Evelyn herself arbitrated. Evelyn had no official role besides her domestic one, but her home was a site of learning and hosted, in person and through their 'paper visits', this group of male friends, fellow readers and intellectual admirers.

Looking at these examples of female engagement with the life of the mind, it is interesting to see that, although women sought individualistic paths to intellectual fulfilment, the encouragement and support of friends were important components in a productive intellectual life. Mary Evelyn relied on male correspondents for her most intense and thoughtful exchanges. Other correspondents studied here sought fellow female correspondents for their most in-depth exchanges. Women in this period had to be responsive to the particulars of their social context in order to develop a life of the mind. Where husbands and family friends proved receptive and supportive, their conversation was eagerly sought. However, there was no need for male mentors in the development of intellectual life, as other women could be found amongst broad social circles who also sought intellectual self-development. Through correspondence, a huge variety of relationships could be fostered, and where there was emotional proximity and shared interest, ideas on diverse topics could be discussed and advanced. It is rare to find correspondence that undermines this process. Whilst conduct books and sermons might have preached female modesty and described the relative weakness of the female mind, letter-writers chose other letter-writers on the basis of shared interest and purpose and not for advice about the limits that should be placed on their exploration of the world of ideas. However, letter-writers had high expectations of what an epistolary relationship could bring them and thus letters became an important discursive space for ideas of love and friendship.

Letters and perfect friendship

Correspondence collections are revealing of contemporary ideals for relationships between two people and the qualities of a perfect *look up!* →

friendship received much attention in the lines of letters. As Frances Harris has highlighted, 'In any society of rigidly prescribed and unequal social roles, friendship was likely to be highly valued for the freedoms and emotional satisfaction it offered'.[22] On 9 March 1666, Mary Beale,[23] eldest daughter of a Puritan rector and a successful London portrait painter, wrote to her friend Elizabeth Tillotson on just this topic. With her letter, she enclosed a short treatise on the meaning and function of friendship, which she described as 'my very imperfect draught after that immortal Beauty Friendship'.[24] 'And so I may shorten the trouble of any further apology by telling you that in the following discourse I have endeavour'd to lay before you my heart, if not what it is, yet what I desire it should bee, and do hope that your Friendship may help to make it.'[25] Beale explicitly framed friendship as a 'Divine thing' and 'the nearest Union which distinct Soules are capable of'.[26] This evocation of an ideal friendship was a theme taken up in contemporary literature. In particular, the poet Katherine Philips (much lauded by women readers at the time, including Mary Evelyn and Elizabeth Elstob) wrote on love and friendship in the mid-seventeenth century and, famously, established a 'society of friendship' amongst a close circle of associates.[27] Philips's own writings drew on a wealth of works devoted to the topic of Platonic friendship, written by authors such as Jeremy Taylor, Francis Finch and Robert Boyle.[28] For Philips, and others, perfect friendship promoted possibilities for spiritual development. This notion of a perfect, divinely sanctioned friendship side-stepped the inequalities of marital relationships and was easily framed as the ideal context for spiritual or cerebral togetherness. Not every letter-writer felt the need to place on paper the tenets of perfect friendship, but many letters referred to the need for equality between correspondents in terms of the emotional energy they invested in their epistolary friendship. When Yorkshire gentlewoman Ann Worsley wrote to her brother in 1737, she made it clear she had high expectations of the personal investment her brother needed to make in their correspondence and, by extension, in his relationship with Ann: 'My Dear Brother What half imperfect Letters you write me, not one out of Course for ye World, just a bare answer & yt is all, I want yr whole heart & soul upon paper, since I cant have em any other way.'[29] In the same letter, Worsley linked her expectations for emotional closeness with her brother to a classical example of perfect friendship, positioning her sisterly plea within a broader cultural framework: 'where is ye openness ye sincerity of a sincere friend, an Antiphilas a Demetrius,[30] yt I just came from reading off, but why should I upbraid you, perhaps ye less Love & friendship for me ye better, & perhaps you wonder at me even for thinking of such things, much more seeming to expect em.'[31] Ann Worsley correctly identified the letter as the only appropriate place for expression of these feelings, and, like Mary Beale, she discussed the facets of perfect friendship in her correspondence. However, where the heart was laid bare, the mind was also actively involved – self-expression, even of an emotional kind, was a thoughtful exercise and one that can frequently be detected in letter-writing of this period.

In the letters exchanged between Mary Evelyn and William Glanville, definitions of love and friendship appear again and again – necessarily being redefined to encompass this unusually intense friendship. Glanville repeatedly declared his strong feelings for Evelyn in his letters and positioned his relationship with her somewhere on the spectrum between Platonic friendship and romantic love. Mary Evelyn addressed this issue in a letter to Glanville on 9 October 1671, which she copied into her letter book (Figure 9):

> Yr last confirms my belief being a very obliging letter Love cannot be the motive from a man prepossessed nor can interest in either of us be the inducement, it must then be concluded a mutuall disposition to like one an others inclinations and tempers, which wee will call friendship, and which from this day forward lett neither piquant raillery nor pleasant interupt, let neither censure nor whisper destroy.[32]

However, only two weeks later, Glanville returned to the subject forcefully, stopping only just short of an extremely controversial declaration of love: 'But should I discover that I am in Love with my friend, It cannot justly offend Her, or any other person, provided my passion bee but platonique.'[33] Glanville, not perturbed by Evelyn's firm rebuttal, pursued this theme doggedly through more than a decade and over many sheets of paper. Very obvious assertions of romantic feeling towards Mary Evelyn began in 1671 and similar sentiments were reiterated until 1684, when their friendship fell into jeopardy. Whilst charging Evelyn to 'Give my Respects what name you please', he explored at length his own feelings towards his friend, and his attitude to becoming an ageing widower.[34]

Although the emotionally charged content of many of Glanville's letters to Mary Evelyn entirely contravened acceptable extra-marital behaviour, they were not alone in this fervent friendship. At this time, Mary Evelyn's husband, John Evelyn, was engaged in a passionate spiritual friendship with a woman at the Restoration court, Margaret Blagge. At this time, Blagge was seriously considering retiring from public life into a private, religious institution. As a Protestant in Reformation

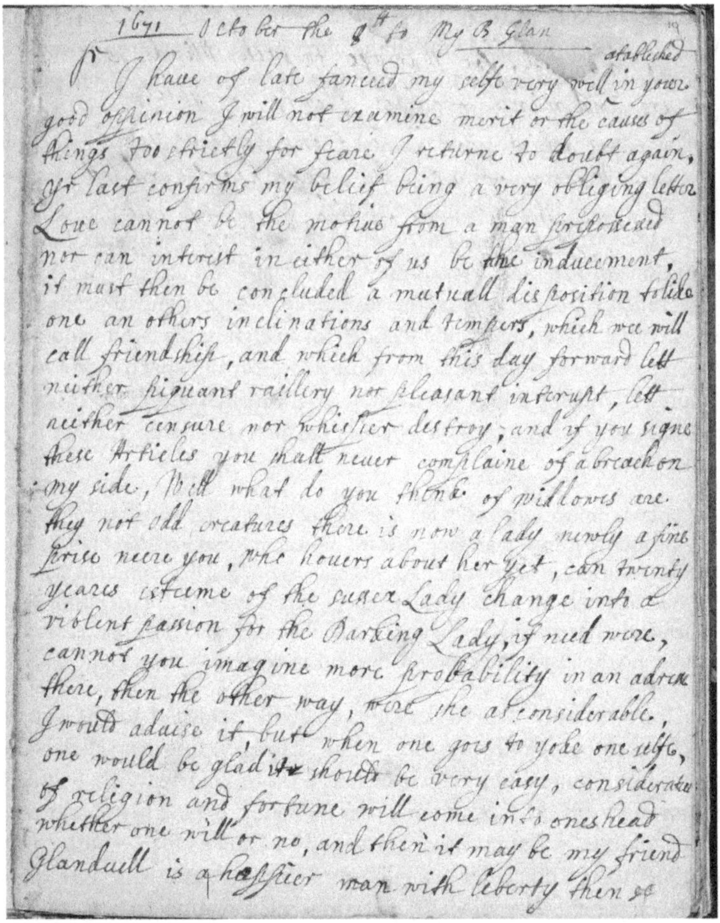

Figure 9: A letter written by Mary Evelyn addressed to her brother-in-law, William Glanville, on 9 October 1671, copied into her letter book for future reference © The British Library Board (Add. MS 78438, fo. 19).

England this was a complicated proposition and, with encouragement from John Evelyn, she decided against this path in favour of marriage to the young courtier, Sydney Godolphin. John Evelyn wrote a guide-book to married life addressed to Margaret Godolphin, to aid her in this transition.[35] At this time, Mary Evelyn was very aware of the spiritual friendship her husband had developed with Margaret Blagge which represented one of the most emotionally intense relationships of his life. John Evelyn's behaviour in this case, no doubt, provided an important backdrop for Mary Evelyn's pursuit of friendship and intellectual exchange outside her marriage.[36]

Glanville's long-held and unrequited romantic interest in Mary Evelyn was evident not only from his overt assertions, but also in his expressions of jealousy and grasping neediness. In August 1673, Glanville was still emphasising 'Love' over 'friendship' and lending an even greater potential to their relationship by imagining a very different history:

> Were I in Love with you, I could not Love you better then I doe, and since I am so perfectly yo[r] fre[nd] I hope you will value mee no Less then if I were yo[r] passionate Lover: Because There is no such thing uppon Earth as Seraphick Love, I dare not wish o[ur] friendship had begun when wee first saw one another, for I am conscious I could not have Trusted my selfe with loving you twenty yeares agoe aswell as I doe now; you in those dayes might have been safe in yo[r] Vertue; But I could not then bee Sure of my Peace: At Wotton I am but merry, but att Deptford I am Happy,[37] And to w[ch] of the two then, I have the greatest Inclinations, is easy For you to determine.[38]

Exactly two years later, Glanville again discussed the nature and parameters of his feelings for Mary Evelyn, returning, once more, to the controversial issue of his physical interest in her. Whereas in 1673 he claimed that he 'could not have Trusted' himself,[39] by 1675 he was hoping that 'Tyme will purify'[40] his feelings for his friend. Speaking about himself in the third person he professed: 'I am certaine [Hee] is intirely yo[rs], and you may bee sure his Fidellity equalls his Affection, w[ch] Tyme will purify, and a few yeeres make as innocent and spirituall as ever were Plato's Amours or any other rigid and religious philosophers.'[41] By October of the same year, he was describing the more day-to-day symptoms of his love sickness, depicting himself at home in low spirits when he was not in Mary Evelyn's company; 'I rise I read, I dine I walke, I thinke I sleepe, and sometimes dreame of you.'[42] Evelyn occasionally gave Glanville some encouragement. In a letter that she copied into her letter book, Evelyn confessed that should she suffer the loss of her husband and consider remarriage, 'I should not only hope but think, my selfe secure when I had twenty yeares knowne & conversed with the freedome honour and friendship permits with a person of so much witt good humour generosity prudence & entegrity as you possess, … and to conclude above all one resolved to love me disenteressedly'.[43] Likewise, on 19 August 1676, Glanville put his position bluntly: 'Were you not another mans wife, I could safely [say] you are my Mistress.'[44]

Despite the frequent affirmations of a secure friendship and emotional closeness within the letters, there was a strong undercurrent of insecurity in Glanville's approaches to Evelyn. By comparison to Glanville's written style, Evelyn maintained a more cautious mode of expression: reassuring but never gushing. Glanville was desperate for greater recognition. Despite Evelyn's best efforts to reassure him of her satisfaction with their friendship (demonstrated in frequent communication via letters and visits), Glanville pushed for more. The necessity to clarify the status of their relationship led to an almost legalistic approach, on Glanville's part, as he attempted to define his feelings for Evelyn and cement their mutual connection. As if nervous of Evelyn retreating from him, he endeavoured, using contractual language, to impose encompassing obligations on his friend and correspondent. Doubting himself and Evelyn's true feelings he protested:

> Madame,
>
> All the Declarations of Respect that I ever made you, have beene very free and Syncere, But when I consider how few of those qualifications are to bee found in Mee; wch you thinks so essentiall and necessary to the friendships you would make; I must then conclude yor Esteeme of Mee cannot bee so great and unfayned as you have profest; For Seeing I come so short of those measures in Reason and Religion, wch a wise and pious Man ought to have; how can you honor that person with yor friendship, who according to yor owne rules Is not worthy of It.[45]

In a more confident mood, he wrote: 'I take you att yor owne Word, Articles are mutually sign'd and seal'd And therefore never thinke of Going back.' This theme was taken up again in December 1673, when Glanville reiterated: 'But the Indentures of perfect Friendship beeing sign'd and seald betweene us, lett us banish all Distrust on either Syde, and Thinke hence forward of Nothing but the performance of Covenants.'[46] It is difficult not to doubt the existence of 'Distrust' in *equal* measures on both sides of this friendship, which was being converted into an extremely emotional exchange. The self-deprecating tone of Glanville's concerns about the inequality of his friendship with Mary Evelyn at times were overturned by transparent attempts to turn the tables and carve for himself a more masterful role:

> you have a single faculty of Discovering iust [*sic*] so much, and no more of yor selfe, then y— please, but whenever you are uppon the Reserve with Mee, I know how to bee quiett with you, for though you beleive you have attain'd to a perfect knowledge of my Temper and Inclinations, I can when I will, make you doubt, and thinke you have taken wrong measures.[47]

Painfully aware of the vulnerable position he had created for himself, Glanville attempted to transfer his own anxieties to Evelyn herself.

Glanville knew that he could not compete with his brother-in-law, John Evelyn, for precedence with Mary Evelyn, but he resented her other close friendships with men, especially with Ralph Bohun. Glanville correctly identified the special nature of Evelyn's correspondence with Bohun and confessed his feelings of inadequacy in 1675: 'I am not yet vaine enough [to] flatter my selfe with an Opinion, that my lett^{rs} are as [hands]ome and gratefull to you as those you receive [from] New College; Myne cannot entertaine you with fine things that M^r B[ohun]'s use to doe.'[48] Commenting on Ralph Bohun, Glanville made his feelings clear and took the opportunity to degrade Bohun's character. He even managed to counsel Evelyn against allowing Bohun to spend further time at Deptford (and in her company), greedily wishing to be the undisputed centre of Mary Evelyn's attention:

> I doe not wish my greatest Enemy ... miserable, and therefore I congratulate Mr Bohuns beeing restored to h[ealth] But crackt Coxcombes[49] are seldome sobberd, and I feare by living ... one Spring or Fall at Deptford, hee would Relapse ... [and] Become as incurable and incorrigible an Ass, as his Brother.[50]

Glanville wished to suggest not only that Ralph Bohun was a man who promoted his academic reputation beyond its true foundations, but also that he was someone who had failed to maintain this false image of himself. This lack of restraint in criticising Evelyn's friend, confidant and refuge for intellectual debate, was revealing of Glanville's immoderate temperament.[51] However, there was little hint in Mary Evelyn's letters, to Glanville or others, that she resented either his charged confessions or his bitter retaliations. Indeed, she appeared to regard Glanville as a true friend and potential second husband.

This exchange gives a clear indication of the difficult path Mary Evelyn trod in relation to her close male correspondents. Much like John Evelyn's infatuation with the pious Margaret Blagge, Glanville also stressed the spiritual aspects of his adoration. Trusted family member as he was, William Glanville's expression of ardent feeling towards his married friend posed a serious challenge to acceptable conduct. Despite this threat, their correspondence continued and Mary Evelyn appeared to field the issue privately and respectably, as might be expected of a sharp intellect, avid correspondent and adept social participant.

William Glanville's relationship with the Evelyns was in part affected by his regular need to petition John Evelyn for help with his professional advancement. His requests for help from John Evelyn were sometimes sent in letters to Mary Evelyn.[52] At times, Glanville voiced to Mary Evelyn his frustration with his lack of progression. He saw his aspirations as having been thwarted and resented the lack of support from those in a position to aid his cause:

> If hee [Captaine Hales][53] bee voted into the House hee sayes hee will owe his Victory to Mee, Should his busines succeed, you will say as you have often, I can prevayle for others but not for my selfe, tis indeed my Fate; and I must bee contented with itt, But when my friends engage as zealously for mee, as I would uppon any occasion for them, I might yet in one thing or other bee fortunate.[54]

This history of disappointments prompted Glanville to react even more vociferously in 1688, when he found himself further diminished, this time by loss of property. He wrote to Mary Evelyn making his position very clear and thereafter ceased his correspondence with the woman to whom he had promised eternal friendship.

> Sister
> A Servant of yo[rs] I suppose by yo[r] order lately sent M[r] Martin to mee, to know whether I would buy Baynerds [a family estate in Surrey]; The message lookd like an intended affront, and hath given mee just occasion to bee dayly more and more sensible, of the great wrong you have done mee and the rest of yo[r] husbands family in depriving us against his express Will of that wch hee intended should descend to the heires of his own bloud.[55]

The family estate, Baynerds, had belonged to John Evelyn's brother, Richard, and was worth '500 pounds per Ann:[um]',[56] but some controversy occurred in the 1680s regarding inheritance of the property. In his anger, Glanville left little room for reconciliation:

> If the Law doe not oblige you to Justification for the injury done us, yet I am sure the Gospell doth; ... It is not only Sister with yo[r] consent, but by yo[r] instigation, that I have been disinherited of a considerable Estate, w[ch] to yo[r] shame is now about to be sold to strangers, to pay scandalous debts. If a man bee condemnd to dye for robbing his neighbo[r] but of ten shillings what doth that woman deserve, who defrauds her brother of ten thousand pounds? Reflect Sister on what you have done in this and some other particulars, then will yor conscience if rightly informd tell you, that without repentance and restitution such as in yo[r] power,

God's justice never can, nor his mercy ever will, forgive the wrong you
and some others have done mee
    Yo[r] allwayes to you kind Brother.[57]

Elsewhere in the surviving Evelyn–Glanville correspondence, there was
evidence of William Glanville's propensity to fall out with those people
closest to him, as he also experienced a troubled relationship with his
son.[58] However, where his connection with his son was reconcilable, his
long-standing friendship with Mary Evelyn was not. The only evidence of
Mary Evelyn's reaction to this sudden severing is gnomic. On the Glanville
letter immediately preceding the one just quoted, the last (surviving) letter
on friendly terms, she had noted: 'From my Br Glan Decem 12th '87, I do
acknowledge the friendship of this Brother was beyond my expectation
and the losse of it unknowne to me.'[59] This claimed lack of comprehension
as to the reasons for the sudden demise in their friendship was echoed
by John Evelyn's later note in his diary at the time of Glanville's death in
1702: 'our Relation and friendship had ben long & greate, but much interrupted by a displeasure he tooke both at me & my Wife, the Cause of which
I could never learn or Imagin, unlesse my not concurring with him, as to
his opinion of the Trinity. … I pray God of his Infinite goodnesse pardon
whatever pass'd between us during the late Settlement in Surry.'[60] Clearly,
the Evelyns did not admit to understanding Glanville's outrage. Even if
they saw his accusations as excessive, it was clear from John Evelyn's entry
that they knew what he was referring to when he mentioned 'the considerable Estate, w[ch] to yo[r] shame is now about to be sold to strangers.'[61]
Whatever their true feelings about the circumstances of the breach, it was
final. John Evelyn preferred to conclude that William Glanville 'Was a
greate friend where he tooke a fancy, & as greate an Enemy when he tooke
displeasure' and a man 'Subject to greate passions'.[62]

Reassured by her friend of over thirty years, that 'Nothing but
death can determine o[ur] friendship', Mary Evelyn must have experienced
Glanville's disavowal in the mid-1680s as a shock.[63] This abrupt termination happened at a stage when the mature familiarity of the correspondence appeared unshakeable. Evelyn saw herself as a 'sceptic in friendship',
and the cautious attitude she took in this regard (so often commented
upon in letters she received from her male friends) transpired to be even
shrewder than she might have expected. The sudden and permanent rift
with Glanville proved beyond doubt that 'Platonic' friendship could be as
precarious a relationship as any other.

Subsequently, the only record of the Evelyn–Glanville feud is exhibited in the correspondence between Mary Evelyn and her nephew,

Glanville's son, William. Characteristically, Evelyn maintained this correspondence, despite its uncomfortable association with her former friend.
The maintenance of friendship, wherever it might fall, and the delivery
of her semi-parental duty towards the young Glanville, prevailed. Mary
Evelyn remained mute on the loss of Glanville as a friend, but she must
have missed the candid exchange of thoughts, feelings and ideas that she
had enjoyed with her brother-in-law for over thirty years.

Evelyn's correspondences open up wider questions about the tone
and content of letters and the gender of correspondents. Whilst Evelyn
attempted to separate reason and emotion, she did not always achieve
this – being pushed to recognise the emotional significance of her thinking life. It seems that Evelyn wished to maintain a dispassionate tone
in her letters in order to uphold her status as a real thinker in the male
mould. Nevertheless, all her intellectual correspondences with male
confidants retain an intense quality with moments of real emotional dis-
closure, giving a more nuanced view of her letter-writing as both performance and friendship.

Letter-writing as self-help

Anne Dormer wished 'to breathe out my soul to thee' in her letters to her
sister.[64] Her declared motivation for letter-writing was to maintain what
she regarded as emotionally supportive contact with her sister. On reading the letters of Anne Dormer, however, it becomes steadily apparent
that her epistles rarely responded to any event or anecdote about which
she may have read in her sister's correspondence. Apart from the assertions of emotional proximity and the well-wishing of family members,
these letters more closely resemble entries in a diary. The many lines of
ink may have been written in letter form, but they might also represent
a writing practice which helped Dormer to cope with her unhappiness.[65]
Moreover, letter-writing for Dormer was not only an opportunity to comfort herself, but also a forum for her incisive self-advocacy. The insights
Dormer presented about her life in her letters represent more than mere
descriptions or complaints; they demonstrate her skill for reasoned argument in defence of her own actions.

Despite the lack of genuine discussion in these letters, Dormer
repeatedly asserted the link between the practice of letter-writing and
the reality of conversation: 'for the only pleasure I have is in thus taulking to my deare friends'.[66] In some cases, the absence of real conversation
in the correspondence was explained by the unreliability of the international postal system. Long gaps between letters, in combination with the

possibility of post going missing, in part justified Dormer's inability to respond more directly to the content of her sister's letters, which were sent from Paris and Constantinople. Dormer wrote on 30 May *c.* 1687: 'the fear of my letters not coming to you makes me not write of my affaires so freely as I would and has kept me from writing many times when it would be an ease to my heart to taulk to thee.'[67] The more convincing conclusion, however, is the one that Dormer herself admits: 'it eases my mind when I fancy I am taulking to thee.'[68] Anne Dormer found writing about her life a cathartic exercise and her letters were less a dialogue than they were a monologue (see, for example, Figure 10). It seems that the lack of companionship in her marriage led Dormer to value her other relationships all the more strenuously, even if they were more imagined in moments of contemplation than directly experienced.

Eliza Worsley's letters to her sister, Frances Robinson, who lived overseas, were also an exercise in writing that could not necessarily expect a reply. On 1 October 1742, she described eloquently her sense of closeness and distance in the relationship with her absent sister. The correspondence was imagined as a physical thread between the two women, upsettingly broken by the unreliability of the international post. In Worsley's case, the act of writing itself was a process of remembrance, even if at times it lost its purpose as a continuation of communicative contact: 'tho I dispair of your recieving this yet I must write for fear I should forget to spell your name, how I wish your affairs was upon a correspondent footing again, you must have quite forgot there is such people in the world, we by holding up our heads can see you both at the end of the room.'[69] Eliza Worsley's generally upbeat style of letter-writing faltered when she wrote to the same sister, then living in Vienna, to confess the importance of writing letters to the state of her mind: 'you'll find I was low spirite'd when I write my last, I allways write to you when I am mightlely pleas'd so you must forgive me if now & then I make you partner of my sorrows, I am allway's easyer after I have write to you.'[70] So letter-writing was not only about active exchange, it also provided a valuable space for expressing difficult or melancholic thoughts, even when a comforting response could not be guaranteed. Letter-writing was often a compulsive activity, and the vagaries of the postal system added urgency to proceedings.[71] However, letter-writers also used the medium to distract from the reality of the wider world, and bring to mind alternative realities. So Jane Johnson confessed in 1756: 'The news papers are full enough of the Dismals, without my adding to them, & I would rather choose to drive all such Ideas far from you than bring them to y^r Remembrance.'[72]

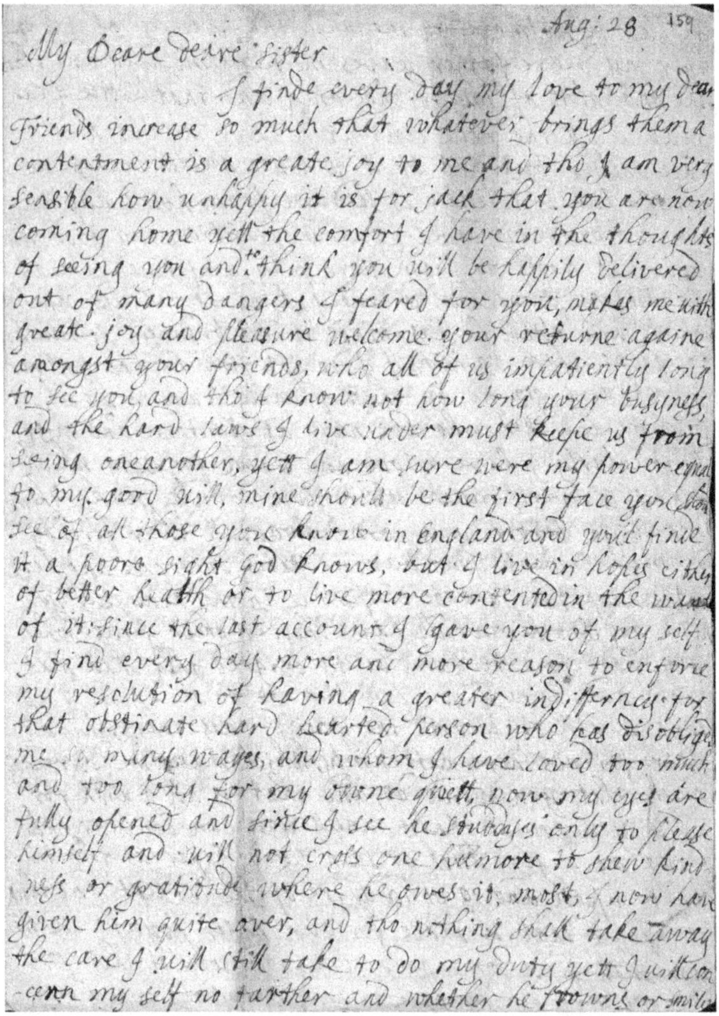

Aug: 28   159

My Deare deare sister

I finde every day my love to my dear
friends increase so much that whatever brings them a
contentment is a greate joy to me and tho I am very
sensible how unhappy it is for Jack that you are now
coming home yett the comfort I have in the thoughts
of seeing you and think you will be happily delivered
out of many dangers I feared for you, makes me with
greate joy and pleasure welcome your returne againe
amongst your friends, who all of us impatiently long
to see you, and tho I know not how long your busyness
and the hard fate I live under must keepe us from
seeing oneanother, yett I am sure were my power equal
to my good will, mine should be the first face you sho
see of all those you know in England and youd finde
it a poore sight god knows, but I live in hopes either
of better health or to live more contentedin the want
of it since the last account I gave you of my self
I finde every day more and more reason to enforce
my resolution of having a greater indifferncy for
that obstinate hard hearted person who has disobligd
me so many wayes, and whom I have loved too much
and too long for my owne quiett, now my eyes are
fully opened and since I see he studyes only to please
himself and will not cross one hayre more to shew kind
ness or gratitude where he owes it most, I now have
given him quite over, and tho nothing shall take away
the care I will still take to do my duty yett I will concern my self no farther and whether he frowne or smile

Figure 10: An example of a letter written by Anne Dormer addressed to her
sister, Elizabeth Trumbull, on 28 August *c.* 1686 © The British Library Board
(Add. MS 72516, fo. 159).

Some correspondents had much greater hope of seeing their friend in person than Anne Dormer or Eliza Worsley did their sisters, but still used letters as reinforcement of their mutual emotional bond. When Sarah Cowper[73] was first forming a close friendship with Anna Maria Mordaunt (later Poyntz) in 1721, she was quick to stress the great affinity she felt existed between the two women: 'I wou'd Dr *Victoria* if possible (till I know yo better) hide from the World how great a progress yo have made in my Esteem, in so short an Acquaintance I wou'd have no one but yr self sensible of the pain I feel from yr being ill.'[74] In this case, short letters were sent in the brief gaps between seeing one another, as if to maintain constant personal contact. The pair used pet names for one another ('Victoria' was Cowper's chosen name for Mordaunt) and a series of pseudonyms for other people, the air of secrecy enhancing the intimacy of their friendship. In this way, Cowper and Mordaunt were able to deepen their new friendship through a high level of contact both in person and via their correspondence.

In women's correspondence of this period, there was a discernible tendency to use letter-writing as a form of escapism. However, this outlet for imaginative thought at times led to depressive introspection. In the early 1740s Jemima Grey counselled her friends, Mary Gregory and Catherine Talbot, on how to maintain a positive outlook:

> We go on Friday, & I am too happy here & have too little Inclination for London not to be sorry for it. I believe I may then in my turn be in the *Hoggle-Groggles* for I'm sure nothing will go right. But while I am still a Philosopher – that is while nothing happens to displease me, let me reproach you for prophaning that Name so much. You Pretenders to Philosophy! Poor Souls! You scarcely know what it means yet, & can be blown about by every Puff as much as the Leaves that are falling in Showers before me: for I will never allow reasoning ones'self into Misory which you call Moralizing, & feeling a thousand Misfortunes in Imagination that may never happen, to be Philosophy.[75]

Grey teased her friends for their pretence to scholarly satisfaction in solitude: 'Then you sit down to Montaigne,[76] – in a great Chair – by the Fireside –& fancy yourself so pleas'd & that you love Quiet so much! When after all, this is not natural to you, you are not the happier for it, & 'tis only indulging a Fit of Indolence & Low Spirits.'[77] Sarah Cowper's letters to Anna Maria Mordaunt betray a similarly paradoxical relationship with solitude. At times she claimed her love of being alone, but at others she bemoaned her lack of company and complained that her isolation robbed her of a lively interest in life. Cowper expressed her upset at being away from her friend:

> I was very angry that I was forc'd to part with yo so soon ys even: I have now vented all my Rage on a piece of cold mutton. I have drunk your Health, & in short my supper has compos'd me, & made me fit for sleep. I wish to dream of being with you because I suppose what makes my Happiness awake, will be so asleep.[78]

Cowper explained, via her letter, the ways by which she maintained her friend's presence in her life, even when the two were apart, through drinking her health and dreaming of their spending time together. The idealised imagined space of Cowper's dreams was contrasted sharply with the frustrated rage which she felt when forced to part with Mordaunt. Despite this strong attachment to her friend, Cowper contended that she had a character well suited to a solitary life: 'It is time I shou'd not be so happy as if I liv'd with yo but believe I cou'd live alone, & that yo are mistaken in thinking I don't love solitude, no one was ever more inclined to a solitary Life'.[79] This comment is reminiscent of Anne Dormer's frequent assertions in her letters that she was resigned to her lonely life, so much so that she had begun to enjoy the serenity of that isolation. Whilst complaining of her husband's 'unreasonable desire of keeping me always at home'[80] she still concluded that: 'for since I love a retired life better than a publick one and find greater enjoyments in a quiett corner then all the bravery of the world could give me' she could be content.[81] Dormer struggled with an unhappy marriage, Sarah Cowper felt emotionally lonely but intellectually thirsty, and for both women letter-writing provided an outlet for their frustration. In September 1726, Cowper claimed 'I am so low spirited that I don't think it possible to think of words enough to fill this Letter'.[82] There was a clear psychological dimension to both Dormer's and Cowper's writing, which suggests that writing was a form of therapy for some women.

Another letter-writer who used correspondence to express her frustration with life was Elizabeth Elstob. Even her gifts to George Ballard of transcriptions from Anglo-Saxon texts communicated her feelings of frustration: 'I can only as knowing you to be a Lover of Antiquity, beg your Acceptance of a small Transcript from the Saxon, written I believe by the first Woman that has studied that language since it was spoke.'[83] Indeed, she openly admitted that her life 'may truly be term'd a life of disappointments, from the Cradle to now'.[84] Having spent her thirties and forties teaching girls in an elementary school, Elizabeth Elstob had dwelt on what education meant for women. In 1752, Elstob wrote to Ballard a short letter, but one with a bitter conclusion on her own lot and that of future generations of women. Here, she referred to Ballard's published work on learned women, which had come into print that same year:

> For your part I am sory to tell you the ch[allenge] you have made for the Honour of Females was the wrongest subject you co[uld] pitch upon. For you can come into no company of Ladies or Gentlemen, who you shall not hear an open and Vehement exclamation against Learned Women, and those women that read much themselves, to what purpose they know best; this I k[now] they wou'd be highly affronted to be thought ignorant. The prospect I have of [the] next age is a melancholy one to me who wish Learning might flourish to the end of th[e] world, both in men and women, but I shall not live to see it; yet I cannot help la[ment] for those that will and who love Learning as well as you do and as dos
>
> S^r
> Your Assured Friend and most
> humble servant Eliz: Elstob[85]

Elstob's statement represents a final acknowledgement that her intellectual abilities had been defeated by her life circumstances. Her words also provide a starkly depressing premonition for the next generation of women, including the many girls whom Elstob had taught in her lifetime. After this point, the Ballard–Elstob correspondence ceased. Within four years, both participants were dead. Despite Elstob's supposition about how her own experiences as a thwarted woman scholar might affect the chances of the next generation, her correspondence with George Ballard had returned a much-needed intellectual friendship to her life. By this time Elstob and Ballard had corresponded for nearly seventeen years. It was on this basis, of long-term and sympathetic letter-writing, that Elizabeth Elstob was able to express her fears for female learning. This stark statement was highly emotionally charged – focused, as it was, on Elstob's most keenly held belief in women's learning and communicated in a letter to an old friend who could empathise with her despair.

Conclusion

Correspondence collections provide the historian with paper artefacts of human relationships, fragmentary and mediated but nonetheless emblematic of friendships fostered in the distant past. These material manifestations of personal relations clearly show that intellectual bonds between individuals could be deeply emotional. They also demonstrate that the intimacy necessary for candid intellectual exchange was often forged through friendship, incorporating qualities of empathy, compatibility and trust. As Elizabeth Elstob confessed to her new friend, George Ballard in August 1735: 'I cannot S^r forbear expressing my Surprize and satisfaction, in meeting with so much Candour and Friendship from a Gentleman unknown. In an Age when even old acquaintance are too often neglected and forgot, and assure you that as long as my memory shall continue with me, [you] will very often be in my thoughts.'[86] The written word, unlike the spoken, required more consideration and, once committed to paper, provided correspondents with texts which were available to read, keep and reread, and to which a considered response was required. This process could provoke both an emotional and a cerebral response. In the case of letter-writing, sense and sensibility worked in tandem, each strengthening the motivation of the correspondent to connect with someone outside their immediate physical reach. Physical distance did not necessarily bequeath mental separation, and keen readers and writers made deft use of correspondence culture to deepen and develop their thinking lives in collaboration with others.

Notes

1 F. Molekamp, 'Therapies for Melancholy and Inordinate Passion in the Letters of Dorothy Osborne to Sir William Temple (1652–1654)', *The Seventeenth Century*, 29:3 (2014), pp. 255–76 at p. 255.

2 As Susan Whyman has pointed out: 'How psychological dependence upon letters affected the emotional lives of people is an important, overlooked topic.' *Pen and the People*, p. 59.

3 BL, HP, Add. MS 382, fo. 177: Anne D'Ewes to Elizabeth Poley, *c*. 1639/40.

4 G. Perry and M. Rossington, *Femininity and Masculinity in Eighteenth-Century Art and Culture* (Manchester: Manchester University Press, 1994), p. 129.

5 d'Ancourt, *Ladys Preceptor*, p. 59.

6 BL, EP, Add. MS 78435, fo. 184: Ralph Bohun to Mary Evelyn, *c*. 1667.

7 BL, EP, Add. MS 78435, fo. 187: Ralph Bohun to Mary Evelyn, *c*. 1667.

8 BL, EP, Add. MS 78434, fo. 9: William Glanville to Mary Evelyn, 4 March 1664.

9 BL, EP, Add. MS 78434, fo. 12: William Glanville to Mary Evelyn, 6 Aug. 1667; Mary Evelyn was pregnant at this time.

10 BL, EP, Add. MS 78539: Mary Evelyn to Ralph Bohun, 23 June 1668.

11 BL, EP, Add. MS 78435, fo. 187: Ralph Bohun to Mary Evelyn, *c*. 1667.

12 BL, EP, Add. MS 78435, fos 10–21: Samuel Tuke to Mary Evelyn, *c*. July 1659–*c*. Sept. 1662.

13 BL, EP, Add. MS 78435, fo. 1: Samuel Tuke to Mary Evelyn, 2 Nov. 1649.

14 BL, EP, Add. MS 78435, fo. 4: Samuel Tuke to Mary Evelyn, 15 Jan. during 1650s.

15 BL, EP, Add. MS 78435, fo. 19: Samuel Tuke to Mary Evelyn, 23 Nov. during 1660s.

16 BL, EP, Add. MS 78435, fo. 15: Samuel Tuke to Mary Evelyn, 21 Sept. during 1660s.

17 BL, EP, Add. MS 78439, fo. 2: Mary Evelyn to Samuel Tuke, first half of 1660s [copy].

18 BL, EP, Add. MS 78435, fo. 36: Samuel Tuke to Mary Evelyn, 22 April 1665.

19 BL, EP, Add. MS 78435, fo. 55: Tuke, a Catholic convert, told Evelyn that he was using a scribe to write out his letters, although no reason was given.

20 BL, EP, Add. MS 78435, fo. 54v: Samuel Tuke to Mary Evelyn, 4 Dec. 1666.

21 BL, EP, Add. MS 78435, fo. 212v: Ralph Bohun to Mary Evelyn, 26 Jan. 1675/6.

22 Harris, *Transformations of Love*, p. 4.

23 Mary Beale's career benefited from the support of premier portrait artist, Sir Peter Lely, see C. Reeve, 'Beale, Mary (*bap.* 1633, *d.* 1699)', in *ODNB*; www.oxforddnb.com/view/article/1803.

24 BL, HP, Add. MS 6828, fo. 510: Mary Beale to Elizabeth Tillotson, 9 March 1666.

25 BL, HP, Add. MS 6828, fo. 510: Mary Beale to Elizabeth Tillotson, 9 March 1666.

26 BL, HP, Add. MS 6828, fos 510–11: Mary Beale to Elizabeth Tillotson, 9 March 1666.

27 W. Chernaik, 'Philips, Katherine (1632–1664)', in *ODNB*; www.oxforddnb.com/view/article/22124.

28 As Mark Llewellyn has pointed out, Jeremy Taylor's *A Discourse of the Nature, Offices and Measures of Friendship, with the rules of conducting it* (London, 1657) was in fact 'Written in answer to a Letter from the most ingenious and virtuous M. K. P.'; see Llewellyn, 'Katherine Philips: Friendship, poetry and Neo-Platonic thought in seventeenth-century England', *Philological Quarterly*, 81:4 (2002), pp. 441–68 at p. 442.

29 WYAS, NH 2822/22: Ann Worsley to Thomas Robinson, *c.* July 1737.

30 Antiphilus and Demetrius constituted a classical Greek example of perfect friendship.

31 WYAS, NH 2822/22, Ann Worsley to Thomas Robinson, *c.* July 1737.

32 BL, EP, Add. MS 78438, fo. 19: Mary Evelyn to William Glanville, 9 Oct. 1671 [copy].

33 BL, EP, Add. MS 78434, fo. 21: William Glanville to Mary Evelyn, 23 Oct. 1671.

34 BL, EP, Add. MS 78434, fo. 21: William Glanville to Mary Evelyn, 23 Oct. 1671.

35 Margaret Godolphin died three years later in September 1678, giving birth to her first child.

36 Seventeenth-century understandings of friendship are discussed fully, in relation to John Evelyn, in Harris, *Transformations*, pp. 1–10.

37 William Glanville lived in Wotton, Surrey, and the Evelyns resided at Sayes Court in Deptford, Kent.

38 BL, EP, Add. MS 78434, fo. 24: William Glanville to Mary Evelyn, 21 Aug. 1673.

39 BL, EP, Add. MS 78434, fo. 24: William Glanville to Mary Evelyn, 21 Aug. 1673.

40 BL, EP, Add. MS 78434, fo. 36: William Glanville to Mary Evelyn, 20 Aug. 1675.

41 BL, EP, Add. MS 78434, fo. 36: William Glanville to Mary Evelyn, 20 Aug. 1675.

42 BL, EP, Add. MS 78434, fo. 41: William Glanville to Mary Evelyn, 1 Oct. 1675.

43 BL, EP, Add. MS 78438, fos 16–16v: Mary Evelyn to William Glanville, Dec. 1670 [copy].

44 BL, EP, Add. MS 78434, fo. 43: William Glanville to Mary Evelyn, 19 Aug. 1676.

45 BL, EP, Add. MS 78434, fo. 26: William Glanville to Mary Evelyn, 29 Aug. 1673.

46 BL, EP, Add. MS 78434, fo. 28: William Glanville to Mary Evelyn, 8 Dec. 1673.

47 BL, EP, Add. MS 78434, fo. 30: William Glanville to Mary Evelyn, 28 April 1674; 'iust' should be read as 'just', William Glanville habitually wrote 'i' in place of 'j'.

48 BL, EP, Add. MS 78434, fo. 36: William Glanville to Mary Evelyn, 20 Aug. 1675.

49 'Coxcombe' is a corruption of 'cock's comb' and was used colloquially to refer to 'A fop; a superficial pretender to knowledge or accomplishments': see S. Johnson, *A Dictionary of the English Language* (London, 1755), *s.v.* coxcomb.

50 BL, EP, Add. MS 78434, fo. 23v: William Glanville to Mary Evelyn, *c.* 1673.

51 See Harris, *Transformations of Love*, pp. 70–4, for more on the character of Ralph Bohun.

52 See BL, EP, Add. MS 78434, fo. 30: William Glanville to Mary Evelyn, 28 April 1684.

53 Sir Edward Hales (1645–95), courtier and convert to Roman Catholicism, was elected in 1679 to the first Exclusion Parliament for Canterbury: see P. Hopkins, 'Hales, Sir Edward, Third Baronet and Jacobite First Earl of Tenterden (1645–1695)', in *ODNB*; www.oxforddnb.com/view/article/11910.

54 BL, EP, Add. MS 78434, fo. 28: William Glanville to Mary Evelyn, 8 Dec. 1673.

55 BL, EP, Add. MS 78434, fo. 62: William Glanville to Mary Evelyn, April 1688.

56 As John Evelyn noted in his diary; see de Beer, *Diary*, p. 880.

57 BL, EP, Add. MS 78434, fo. 62: William Glanville to Mary Evelyn, April 1688.

58 See BL, EP, Add. MS 78434, fo. 32: William Glanville (junior) to Mary Evelyn, 1674.

59 BL, EP, Add. MS 78434, fo. 60v: William Glanville to Mary Evelyn, 12 Dec. 1687.

60 de Beer, *Diary*, p. 1081.

61 BL, EP, Add. MS 78434, fo. 62: William Glanville to Mary Evelyn, April 1688.

62 de Beer, *Diary*, p. 1082.

63 BL, EP, Add. MS 78434, fo. 30: William Glanville to Mary Evelyn, 28 April 1674.

64 BL, TP, Add. MS 72516, fo. 157: Anne Dormer to Elizabeth Trumbull, 9 Aug. *c.* 1686.

65 For a study of another seventeenth-century letter-writer's discussion of strategies for dealing with melancholy, see Molekamp, 'Therapies for Melancholy'.

66 BL, TP, Add. MS 72516, fo. 199: Anne Dormer to Elizabeth Trumbull, 2 Jan. 1688.

67 BL, TP, Add. MS 72516, fo. 161v: Anne Dormer to Elizabeth Trumbull, 30 May *c.* 1687.

68 BL, TP, Add. MS 72516, fo. 199: Anne Dormer to Elizabeth Trumbull, 2 Jan 1688.

69 WYAS, NH 2828/34: Eliza Worsley to Frances Robinson, 1 Oct. 1742.

70 WYAS, NH 2825/10: Eliza Worsley to Frances Robinson, 12 Feb. 1739.

71 R. M. Willcocks, *England's Postal History to 1840: With notes on Scotland, Wales and Ireland* (London: Author, 1975).

72 Bodl., MS Don c 190, fo. 13v: Jane Johnson to Rebecca Brompton, 28 Feb. 1756.

73 Sarah Cowper was the granddaughter of the diary-writer, Sarah Cowper, discussed briefly in the Introduction and Chapter 3.

74 BL, AP, Add. MS 75460: Sarah Cowper to Anna Maria Mordaunt, 1721.

75 BLA, LP, L 30/9a/1, fo. 15: Jemima Grey to Catherine Talbot, 30 Oct. 1743 [copy].

76 Michel de Montaigne (1533–92), the influential writer of the French Renaissance.

77 BLA, LP, L 30/9a/1, fo. 16: Jemima Grey to Catherine Talbot, 30 Oct. 1743 [copy].

78 BL, AP, Add. MS 75460: Sarah Cowper to Anna Maria Mordaunt, 'Thurs: night', 1721.

79 BL, AP, Add. MS 75460: Sarah Cowper to Anna Maria Mordaunt, 1 Sept. 1726.

80 BL, TP, Add. MS 72516, fo. 191: Anne Dormer to Elizabeth Trumbull, *c.* Oct. 1688.

81 BL, TP, Add. MS 72516, fo. 214: Anne Dormer to Elizabeth Trumbull, 10 Dec. c. 1689.

82 BL, AP, Add. MS 75460: Sarah Cowper to Anna Maria Mordaunt, Sept. 1726.

83 Bodl., Ballard 43, fo. 5: Elizabeth Elstob to George Ballard, 29 Aug. 1735.

84 Bodl., Ballard 43, fo. 17: Elizabeth Elstob to George Ballard, 7 March 1735/36.

85 Bodl., Ballard 43, fo. 89: Elizabeth Elstob to George Ballard, 16 Jan. 1752.

86 Bodl., Ballard 43, fo. 3: Elizabeth Elstob to George Ballard, 17 Aug. 1735.

6

A seedbed for change

I n the preceding pages, hundreds of letters have yielded their insights into women's experiences of a life of the mind in early modern England. Through the medium of correspondence, literate women put pen to paper and revealed their motivation to read, write and think. Women did so determinedly and consistently over the period in question and, in this way, made their contribution to the traffic of ideas. Here, conclusions will be drawn about the role of letters, gender and space on women's experiences of the life of the mind over a period of 100 years, from the mid-seventeenth to the mid-eighteenth century.

Letters

Letters are an extremely rewarding historical source for those of us who wish to understand the lives of early modern people. More particularly, they are underused for their insight into the intellectual practices and experiences of women in this period. However, they also require patience, as each letter presents the reader with a complicated tangle of topics, and evidence of intellectual work is only to be found between family news, remedies for the sick and any number of other subjects pertinent to daily life. But in letters it is possible not only to see what women read, thought and discussed with friends, but also exactly how these activities related to other spheres of their lives. Letters show us where reading fitted into the domestic routine and, conversely, where intellectual pursuits fought with other demands for pre-eminence in a busy household schedule. Correspondence is revealing of how women negotiated a sense of their own intellectual identity, and how this identity related to other facts of their existence, such as marriage, work, motherhood or childlessness. Letters make connections between the emotional and the intellectual, demonstrating the intense personal and epistolary relationships that garnered intellectual fruit. Through reading correspondence it is possible to learn how critical reading and writing could be to women's feelings of personal happiness, and how these activities could also act as coping strategies in circumstances of personal difficulty. Letters reveal interior worlds by connecting different facets of life in one document, by being domestically situated and yet destined to travel, and by allowing correspondents to write about the quotidian and the extraordinary in the same line of ink.

The confident letter-writer learned to adapt this flexible medium to her own purposes, seeming little concerned by the rigid rules for epistolary conduct published in advice manuals of the period. Whilst social codes were important, they have sometimes been overemphasised in historical studies of letter-writing and it is important to recognise the expansive framework for expression that was encompassed by correspondence culture at this time. Flexible, accessible and socially acceptable: letter-writing proved a vital tool for many women who wished to develop a life of the mind. Whether correspondence provided the key space for intellectual work or the catalyst for engagement with writing, or represented just one of many fora for the discussion of ideas, letters nevertheless played their part. For some, letters were a place for rehearsal of ideas that would later find themselves in print, but for many, correspondence is the only surviving evidence of a life lived for ideas. By using these collections of unpublished letters, a whole range of intellectual activity – unacknowledged by scholarship – becomes suddenly visible. Letter collections also reveal the networks that linked the intellectually curious – connections that operated locally or transnationally, at some times connected with academic institutions and at others distinct and distant from universities and scholarly societies. By tracing epistolary networks of the kind discussed here, a new geography of intellectual activity can be drawn for early modern England – one that encompasses the home as a site of learning.

Whilst letters may have become the product of a woman's thinking life, they might also have been instrumental in the early years of her education. Female learning most often took place in the home, and evidence shows that mothers and home tutors emphasised edifying conversation (both spoken and written) as a pathway to successful adult life. Childhood lessons could, therefore, pave the way for an intellectual life expressed exclusively through personal and epistolary conversation. The quality of childhood schooling might open or close doors to adult achievement, but it was women themselves who most often acted as educators of girls. To take two exceptional examples discussed here: Jane Johnson and Elizabeth Elstob. The former thought seriously about issues of piety, scholarship, motherhood and education, and in teaching her daughter, Barbara, presented the young girl with a model of motherhood which was deeply intellectually engaged. Likewise, as the scholar Elizabeth Elstob slipped into old age as governess in the Duchess of Portland's household, her young charges acted as scribe, relaying letters concerned with antiquarian research and publication for their infirm mistress. Whilst a story of steady progression cannot be told for female education of this period, women who educated the next generation offered opportunities for female aspiration beyond the scope of societal expectation.

In the twenty-first century, digitisation projects – ambitious in scope – have attempted both to capture the content of letters and to map epistolary networks on a global scale. Extensive use of these resources is likely to become the mainstay of research in this field. However, the under-representation of women letter-writers in historical studies is mirrored by the comparatively small numbers of women's letters making their way into the pages of online repositories. Thus, whilst digital resources can highlight hidden finds, they may also magnify original absences. The examples discussed here show that women were equal participants in the epistolary culture of their day and that the practice of letter-writing was integral to their development of a life of the mind. This finding may also have a bearing on broader cultures of male intellectual thought in this era. As our ability to engage with quantitative studies of seventeenth- and eighteenth-century letter-writing improves, the physical processes, methods and procedures of correspondence, the spaces, places and materialities should not be lost. It is these sources of evidence that provide an invaluable insight into the relationships women had with letter-writing and their experiences, through this medium, of the life of the mind.

Gender

Gender shaped an individual's experience of intellectual life, from its locations and networks to its opportunities and rewards. Gender also played its part in defining the character of intellectual friendships. As we have seen, women developed extremely close, mutually supportive alliances with other women that could cohere around intellectual interests. Specific dynamics were also discernible amongst examples of cross-gender intellectual exchange, illuminating the conditions under which men and women were able to openly discuss ideas. In some cases, differentiated modes of communication between the sexes – the specific deployment of flattery or modest refusal of compliment – were evident on the page. But, conversely, the epistolary arena also provided a space that could be negotiated differently from the curtseying codes of politeness common to other sites of social exchange.

Being a woman in this period predicated against the consistent production of intellectual work, most especially so in the historically resilient format of print publication. Deficient educations and wifely obligations have often been blamed for the intellectual underachievement of women, but most women of the middling sort, gentry or aristocracy, received an education that equipped them to read sophisticated texts written in, or translated into, English, putting a vast literature at their disposal. Instead, it was women's lack of financial autonomy that most significantly hindered their intellectual production. But despite this disadvantage, women were resourceful, placing their thoughts in more ephemeral but infinitely more accessible media such as letters and diaries, and commonly circulated their writings in this manuscript form. Nevertheless, the impermanence of female textual production combined with the rigours of a life focused on child-bearing and child-rearing took its toll and, at the very least, rendered it near impossible to commit a consistent level of attention to intellectual work over the course of a lifetime. The consequent lack of a biography clearly demarcated by regular publications makes female contributions to the history of ideas all the more difficult to trace. Women did act as helpmates to male thinkers, but female talent could be recognised in its own right, even when this talent was only expressed in epistolary form and steered a path distinct from print culture.

Space

The home was an important location for intellectual work for both men and women, but it occupied a particularly central space in women's experiences of the life of the mind. Homes provided closets, corners, table-tops and firesides for reading and writing but they also offered distractions. Reading and writing were practices that could form a perfectly legitimate part of the daily routine, be that private reading or reading in company, completing domestic accounting or writing letters to friends. Homes were also places where collections of books could be found, luckier households accommodating extensive and diverse libraries. But, likewise, the time and space necessary for serious intellectual endeavour were often compromised by the demands of running a household. Domestic space had implications for psychological well-being, not least because it shaped women's access to privacy and autonomy. It is perhaps unsurprising, therefore, that women used letters to take imagined journeys that escaped the specificities of their domestic context, using letter-writing as a space for creative writing.

For most women, the life of the mind was simultaneously domestically rooted and outward reaching. In a letter written in December 1669, Mary Evelyn described her home in terms that contrasted dramatically with her usual descriptions of domestic work and social hubbub. In this letter, Evelyn described a silent household made snug but isolated by the winter snow.

> You will not expect an account in this season of the yeare, how the flowers, and greens, prosper in the garden since they are candying, in snow; to be preserved for the spring, and our delights, confined, to the litle wooden Roome, which could yr perspective, reach, would for variety, be noe unpleasing divertion, then to see a Dull fire, cirled with a philosopher, a woeman, and a child, heapes of bookes, our food, and entertainment, silence our law, soe strictly observed that neither Dog nor Cat dares transgresse it, The Crackling of the Ice, and whistling winds are our Musick, which if continued long in the same quarter may possibly freese our witts as well as our penns, though Apollo were himselfe amongst us, in fine the whole house containes not soe many living creatures in it, as Noahs Ark, and to looke out of the window, one would judge us unlikly to recover the habitable earth againe, yet still we live, and the dayes passe not the least part of our happinesse, though wee hardly disserve the name of Animalls, for wee neither feare, wish, nor Envie.[1]

This passage is unusual in Mary Evelyn's letter-writing. Her descriptions of home were generally confined to brief comments that hinted at the flurry of domestic work and child-rearing that she oversaw and which took her away from her books. But on this winter day at least, the Evelyn household was most certainly the refuge of the scholarly – a scene reminiscent of other cloistered communities of spiritual or academic note. Through letters, Mary Evelyn was positioned at the centre of a network of three male confidants, all of whom avidly courted her attention through epistolary contact. Yet ultimately, it was Evelyn's 'wooden parlour' at her home in Sayes Court in Deptford that rooted the intellectual connections of each of these men to Evelyn – a wooden parlour in which Evelyn herself presided over the discourse.[2]

In order to develop a life of the mind, women had to operate within their given domestic environment and respond to its demands. Domestic space and the activities it engendered therefore had an important influence on female intellectual identity. Letters were also spaces where idealised visions of friendship were projected and, it was hoped, enacted. But for each plea for perfect friendship there were many more letters betraying the slights upon which friendship foundered and the disappointed expectations of optimistic letter-writers.

The next generation

The letters and letter-writers explored in this book point towards a diffuse intellectual culture in this period that incorporated, and sometimes even welcomed, the contributions of women. Whilst barriers to achievement existed, epistolary culture opened doors to literate women and many readily took up the pen to engage with communities of knowledge production and exchange – communities that often lay out of physical reach. In these letters, we can see spaces open to women for intellectual thought and exchange.

The evidence presented here shows the obstacles and opportunities that women encountered in their efforts to engage with a life of the mind. However, within these diverse experiences of intellectual aspiration, it is clear that even unfavourable personal circumstances did not extinguish motivations to learn. It is within these examples of female letter-writing that a seedbed for social change can be located. Where women tried and failed to pursue their intellectual goals, they may have educated their own or other people's daughters to expect more. Indeed, the next generation of women in the later eighteenth century were emboldened to produce radical arguments in favour of female education and freedom. Hannah More famously railed against the 'singular injustice which is often exercised towards women, first to give them a very defective Education, ... and then to censure them for not proving faultless.'[3] Mary Wollstonecraft argued that the female rational mind should be freed by equal educational opportunity.[4] The examples discussed here show that the drive to aspire existed and that access to paper, pen, books and friends could secure a life of the mind for very many women in early modern England.

Notes

1 BL, EP, Add. MS 78435, fo. 60: Mary Evelyn to Samuel Tuke, *c.* Dec. 1669.

2 See Chapter 5, p. 159.

3 H. More, *Strictures on the Modern System of Female Education* (London, 1799), p. i.

4 See M. Wollstonecraft, *Vindication of the Rights of Woman* (Dublin, 1792).

Appendix

Table 1 Content analysis: selected letters of Mary Grey, 1740–41
The figures in the table represent the percentage (%) of the total number of words spent on a subject category in each letter.

Letter	Reading/ academic exchange	Friendship/ mental proximity	Other friends/ visits	Daily life/ health	Thanks/ apology/ well-wishing	Expectations of epistolary contact	Local news
1: 10 Aug. 1740	1.2	23.6	4.6	54.4	4.3	11.9	0
2: 17 Aug. 1740	16.0	24.6	12.5	19.8	14.4	6.5	6.2
3: Aug. 1740	9.2	0	0	72.5	18.3	0	0
4: 30 Aug. 1741	14.7	11.8	17.5	49.3	5.0	1.7	0
5: 5 Sept. 1741	15.1	16.5	24.3	32.6	11.4	0	0

Average percentages for each subject category across all five letters
(in descending order):
Daily life/health: 45.72
Friendship/mental proximity: 15.3
Other friends/visits: 11.76
Reading/academic exchange: 11.24
Thanks/apology/well-wishing: 10.68
Expectations of epistolary contact: 4.02
Local news: 1.24

Table 2 Content analysis: selected letters of Elizabeth Elstob, 1736–37

The figures in the table represent the percentage (%) of the total number of words spent on a subject category in each letter.

Letter	Books/ academic exchange	Intellectual contacts	Private contemplation	Daily life/work/ health	Future prospects	Thanks/ apology/ well-wishing	Meeting in person
1: 9 May 1736	23.0	35.0	5.5	18.0	12.5	6.0	0
2: 12 Sept. 1736	51.4	29.1	0	14.1	0	5.4	0
3: 4 Dec. 1736	45.0	6.0	0	9.0	19.0	12.0	9.0
4: 7 March 1737	64.0	12.5	0	0	0	23.5	0
5: 10 July 1737	73.2	0	0	0	0	11.3	15.5

Average percentages for each subject category across all five letters (in descending order):

Books/academic exchange: 51.32
Intellectual contacts: 16.52
Thanks/apology/well-wishing: 11.64
Daily life/work/health: 8.22
Future prospects: 6.3
Meeting in person: 4.9
Private contemplation: 1.1

Table 3 Content analysis: selected letters of Mary Evelyn, 1667–68
The figures in the table represent the percentage (%) of the total number of words spent on a subject category in each letter.

Letter	Discussion of ideas	Review of cultural production	Discussion of intellectual personalities	News	Demonstration of epistolary style	Daily life/family health amd education	Thanks/apology/well-wishing	Comment on epistolary contact
1: 3 April 1667	31.83	0	12.95	10.61	39.21	0	5.4	0
2: 3 Feb. 1668	5.31	50.94	4.69	6.56	0	20.94	0	11.56
3: 12 April 1668	34.47	0	0	10.53	0	30.53	7.11	17.37
4: 14 May 1668	38.99	0	0	11.39	0	45.32	4.3	0
5: 21 May 1668	13.94	16.06	4.7	11.36	13.48	36.67	0	3.94

Average percentages for each subject category across all five letters (in descending order):
Daily life/family health and education: 26.69
Discussion of ideas: 24.91
Review of cultural production: 13.4
Demonstration of epistolary style: 10.54
News: 10.09
Comment on epistolary contact: 6.57
Discussion of intellectual personalities: 4.47
Thanks/apology/well-wishing: 3.36

Bibliography

Primary sources

Manuscript

BEDFORDSHIRE AND LUTON ARCHIVE SERVICE

Lucas Papers: L 30/8/31/1–17, L 30/9/3/1–116, L 30/9/50/1–43, L 30/9/53/1–19, L 30/9/84/1–9, L 30/9a/1–9, modern transcripts, numbered by letter (3 vols)

BODLEIAN LIBRARY

Ballard Papers: Ballard 43
Coleridge Papers: MS Eng letter c 142
Johnson Papers: MS Don c 190
Madan Papers: MSS Eng d 286–7

BRITISH LIBRARY

Althorp Papers: Add. MS 75460
Birch Collection: Add. MS 4454
Conway Papers: Add. MS 23214
Evelyn Papers: Add. MS 78221, Add. MS 78300, Add. MS 78431, Add. MS 78432, Add. MS 78433, Add. MS 78434, Add. MS 78435, Add. MS 78438, Add. MS 78439, Add. MS 78539
Harley Papers: Add. MS 6828
Osborne and Temple: Add. MS 33975
Petty Papers: Add. MS 72857
Portland Papers: Add. MS 70493
Trumbull Papers: Add. MS 72516

DERBYSHIRE RECORD OFFICE

Soresby Papers: D331/12/26/1–12, D5202/10/1–2

EAST SUSSEX RECORD OFFICE, THE KEEP ARCHIVES

Sayer Papers: Say/1555, Say/1569, Say/1667, Say/1674, Say/1740, Say/1761

HERTFORDSHIRE ARCHIVES AND LOCAL STUDIES

Cowper Papers: D/EP

LIBRARY OF THE SOCIETY OF FRIENDS

Follows Papers: Temp MSS 127/1/1
Isham Papers: I.C.3415, I.C. 4213, I.C. 4214, I.C. 4829, I.C. 5111
Newby Hall Papers: 2822, 2825, 2828
Northamptonshire Record Office
Portland Papers: PwE8, PwE9
Sanford Estate Papers: DD\SF/7/1/31
Somerset Archive and Record Office
University of Nottingham Manuscripts and Special Collections
West Yorkshire Archive Service

Print

d'Ancourt, A., *The Ladys Preceptor: Or, a letter to a lady of distinction upon politeness* (London, 1743).

Anon., *Polite Epistolary Correspondence: A collection of letters, on the most instructive and entertaining subjects* (London, 1751).

——. *The Accomplished Letter-Writer; Or, Universal Correspondent. Containing familiar letters on the most common occasions in life* (London, 1779).

Astell, M., *A Serious Proposal to the Ladies, for the Advancement of Their True and Greatest Interest* (London, 1694).

Fénelon, F., *Instructions for the Education of a Daughter Done into English, and Revised by Dr. Hickes* (London, 1713).

——. *The Accomplish'd Governess: Or, short instructions for the education of the fair sex* (London, 1752).

Locke, J., *Some Thoughts Concerning Education* (London, 1693).

More, H., *Strictures on the Modern System of Female Education* (London, 1799).

Talbot, C., *Reflections on the Seven Days of the Week* (London, 1770).

Wollstonecraft, M., *Vindication of the Rights of Woman* (Dublin, 1792).

Yorke, P., *Athenian Letters* (London, 1741).

Secondary sources

Arendt, H., *The Life of the Mind*, vols 1–2 (London: Secker and Warburg, 1978).

Arizpe, E. and Styles, M., *Reading Lessons from the Eighteenth Century: Mothers, Children and Texts* (Shenstone: Pied Piper, 2006).

Atherton, M. (ed.), *Women Philosophers of the Early Modern Period* (Indianapolis: Hackett Pub., 1994).

Baines, P., *The House of Forgery in Eighteenth-Century Britain* (Aldershot: Ashgate, 1999).

Baird, R., *Mistress of the House: Great ladies and grand houses, 1670–1830* (London: Weidenfeld & Nicolson, 2003).

Ballaster, R., 'Women and the Rise of the Novel: Sexual prescripts', in V. Jones (ed.), *Women and Literature in Britain, 1700–1800* (Cambridge: Cambridge University Press, 2000), pp. 197–216.

Ballaster, R. (ed.) *The History of British Women's Writing, 1690–1750* (Basingstoke: Palgrave Macmillan, 2010).

Barczewski, S. L., 'Yorke, Philip, Second Earl of Hardwicke (1720–1790)', in *Oxford Dictionary of National Biography* (Oxford: Oxford University Press, 2004); www .oxforddnb.com/view/article/30246.

Barker, H., *The Business of Women: Female enterprise and urban development in northern England, 1760–1830* (Oxford: Oxford University Press, 2006).

Batchelor, J. and Kaplan, C. (eds), *Women and Material Culture, 1660–1830* (Basingstoke: Palgrave Macmillan, 2007).

Beal, P. and Ezell, M. J. M. (eds), *English Manuscript Studies, 1100–1700*, vol. 9 (London: British Library, 2000).

Beal, P. and Griffiths, J. (eds), *English Manuscript Studies, 1100–1700*, vol. 7 (London: British Library, 1998).

Bédoyère, G. de la (ed.), *Particular Friends: The correspondence of Samuel Pepys and John Evelyn* (Woodbridge: The Boydell Press, 1997).

Beer, E. S. de (ed.), *The Correspondence of John Locke*, 8 vols (Oxford: Clarendon Press, 1989).

Berg, T. F., *The Lives and Letters of an Eighteenth-Century Circle of Acquaintance* (Aldershot: Ashgate, 2006).

Bergen Brophy, E., *Women's Lives and the 18th-Century English Novel* (Tampa: University of South Florida Press, 1991).

Bigold, M., 'Letters and Learning', in R. Ballaster (ed.), *The History of British Women's Writing, 1690–1750* (Basingstoke: Palgrave Macmillan, 2010), pp. 173–86.

——. *Women of Letters, Manuscript Circulation, and Print Afterlives in the Eighteenth Century* (Basingstoke: Palgrave Macmillan, 2013).

Blake, N. F. and Jones, C. (eds), *English Historical Linguistics: Studies in development* (Sheffield: The Centre for English Cultural Tradition and Language University of Sheffield, 1984).

Bradley, E. T., 'Gregory, David (1695/6–1767)', rev. S. J. Skedd, in *Oxford Dictionary of National Biography* (Oxford: Oxford University Press, 2004); www.oxforddnb.com/view/article/11458.

Brant, C., *Eighteenth-Century Letters and British Culture* (Basingstoke: Palgrave Macmillan, 2006).

Brayman Hackel, H. and Kelly, C. E. (eds), *Reading Women: Literacy, authorship, and culture in the Atlantic World, 1500–1800* (Philadelphia: University of Pennsylvania Press, 2008).

Brewer, J., 'This, That and the Other: Public, social and private in the seventeenth and eighteenth centuries', in D. Castiglione and L. Sharpe (eds), *Shifting the Boundaries – Transformations of the language of public and private in the eighteenth century* (Exeter: University of Exeter Press, 1995), pp. 1–21.

Carroll, B. A., 'The Politics of "Originality": Women and the Class System of the Intellect', *Journal of Women's History*, 2 (1990), pp. 136–63.

Castiglione, D. and Sharpe, L. (eds), *Shifting the Boundaries – Transformations of the language of public and private in the eighteenth century* (Exeter: University of Exeter Press, 1995).

Champion, J. A. I., 'Enlightened Erudition and the Politics of Reading in John Toland's Circle', *Historical Journal*, 49 (2006), pp. 111–41.

Chartier, R., *Cultural History: Between practices and representations* (Cambridge: Cambridge University Press, 1988).

Chernaik, W., 'Philips, Katherine (1632–1664)', in *Oxford Dictionary of National Biography* (Oxford: Oxford University Press, 2004); www.oxforddnb.com/view/article/22124.

Chico, T., *Designing Women: The dressing room in eighteenth-century English literature and culture* (Lewisburg, Pa.: Bucknell University Press, 2005).

Childs, J., 'The Williamite War, 1689–91', in T. Bartlett and K. Jeffery (eds), *A Military History of Ireland* (Cambridge: Cambridge University Press, 1996), pp. 188–210.

Christie, C., *The British Country House in the Eighteenth Century* (Manchester: Manchester University Press, 2000).

Clark, R., *Sir William Trumbull in Paris, 1685–86* (Cambridge: Cambridge University Press, 1938).

Clarke, N., 'Elizabeth Elstob (1674–1752): England's first professional woman historian?', *Gender & History*, 17:1 (2005) pp. 210–20.

Clucas, S. (ed.), *A Princely Brave Woman: Essays on Margaret Cavendish, Duchess of Newcastle* (Aldershot: Ashgate, 2003).

Cohen, M., '"Familiar Conversation": The role of the "familiar format" in education in eighteenth-century England', in M. Hilton and J. Shefrin (eds), *Educating the Child in Enlightenment Britain: Beliefs, cultures, practices* (Farnham: Ashgate, 2009), pp. 99–116.

Colclough, S., 'Procuring Books and Consuming Texts: The reading experience of a Sheffield apprentice, 1798', *Book History*, 3 (2000), pp. 21–44.

Coleman, P., Lewis, J. and Kowalik, J. (eds), *Representations of the Self from the Renaissance to Romanticism* (Cambridge: Cambridge University Press, 2000).

Collett-White, J., 'My Choice: A Poem Written in 1751 by Mary Orlebar', *Bedfordshire Historical Miscellany*, 72 (1993), pp. 129–41.

——. 'Yorke, Jemima, suo jure Marchioness Grey (1722–1797)', in *Oxford Dictionary of National Biography* (Oxford: Oxford University Press, 2004); www.oxforddnb.com/view/article/68351.

Cook, D. and Culley, A. (eds), *Women's Life Writing, 1700–1850: Gender, genre and authorship* (Basingstoke: Palgrave Macmillan, 2012).

Corfield, P. J., 'History and the Challenge of Gender History', *Rethinking History*, 1 (1997), pp. 241–58.

Crangle, S., Epistolarity, Audience, Selfhood: The letters of Dorothy Osborne to William Temple', *Women's Writing*, 12:3 (2005), pp. 433–52.

Crawford, P., 'Women's Dreams in Early Modern England', in D. Pick and L. Roper (eds), *Dreams and History: The interpretation of dreams from ancient Greece to modern psychoanalysis* (Hove: Brunner Routledge, 2004), pp. 91–104.

Cressy, D., *Literacy and the Social Order: Reading and writing in Tudor and Stuart England* (Cambridge: Cambridge University Press, 1980).

Cunningham, B. and Kennedy, M. (eds), *The Experience of Reading: Irish historical perspectives* (Dublin: Rare Books Group of the Library Association of Ireland and Economic and Social History Society of Ireland, 1999).

Daly Groggin, M. and Fowkes Tobin, B. (eds), *Women and Things, 1750–1950: Gendered material strategies* (Farnham: Ashgate, 2009).

Daybell, J. 'Interpreting Letters and Reading Script: Evidence for female education and literacy in Tudor England', *History of Education: Journal of the History of Education Society*, 34:6 (2005), pp. 695–715.

——. *Women Letter-Writers in Tudor England* (Oxford: Oxford University Press, 2006).

——. (ed.), *Early Modern Women's Letter-Writing, 1450–1700* (Basingstoke: Palgrave Macmillan, 2001).

Daybell, J. and Hinds, P. (eds), *Material Readings of Early Modern Culture: Texts and social practices, 1580–1730* (Basingstoke: Palgrave Macmillan, 2010).

Deane, D., 'Reading Romantic Letters: Charlotte Smith at the Huntington', *Huntington Library Quarterly*, 66:3/4 (2003), pp. 393–410.

Dierks, K., 'Letter Writing, Stationery Supplies, and Consumer Modernity in the Eighteenth-Century Atlantic World', *Early American Literature*, 41:3 (2006), pp. 473–94.

——. *In My Power: Letter writing and communications in early America* (Philadelphia: University of Pennsylvania Press, 2009).

Ditz, T. L., 'Formative Ventures: Eighteenth-century commercial letters and the articulation of experience', in R. Earle (ed.), *Epistolary Selves: Letters and letter-writers, 1600–1945* (Aldershot: Ashgate, 1999), pp. 59–78.

Dow, G., 'A Model for the British Fair? French women's life writing in Britain, 1680–1830', in D. Cook and A Culley (eds), *Women's Life Writing, 1700–1850: Gender, genre and authorship* (Basingstoke: Palgrave Macmillan, 2012), pp. 86–102.

Dowd, M. M. and Eckerle, J. A., *Genre and Women's Life-Writing in Early Modern England* (Aldershot: Ashgate, 2007).

Dragstra, H., Ottway, S. and Wilcox, H. (eds), *Betraying Our Selves: Forms of self-representation in early modern English texts* (Basingstoke: Macmillan, 2000).

Dussinger, J. A., 'Middleton, Conyers (1683–1750)', in *Oxford Dictionary of National Biography* (Oxford: Oxford University Press, 2004); www.oxforddnb.com/view/article/18669.

——. 'Edwards, Thomas (d. 1757)', in *Oxford Dictionary of National Biography* (Oxford: Oxford University Press, 2004); www.oxforddnb.com/view/article/8558.

Eales, J., 'Female Literacy and the Social Identity of the Clergy Family in the Seventeenth Century', *Archaeologia Cantiana*, 133 (2013), pp. 67–81.

Earle, R. (ed.), *Epistolary Selves: Letters and letter-writers, 1600–1945* (Aldershot: Ashgate, 1999).

Eger, E., *Bluestockings: Women of reason from Enlightenment to Romanticism* (Basingstoke: Palgrave Macmillan, 2010).

Eger, E., Grant, C., Ó Gallchoir, C. and Wharburton, P. (eds), *Women, Writing and the Public Sphere, 1700–1830* (Cambridge: Cambridge University Press, 2006).

Ellis, M., 'Coffee-Women, *The Spectator* and the Public Sphere in the Early Eighteenth Century', in E. Eger, C. Grant, C. O Gallchoir and P. Wharburton (eds), *Women, Writing and the Public Sphere, 1700–1830* (Cambridge: Cambridge University Press, 2006), pp. 27–52.

——. 'Coffee-House Libraries in Mid-Eighteenth-Century London', *The Library: Transactions of the Bibliographical Society*, 10:1 (2009), pp. 3–40.

Erskine-Hill, H. (ed.), *Alexander Pope: Selected letters* (Oxford: Oxford University Press, 2000).

Feingold, M., 'Barrow, Isaac (1630–1677)', in *Oxford Dictionary of National Biography* (Oxford: Oxford University Press, 2004); www.oxforddnb.com/view/article/1541.

Fergus, J., *Provincial Readers in Eighteenth-Century England* (Oxford: Oxford University Press, 2006).

Findlay, E., 'Ralph Thoresby the Diarist: The late seventeenth century pious diary and its demise', *The Seventeenth Century*, 17 (2002) pp. 108–30.

Fitzmaurice, S. M., *The Familiar Letter in Early Modern English* (Amsterdam: John Benjamins, 2002).

Garrard, G., *Counter-Enlightenments: From the eighteenth century to the present* (London: Routledge, 2006).

Girouard, M., in *Life in the English Country House: A social and architectural history* (Harmondsworth: Penguin, 1980).

Godber, J., *The Marchioness Grey of Wrest Park* (Bedford: The Bedfordshire Historical Record Society, 1968).

Goldgar, A., *Impolite Learning: Conduct and community in the Republic of Letters, 1680–1750* (London: Yale University Press, 1995).

Goldie, M., 'Clarke, Edward (1649/51–1710)', *Oxford Dictionary of National Biography* (Oxford: Oxford University Press, 2004); www.oxforddnb.com/view/article/37290.

Goldie, M. (ed.), *John Locke: Selected correspondence* (Oxford: Oxford University Press, 2002).

Goodman, D., 'Pigalle's *Voltair nu*: The Republic of Letters presents itself to the world', *Representations*, 16 (1986), pp. 86–109.

Goodman, D., 'Public Sphere and Private Life: Toward a synthesis of current historiographical approaches to the Old Regime', *History and Theory*, 31:1 (1992), pp. 1–20.

——. *Becoming a Woman in the Age of Letters* (London: Cornell University Press, 2009).

Grazia, M. de, Quilligan, M. and Stallybrass, P. (eds), *Subject and Object in Renaissance Culture* (Cambridge: Cambridge University Press, 1996).

Gregory, J., 'Writing Women in(to) the Long Eighteenth Century', *Literature and History*, 11:1 (2001), pp. 83–4.

Gretsch, M., 'Elizabeth Elstob: A scholar's fight for Anglo-Saxon studies, part I', *Anglia*, 117:2 (1999), pp. 163–200.

——. 'Elizabeth Elstob: A scholar's fight for Anglo-Saxon studies, part II', *Anglia*, 117:4 (1999), pp. 481–524.

Guest, H., *Small Change: Women, learning, patriotism, 1750–1810* (Chicago: University of Chicago Press, 2000).

Habermas, J., *The Structural Transformation of the Public Sphere: An enquiry into a category of bourgeois society* (Cambridge, Mass.: MIT Press, 1991).

Hanham, A. A., 'Trumbull, Sir William (1639–1716)', in *Oxford Dictionary of National Biography* (Oxford: Oxford University Press, 2004); www.oxforddnb.com/view/article/27776.

Hannan, L., 'Collaborative Scholarship on the Margins: An epistolary network', *Women's Writing*, 21:3 (2014), pp. 290–315.

Harcstark Myers, S., *The Bluestocking Circle: Women, friendship, and the life of the mind in eighteenth-century England* (Oxford: Clarendon Press, 1990).

Harmsen, T., 'George Hickes (1642–1715)', *Oxford Dictionary of National Biography* (Oxford: Oxford University Press, 2004); www.oxforddnb.com/view/article/13203.

Harris, F., 'Living in the Neighbourhood of Science: Mary Evelyn, Margaret Cavendish and the Greshamites', in L. Hunter and S. Hutton (eds), *Women, Science and Medicine 1500–1700: Mothers and sisters of the Royal Society* (Stroud: Sutton, 1997), pp. 198–217.

——. 'The Letterbooks of Mary Evelyn', in P. Beal and J. Griffiths (eds), *English Manuscript Studies, 1100–1700*, vol. 7 (London: British Library, 1998), pp. 202–15.

——. *Transformations of Love: The friendship of John Evelyn and Margaret Godolphin* (Oxford: Oxford University Press, 2002).

Harvey, K., *The Little Republic: Masculinity and domestic authority in eighteenth-century Britain* (Oxford: Oxford University Press, 2012).

Hayes, K. J., *A Colonial Woman's Bookshelf* (Knoxville: University of Tennessee Press, 1996).

Hesse, C., 'Women Intellectuals in the Enlightened Republic of Letters: Introduction', in S. Knott and B. Taylor (eds), *Women, Gender and Enlightenment* (Basingstoke: Palgrave Macmillan, 2005), pp. 259–64.

Heyd, U., *Reading Newspapers: Press and public in eighteenth-century Britain and America* (Oxford: Voltaire Foundation, 2012).

Hilton, M., *Women and the Shaping of the Nation's Young: Education and public doctrine in Britain, 1750–1850* (Aldershot: Ashgate, 2007).

Hilton, M. and Shefrin, J. (eds), *Educating the Child in Enlightenment Britain: Beliefs, cultures, practices* (Farnham: Ashgate, 2009).

Hintz, C., 'A Second Reference to Marin le Roy de Gomberville's *Polexandre* in Dorothy Osborne's Letters', *Notes and Queries*, 46:3 (1999), pp. 339–40.

——. *An Audience of One: Dorothy Osborne's letters to Sir William Temple, 1652–1654* (London: University of Toronto Press, 2005).

Hodgson Anderson, E., *Eighteenth-Century Authorship and the Play of Fiction: Novels and the theater, Haywood to Austen* (London: Routledge, 2009).

Hopkins, P., 'Hales, Sir Edward, Third Baronet and Jacobite First Earl of Tenterden (1645–1695)', in *Oxford Dictionary of National Biography* (Oxford: Oxford University Press, 2004); www.oxforddnb.com/view/article/11910.

Houston, R. A., *Literacy in Early Modern Europe: Culture and education, 1500–1800* (Harlow: Longman, 1988).

How, J., *Epistolary Spaces: English letter-writing from the foundation of the Post Office to Richardson's Clarissa* (Aldershot: Ashgate, 2003).

Hume, R. D., 'Diversity and Development in Restoration Comedy, 1660–79', *Eighteenth-Century Studies*, 5 (1972), pp. 365–97.

Hunter, L., 'Sisters of the Royal Society: The circle of Katherine Jones, Lady Ranelagh', in L. Hunter and S. Hutton (eds), *Women, Science and Medicine 1500–1700: Mothers and sisters of the Royal Society* (Stroud: Sutton, 1997), pp. 178–97.

——. *The Letters of Dorothy Moore, 1612–64: The friendships, marriage, and intellectual life of a seventeenth-century woman* (Aldershot: Ashgate, 2004).

Hunter, L. and Hutton, S. (eds), *Women, Science and Medicine 1500–1700: Mothers and sisters of the Royal Society* (Stroud: Sutton, 1997).

Hunter, M. C. W., *The Royal Society and Its Fellows, 1660–1700: The morphology of an early scientific institution* (Chalfont St Giles: British Society for the History of Science, 1982).

Hutton, S., 'Damaris Cudworth, Lady Masham: Between Platonism and Enlightenment', *British Journal for the History of Philosophy*, 1 (1993), pp. 29–54.

——. *Anne Conway: A woman philosopher* (Cambridge: Cambridge University Press, 2004).

Israel, J., *Enlightenment Contested: Philosophy, modernity, and the emancipation of man, 1670–1752* (Oxford: Oxford University Press, 2006).

Italia, I., *The Rise of Literary Journalism in the Eighteenth Century: Anxious employment* (London: Routledge, 2005).

Jackson, I., 'Approaches to the History of Readers and Reading in Eighteenth-Century Britain', *Historical Journal*, 47:4 (2004), pp. 1041–54.

Jones, V., 'The Seductions of Conduct: Pleasure and conduct literature', in R. Porter and M. Mulvey Roberts (eds), *Pleasure in the Eighteenth Century* (Basingstoke: Macmillan, 1996), pp. 108–32.

Jones, V. (ed.), *Women and Literature in Britain, 1700–1800* (Cambridge: Cambridge University Press, 2000).

Kerber, L. K., *Toward an Intellectual History of Women* (Chapel Hill: University of North Carolina Press, 1997).

Klein, L., 'Gender and the Public/Private Distinction in the Eighteenth Century: Some questions about evidence and analytic procedure', *Eighteenth-Century Studies*, 29:1 (1995), pp. 97–109.

Knott, S. and Taylor, B. (eds), *Women, Gender and Enlightenment* (Basingstoke, 2005).

Kugler, A., *Errant Plagiary: The life and writing of Lady Sarah Cowper, 1644–1720* (Stanford, Calif.: Stanford University Press, 2002).

Laurence, A., 'Women Using Building in Seventeenth-Century England: A question of sources?' *Transactions of the Royal Historical Society*, 13 (2003), pp. 293–303.

Laurence A., 'Real and Imagined Communities in the Lives of Women in Seventeenth-Century Ireland: Identity and gender', in S. Tarbin and S. Broomhall (eds), *Women, Identities and Communities in Early Modern Europe* (Aldershot: Ashgate, 2008), pp. 13–27.

Lawrence-Mathers, A. and P. Hardman (eds), *Women and Writing, c. 1350–c. 1650: The domestication of print culture* (Woodbridge: York Medieval Press in association with The Boydell Press, 2010).

Lenz, K. and Möhlig, R. (eds), *Of Dyuersite & Chaunge of Language: Essays presented to Manfred Görlach on the occasion of his 65th birthday* (Heidelberg: C. Winter, 2002).

Lipsedge, K., '"Enter into thy Closet": Women, closet culture, and the eighteenth-century English novel', in J. Styles and A. Vickery (eds), *Gender, Taste, and Material Culture in Britain and North America, 1700–1830* (London: The Paul Mellon Centre for Studies in British Art, 2006), pp. 107–22.

Llewellyn, M., 'Katherine Philips: Friendship, poetry and Neo-Platonic thought in seventeenth-century England', *Philological Quarterly*, 81:4 (2002), pp. 441–68.

Longfellow, E., *Women and Religious Writing in Early Modern England* (Cambridge: Cambridge University Press, 2004).

Lorraine de Montluzin, E., *Daily Life in Georgian England as Reported in the Gentleman's Magazine* (Lewiston, NY: Edwin Mellen Press, 2002).

Mandelbrote, S., 'The English Bible and Its Readers in the Eighteenth Century', in I. Rivers (ed.), *Books and Their Readers in Eighteenth-Century England: New essays* (London: Leicester University Press, 2001), pp. 35–78.

Martin, R. and Barresi, J., *Naturalization of the Soul: Self and personal identity in the eighteenth century* (London: Routledge, 2000).

McDowell, P., *The Women of Grub Street: Press, politics and gender in the London literary marketplace, 1678–1730* (Oxford: Clarendon Press, 1998).

Mechling, J., 'Advice to Historians on Advice to Mothers', *Journal of Social History*, 9 (1975), pp. 44–63.

Meldrum, T., 'Domestic Service, Privacy and the Eighteenth-Century Metropolitan Household', *Urban History*, 26:1 (1999), pp. 27–39.

Mendelson, M., 'Neighbourhood as Female Community in the Life of Anne Dormer', in S. Tarbin and S. Broomhall (eds), *Women, Identities and Communities in Early Modern Europe* (Aldershot: Ashgate, 2008), pp. 153–64.

Mendelson, S. H., 'Stuart Women's Diaries and Occasional Memoirs', in M. Prior (ed.), *Women in English Society, 1500–1800* (London: Methuen, 1985), pp. 136–57.

——. 'Clarke, Mary (d. 1705)', in *Oxford Dictionary of National Biography* (Oxford: Oxford University Press, 2004); www.oxforddnb.com/view/article/66720.

——. 'Child-Rearing in Theory and Practice: The Letters of John Locke and Mary Clarke', *Women's History Review*, 19:2 (2010), pp. 231–43.

Mendelson, S. H. (ed.), *Margaret Cavendish* (Farnham: Ashgate, 2009).

Mendelson, S. and O'Connor, M., '"Thy Passionately Loving Sister and Faithfull Friend": Anne Dormer's letters to her sister Lady Trumbull', in N. J. Miller and N. Yavneh, *Sibling Relations and Gender in the Early Modern World* (Aldershot: Ashgate, 2004), pp. 206–15.

Miller, N. J. and Yavneh, N. (eds), *Sibling Relations and Gender in the Early Modern World* (Aldershot: Ashgate, 2004).

Milton, J. R., 'Locke, John (1632–1704)', in *Oxford Dictionary of National Biography* (Oxford: Oxford University Press, 2004); www.oxforddnb.com/view/article/16885.

Mitchell, L. C., 'Entertainment and Instruction: Women's roles in the English epistolary tradition', *Huntington Library Quarterly*, 66:3/4 (2003), pp. 331–47.

Moessner, L., 'The Influence of the Royal Society on 17th-Century Scientific Writing', *International Computer Archive of Modern and Medieval English*, 33 (2009), pp. 65–87.

Molekamp, F., 'Early Modern Women and Affective Devotional Reading', *European Review of History*, 17:1 (2010), pp. 53–74.

——. *Women and the Bible in Early Modern England: Religious reading and writing* (Oxford: Oxford University Press, 2013).

——. 'Therapies for Melancholy and Inordinate Passion in the Letters of Dorothy Osborne to Sir William Temple (1652–1654)', *The Seventeenth Century*, 29:3 (2014), pp. 255–76.

Morgan, S. (ed.), *Women, Religion and Feminism in Britain, 1750–1900* (Basingstoke: Palgrave Macmillan, 2002).

Moseley, A., *John Locke* (London: Continuum, 2007).

Nevala, M., *Address in Early Modern English Correspondence: Its forms and socio-pragmatic functions* (Helsinki: Société Néophilologique, 2004).

Norbrook, D., 'Women, the Republic of Letters, and the Public Sphere in the Mid-Seventeenth Century', *Criticism*, 46:2 (2004), pp. 223–40.

Norton, R. E., 'The Myth of the Counter-Enlightenment', *Journal of the History of Ideas*, 68:4 (2007), pp. 635–58.

O'Connor, M., 'Representations of Intimacy in the Life-Writing of Anne Clifford and Anne Dormer', in P. Coleman, J. Lewis and J. Kowalik (eds), *Representations of the Self from the Renaissance to Romanticism* (Cambridge: Cambridge University Press, 2000), pp. 79–96.

——. 'Interpreting Early Modern Woman Abuse: The case of Anne Dormer', *Quidditas*, 23 (2002), pp. 49–66.

Osselton, N. E., 'Informal Spelling Systems in Early Modern English: 1500–1800', in N. F. Blake and C. Jones (eds), *English Historical Linguistics: Studies in development* (Sheffield: The Centre for English Cultural Tradition and Language, University of Sheffield, 1984), pp. 123–37.

Pagden, A., *The Enlightenment: And why it still matters* (Oxford: Oxford University Press, 2013).

Pal, C., *Republic of Women: Rethinking the Republic of Letters in the Seventeenth Century* (Cambridge: Cambridge University Press, 2012).

Parker, K. (ed.), *Dorothy Osborne: Letters to Sir William Temple, 1652–54: Observations on love, literature, politics, and religion* (Aldershot: Ashgate, 2002).

Pearson, J., *Women's Reading in Britain 1750–1835* (Cambridge: Cambridge University Press, 1999).

Perry, G. and Rossington, M., *Femininity and Masculinity in Eighteenth-Century Art and Culture* (Manchester: Manchester University Press, 1994).

Perry, R., *Women, Letters and the Novel* (New York: AMS Press, 1980).

Phillips, N., *Women in Business, 1700–1850* (Woodbridge: Boydell Press, 2006).

Pick, D. and Roper, L. (eds), *Dreams and History: The interpretation of dreams from ancient Greece to modern psychoanalysis* (Hove: Brunner Routledge, 2004).

Pickering, S. F., *John Locke and Children's Books in Eighteenth-Century England* (Knoxville: University of Tennessee Press, 1981).

Pollock, L. A., 'Rethinking Patriarchy and the Family in Seventeenth-Century England', *Journal of Family History*, 23 (2000), pp. 3–27.

Popiel, J. J., *Rousseau's Daughters: Domesticity, education, and autonomy in modern France* (Lebanon: University of New Hampshire Press, 2008).

Porter, R. and Mulvey Roberts, M. (eds), *Pleasure in the Eighteenth Century* (Basingstoke: Macmillan, 1996).

Prior, M. (ed.), *Women in English Society, 1500–1800* (London: Methuen, 1985).

Purcell, M., 'The Private Library in Seventeenth- and Eighteenth-Century Surrey', *Library History*, 19 (2003), pp. 119–28.

Raftery, D., *Women and Learning in English Writing, 1600–1900* (Dublin: Four Courts, 1997).

Rand, B. (ed.), *The Correspondence of John Locke and Edward Clarke* (London: Humphrey Milford, 1927).

Rasmussen, C. B., '"Speaking on the Edge of my Tomb": The epistolary life and death of Catherine Talbot', *Partial Answers: Journal of Literature and the History of Ideas*, 8:2 (2010), pp. 255–75.

Raven, J., 'From Promotion to Proscription: Arrangements for reading and eighteenth-century libraries' in J. Raven, H. Small and N. Tadmor (eds), *Practice and Representation of Reading* (Cambridge: Cambridge University Press, 1996), pp. 175–201.

——. 'New Reading Histories, Print Culture and the Identification of Change: The case of eighteenth-century England', *Social History* 23:3 (1998), pp. 268–87.

Raven, J., Small, H. and Tadmor, N. (eds), *The Practice and Representation of Reading in England* (Cambridge: Cambridge University Press, 1996).

Reeve, C., 'Beale, Mary (bap. 1633, d. 1699)', in *Oxford Dictionary of National Biography* (Oxford: Oxford University Press, 2004); www.oxforddnb.com/view/article/1803.

Ritchie, R. C., 'Coote, Richard, First Earl of Bellamont (1636–1701)', in *Oxford Dictionary of National Biography* (Oxford: Oxford University Press, 2004); www.oxforddnb.com /view/article/6247.

Rivers, I., 'Tillotson, John (1630–1694)', in *Oxford Dictionary of National Biography* (Oxford: Oxford University Press, 2004); www.oxforddnb.com/view/article/27449.

Rivers, I. (ed.), *Books and Their Readers in Eighteenth-Century England: New essays* (London: Leicester University Press, 2001).

Ross, S., 'Austen, Katherine (b. 1629, d. in or before 1683)', in *Oxford Dictionary of National Biography* (Oxford: Oxford University Press, 2004); www.oxforddnb.com/view /article/68248.

Scott, J. W., *Feminism and History* (Oxford: Oxford University Press, 1996).

Seaward, P., 'Hyde, Edward, First Earl of Clarendon (1609–1674)', in *Oxford Dictionary of National Biography* (Oxford: Oxford University Press, 2004); www.oxforddnb.com/ view/article/14328.

Shapin, S., 'The House of Experiment in Seventeenth-Century England', *Isis*, 79:3 (1988), pp. 373–404.

Sheppard, S., *Pharsalus 48 BC: Caesar and Pompey – clash of the titans* (Oxford: Osprey, 2006).

Sheridan, P. (ed.), *Catherine Trotter Cockburn: Philosophical writings* (Peterborough, ON: Broadview Press, 2006).

Skidmore, G., *Strength in Weakness: Writings of eighteenth-century Quaker women* (Oxford: Altamira Press, 2003).

——. 'Follows, Ruth (1718–1808)', in *Oxford Dictionary of National Biography* (Oxford: Oxford University Press, 2004); www.oxforddnb.com/view/article/9797.

Smith, H. L., 'Women Intellectuals and Intellectual History: Their paradigmatic separation', *Women's History Review*, 16:3 (2007), pp. 353–68.

Smith, H. L. (ed.), *Women Writers and the Early Modern British Political Tradition* (Cambridge: Cambridge University Press, 1998).

Smyth, A., *Autobiography in Early Modern England* (Cambridge: Cambridge University Press, 2010).

Spacks, P. M., *Imagining a Self: Autobiography and novel in eighteenth-century England* (London: Harvard University Press, 1976).

Spacks, P., *Privacy: Concealing the eighteenth-century self* (Chicago: University of Chicago Press, 2003).

Spufford, M., *Small Books and Pleasant Histories: Popular fiction and its readership in seventeenth-century England* (London: Methuen, 1981).

Spurr, J., 'Taylor, Jeremy (*bap.* 1613, *d.* 1667)', in *Oxford Dictionary of National Biography* (Oxford: Oxford University Press, 2004); www.oxforddnb.com/view/article/27041.

——. *The Post-Reformation: Religion, politics and society in Britain, 1603–1714* (Harlow: Pearson Education Limited, 2006).

Stevenson, J., 'Women Writing and Scribal Publication in the Sixteenth Century', in P. Beal and M. J. M. Ezell (eds), *English Manuscript Studies, 1100–1700*, vol. 9 (London: British Library, 2000), pp. 1–32.

Stewart, A., 'The Early Modern Closet Discovered', *Representations*, 50 (1995), pp. 76–100.

Stone, L., 'Literacy and Education in England, 1640–1900', *Past and Present*, 42 (1969), pp. 69–139.

——. *The Family, Sex and Marriage in England, 1500–1800* (London: Weidenfeld and Nicolson, 1977).

Stubbs, J., *John Donne: The reformed soul* (London: Viking, 2006).

Styles, J. and Vickery, A. (eds), *Gender, Taste, and Material Culture in Britain and North America, 1700–1830* (London: The Paul Mellon Centre for Studies in British Art, 2006).

Summit, J., 'Hannah Wolley, the Oxinden Letters, and Household Epistolary Practice', in N. E. Wright, M. W. Ferguson and A. R. Buck (eds), *Women, Property, and the Letters of the Law in Early Modern England* (Toronto: University of Toronto Press, 2004), pp. 201–18.

Sweet, R., *Antiquaries: The discovery of the past in eighteenth-century Britain* (London: Hambledon and London, 2004).

Tadmor, N., ' "In the even my wife read to me": Women, reading and household life in the eighteenth century', in J. Raven, H. Small and N. Tadmor (eds), *The Practice and Representation of Reading in England* (Cambridge: Cambridge University Press, 1996), pp. 162–74.

Tarbin, S. and Broomhall, S. (eds), *Women, Identities and Communities in Early Modern Europe* (Aldershot: Ashgate, 2008).

Tavor Bannet, E., *Empire of Letters: Letter manuals and transatlantic correspondence, 1680–1820* (Cambridge: Cambridge University Press, 2005).

Thiel, U., *The Early Modern Subject: Self-consciousness and personal identity from Descartes to Hume* (Oxford: Oxford University Press, 2011).

Thomas, P., *Katherine Philips, 'Orinda'* (Cardiff: University of Wales Press, 1988).

Tieken-Boon van Ostade, I., ' "You was" and Eighteenth-Century Normative Grammar', in K. Lenz and R. Möhlig (eds), *Of Dyuersite & Chaunge of Language: Essays presented to Manfred Görlach on the occasion of his 65th birthday* (Heidelberg: C. Winter, 2002), pp. 88–102.

Trentmann, F., 'Materiality in the Future of History', *Journal of British Studies*, 48:2 (2009), pp. 283–307.

Vickery, A., *The Gentleman's Daughter: Women's lives in Georgian England* (London: Yale University Press, 1998).

Vickery, A. (ed.), *Women, Privilege and Power: British politics, 1750 to the present* (Stanford, Calif.: Stanford University Press, 2001).

Wahrman, D., *The Making of the Modern Self: Identity and culture in eighteenth-century England* (London: Yale University Press, 2004).

Walker, S., 'Prescription and Practice in the Visual Organization of Correspondence', *Huntington Library Quarterly*, 66:3/4 (2003), pp. 307–29.

Wallwork, J. and Salzman, P. (eds), *Early Modern Englishwomen Testing Ideas* (Farnham: Ashgate, 2011).

Wayne White, C., *The Legacy of Anne Conway (1631–1679): Reverberations from a mystical naturalism* (Albany: State University of New York Press, 2008).

Whyman, S., '"Paper visits": The post-Reformation letter as seen through the Verney archive', in R. Earle (ed.), *Epistolary Selves: Letters and letter writers, 1600–1945* (Aldershot: Ashgate, 1999), pp. 15–36.

——. 'Letter Writing and the Rise of the Novel: The Epistolary Literacy of Jane Johnson and Samuel Richardson', *Huntington Library Quarterly*, 70 (2007), pp. 577–606.

——. *The Pen and the People: English letter-writers, 1660–1800* (Oxford: Oxford University Press, 2009).

Willcocks, R. M., *England's Postal History to 1840* (London: Author, 1975).

Wright, N. E., Ferguson, M. W. and Buck, A. R. (eds), *Women, Property, and the Letters of the Law in Early Modern England* (Toronto: University of Toronto Press, 2004).

Zimmerman, S. M., 'Smith, Charlotte (1749–1806)', in *Oxford Dictionary of National Biography* (Oxford: Oxford University Press, 2004); www.oxforddnb.com/view/article/25790.

Zuk, R., *Bluestocking Feminism: Writings of the Bluestocking Circle, 1738–1785*, vol. 3 (London: Pickering & Chatto, 1999).

——. 'Talbot, Catherine (1721–1770)', in *Oxford Dictionary of National Biography* (Oxford: Oxford University Press, 2004); www.oxforddnb.com/view/article/26921.

Unpublished

Brodie, A., 'Correspondence: The materiality and practice of letter-writing in England, 1650–1750' (MA dissertation, V&A/RCA, 2002).

Soenmez, M. J.-M., 'English Spelling in the Seventeenth Century: A study of the nature of standardisation as seen through the MS and printed versions of the Duke of Newcastle's "A New Method ..."' (PhD thesis, Durham University, 1993).

Weir, G., 'Orthography in the Correspondence of Lady Katherine Paston, 1603–1627' (MPhil thesis, University of Glasgow, 2010).

Index

access to books 5, 50–3, 119
accomplishments 37, 66, 99, 126–7, 138
  needlework 37, 46, 49, 138
  address 99, 105–6, 107–8
  see also formality and style;
    letter-writing: conventions
advice literature 11–12, 29n.63, 35,
  37–8, 109, 179
antiquarianism 14–15, 72–6
antiquaries 52, 70, 72–6, 79, 82
artefacts and texts 42, 52, 53, 79, 172
Society of Antiquaries 42
archives 4, 7, 9, 16, 21, 70–1, 73, 74, 77,
  102, 116–19
  archival research 7, 9, 15–19
  digital 6, 180
  letter collections 15–16, 70–1,
    116–19, 124
Astell, Mary 5, 7, 37

Ballard, George 52–3, 70–2, 74–6,
  77–80, 112–13, 115, 119,
  139, 172–4
Balzac, Jean-Louis Guez de 12, 67
Barrow, Isaac 129, 131, 147n.29
Bathurst, Dr Ralph 66, 67
Beale, Mary 160–1
Beck, Sarah 110–11
Bluestockings 5, 8, 17–18, 38, 40, 51, 78–9
Bohun, Ralph 20, 66–9, 83–6, 87, 89,
  113, 115, 116, 117, 155–8, 165
booksellers 4, 52, 58
Brompton, Rebecca see Garth,
  Rebecca
Browne, Richard 17, 66–7, 118

Campbell, Jemima see Grey, Jemima
  Marchioness
Carter, Elizabeth 7, 40, 82, 92n.54
Cavendish, Margaret, Duchess of
  Newcastle 7, 51–2, 69, 86,
  87–8

Cavendish Bentinck, Margaret,
  Duchess of Portland 76–8, 180
Chapone, Sarah 76, 91n.43, 119
Charles I 48, 65
Charles II 127
Chesterfield, Earl of 98
Chicksands Priory, Bedfordshire 141
Church 73
  clergy 17–18, 41, 66, 72, 79, 97,
    110–11, 119, 130
  clerical families 3, 17, 72, 102, 133
Clandon Park, Surrey 133
Clarendon, Earl of see Hyde, Edward,
  first Earl of
Clarke, Edward 18, 53–7, 104–5, 143–4
Clarke, Mary 17, 18, 53–7, 98, 104–5,
  115, 143–4, 145
class 4, 17–18
  aristocracy 14, 17–18, 42, 105, 127
  gentry 4, 14, 17–19, 97, 99, 104,
    105, 135
  middling sort 4, 17–18, 99, 105
  professions 99, 104
  trade 5, 70, 74, 79, 110
clothing see dress
Collier family 99–101, 108, 109–10
  Collier, Cordelia 99–101
  Collier, John (junior) 99
  Collier, John (senior) 99–100
  Collier, Mary (junior) 100
  Collier, Mary (senior) 108, 109
  see also Cranston, William;
    Denham, Elizabeth
community 14–15, 70, 72, 138, 139
compliments 157, 181 see also
    letter-writing: conventions
conduct books see advice literature
conversation 109–10, 154, 168–9, 179–80
copyright 13
Cotterell, Sir Charles 127
Cowper, Sarah 135, 148n.61, 171–2,
  176n.73

Cowper, Sarah (diarist) 13, 65, 97, 110
  diary 13, 65
Cranston, William 108
cross roads *see* postal service: routes
Cuddesden, Oxfordshire 43, 49, 133,
  137, 148n.52
  see also Secker, Reverend/
  Bishop Thomas

Delany, Mary 76-7
Denham, Elizabeth 109-10
D'Ewes, Anne 153
diaries and journals *see* life writing
Dormer, Anne 17, 97, 110, 115, 127-31,
  142-3, 168-71, 172
Dormer, Robert 127-8, 130-1,
  142-3, 172
dreams 144-5, 172
dress 84, 99-100, 101, 118, 138
Dryden, John 83, 92n.57

education 3-4, 25n.15, 35-41, 50,
  66, 72, 77, 86, 98-105, 172-3,
  179-80, 183
  educators 4, 38, 72, 77, 84, 100,
    102-5, 138, 180
  epistolary 98-103, 105
  at home 4, 35, 37, 104-5, 179
  at school 4, 72, 99, 105
  self- 35, 42, 46-58, 87, 123
    see also access to books
  social 98-100, 101-2
Elizabeth I 38
Elstob, Elizabeth 17, 52-3, 71-80, 87, 112-13,
  115, 119, 139, 160, 172-4, 180
Elstob, William 72-3, 79
Enlightenment 4, 5, 8, 13, 26n.28, 123
Evelyn, John 17, 66, 116, 144, 156,
  161-3, 165-7
  diary 116, 167
  and Margaret Blagge 161-3, 165
Evelyn, Mary 12, 17, 20, 65-70, 83-9,
  113, 115, 116-19, 137, 138, 144,
  155-68, 182-3

children of 83, 84, 118

family life 18, 53, 84-5, 137, 143-4
femininity 37, 40, 54, 86, 124, 154-5
Fénelon, François 37-8
Follows, Ruth 110-11
formality and style 12, 13, 67, 105-9,
  113, 116, 154, 164
  see also address; letter-writing:
  conventions
friendship 40, 45, 80, 112, 116-18,
  124-5, 135, 156-74
  broken 166-8
  female 45, 112, 135, 171-2
  with men 117-18, 156-9, 163-8
  perfect 8, 159-63, 183
  Platonic 160-1, 163
  sibling 108, 124-6, 127, 129, 153-4,
    160-1, 168-70

Garth, Rebecca 138, 144-5
gender 6, 8, 11, 12, 13, 18, 39-40, 56-7,
  84-6, 154-6, 156-7, 168, 180-1
  and history 6-9
  roles 12, 13, 39-40, 84-6, 181
  and space 128-9
Glanville, William 117, 155-9, 161-8
Granville, Ann 76-7
Gregory, Dr David 42, 60n.30
Gregory, Mary *see* Grey, Mary
Grey, Amabel 57
Grey, Jemima, Marchioness 17, 18, 38,
  40-50, 51-2, 70, 80-2, 107, 112,
  119, 125-7, 131-4, 136-7, 171
Grey, Mary 17, 18, 40-50, 80-2, 107,
  112, 119, 124, 125, 132, 133-4,
  136-7, 171

Ham House, Richmond 133
handwriting 20, 36, 37, 100, 103, 116,
  118, 141, 157, 158
Hickes, George 73, 74
Hinwick Hall, Bedfordshire 125
home *see* household

household 15, 21–2, 131, 182
  as a site of learning 15, 22, 125–7,
    159, 182
  space 21–2, 124–5, 127–9, 131–4,
    139–41, 142–3, 182–3
    closet 22, 123, 127, 128–9,
      131–2, 142
    fireside 49, 125, 133, 136, 171
    garden 44, 131, 132–3, 142, 182
    nursery 82, 85, 142
    psychology of 124, 128, 139–41, 143
    still house 66, 83, 85
  work or duties 15, 41, 57, 66, 70, 82,
    83–6, 138–9
Hovingham Hall, North Yorkshire
  124, 125, 135
Hyde, Edward, first Earl of Clarendon
  45–6, 48–9, 70

identity 10, 13, 15, 64–5, 69–70, 76, 79,
  124, 178, 183
illness 130, 143–4, 158
Isham family 38–40, 51, 53, 137
Isham, Lady Elizabeth 137
Isham, Sir Justinian 38–40, 53, 137

James II 56
Johnson, Jane 4, 17, 18, 38, 102–3, 115,
  121n.20, 138, 144–5, 169, 180

Lamport Hall, Northamptonshire 53
letters
  of advice 35, 39, 98
  childhood 37, 97–103
  circulation of 9, 28n.48, 66
  collecting of 21, 66, 116, 118,
    153–4, 157
  courtship 65, 141–2
  creative writing in 12, 107, 143–5
  of friendship 40, 45, 80, 112, 116–18,
    124–5, 135, 156–74
    see also friendship
  intellectual 40, 45–50, 74–80, 112,
    116–19, 156–9, 168, 173–4

manuscript 7, 9–10, 36
  see also archives: archival research;
    archives: letter collections
marital 53–7, 98, 104–5, 115, 135–6,
  137, 143–4
  as mementos 21, 154
  in print 11, 12, 23, 51, 67, 69
  seeking support 13, 71, 76–8, 91n.43,
    118–19, 157–8, 166, 168–9
    emotional 118–19, 157–8, 168–72
    material or financial 71, 76–8,
      91n.43, 166
    spiritual 110–11, 130, 138–9, 165
letter-writing
  conventions 12, 13, 67, 99, 105–9, 113,
    116, 154, 164
    see also address; compliments;
      formality and style; handwriting
  democratisation of 3, 38, 58,
    89, 134–5
  equipment 20–1, 69, 101
  making copies 21, 66, 116, 118, 157,
    158, 161, 163
    letter books 66, 71, 77, 79, 87, 116,
      118, 157, 158, 161, 162, 163
  manuals see advice literature
  materiality of 19–21
libraries 5, 40, 47, 50, 51, 72, 133
  access to 72, 73, 77
  Bodleian Library, the 70, 72, 77
  circulating or subscription 5, 50, 57
  private 11, 47, 51, 53, 133
life writing 2, 13, 23, 65, 81, 114, 116,
  167, 168
literacy 2–3, 16, 36–7, 38, 58, 89, 98, 105
  epistolary 3, 16, 36, 134
  female 3, 36–7, 58, 89
  in multiple languages 72–3, 76, 105
    ancient 73, 76
    Anglo-Saxon 52, 72–4, 76, 172
    classical 41, 73
    French 12, 30n.72, 41, 46, 66, 72,
      98, 101, 102, 104–5
    German 72, 82

literacy (*cont.*)
  Greek 72
  Hebrew 72
  Italian 41, 46, 66
  Latin 72–3, 102
  Old English 72–3
  rates of 3, 25n.6
  spelling 3, 25n.11, 36–7, 77, 105,
    121n.35
literary criticism 8, 46–7, 51, 66–8, 83,
    88–9, 113
literary culture 1, 2, 4, 13–14, 28n.48,
    40, 42, 82, 124, 149n.83
  coffee-shops 50, 89, 123–4
Locke, John 18, 37, 38, 65, 104–5, 115,
    121n.29, 126
London 3, 14, 15, 17, 40, 44, 48, 54, 57,
    72, 76, 81, 99, 101–2, 132, 134–5,
    141, 160, 171

Maintenon, Madame de 12
Maitland, John, first Duke of
    Lauderdale 133
marriage 42, 66, 119, 142–3, 163
  market 39, 42
  unhappy 17, 97, 127–8, 142, 169, 172
  unmarried women 17–18, 42,
    43, 80, 82
Mary, Queen of Scots 48–9
material culture 19–21
  letters as 153–4
  of letter-writing 20–1
melancholy and low spirits 77,
    163, 168–73
Montagu, Elizabeth 38, 40, 51, 78
Mordaunt, Anna Maria 135,
    148n.62, 171–2
motherhood 81–2, 83–5, 118, 128, 137,
    138, 180

neighbourhood *see* community
networks 1, 6, 13–15, 53, 58, 74, 76–80,
    89, 90n.23, 114–19, 122n.57, 179,
    180, 182

newspapers *see* periodicals

occupation
  artist 160
  clerical *see* Church: clergy
  diplomat 17, 127
  legal 97, 99, 150n.112
  playwright 83, 87, 156
  political 18, 38, 53, 97, 148n.61,
    150n.107
  in trade 5, 70, 74, 79, 110
  yeoman 39
Onslow, Arthur 133
Orlebar, Mary 125–6
orthography 37, 121n.35
  see also literacy
Osborne, Dorothy 12, 65, 141–2
Osborne, Henry 141–2
Oxford, University of 42, 48, 66, 67,
    72, 77, 155
  Magdalen College 77
  New College 165
  Queen's College 74

Parliament 48, 53–7
  news of 48, 54–7
  Tories 48
  Whigs 97, 150n.107
patronage 6, 14, 30n.79, 77, 80
periodicals 12, 30n.74, 47, 50–1, 58, 81
Petty family 101–2
  Petty, Anne 101
  Petty, Elizabeth 101
  Petty, William 101
Philips, Katherine 74, 88–9,
    93n.82, 160
Poley, Elizabeth 153
Pope, Alexander 51, 70
post roads *see* postal service: routes
postal service 10, 20, 49, 54, 98, 102,
    134–5, 153, 168–9
  carriers 51, 134, 136, 141
  cost of 102
  General Letter Office 134

international 168–9
knowledge of 20, 54, 98, 135–6
in London 134–5
Post Office 10, 134
regularity of 135, 168–9
routes 134–5, 148n.58
Poyntz, Anna Maria *see* Mordaunt,
  Anna Maria
pregnancy 137, 157
print culture 1, 9, 11, 23, 57–8, 89
  see also periodicals; publishing
privacy 21, 22, 124, 128–9, 134, 139–43,
  145, 149n.91
of letters 9–10, 20, 141–2
loss of 141–3
publishing 46, 52, 58, 72, 74, 76, 79, 82,
  86–8, 104, 129, 173

readers 2, 4–5, 8, 50–1, 53, 73, 130
reading 2, 4–5, 8, 38, 40, 45–53, 80,
  125–6, 128, 129–31, 132–3, 136–7,
  140, 181
  novels 4–5, 47, 58
  plays 4, 12, 53, 69, 83
  religious 4–5, 40, 49, 129–31, 138
  sermons 12, 30n.74, 40, 46,
    49, 129–30
  shared 40, 45–6, 48, 136
  in translation 66
relationships
  courting couple 65, 141–2
  friends *see* friendship
  husband and wife 42, 52, 53–7, 98,
    104–5, 127–9, 130–1, 136, 137,
    142–3, 143–4, 161–3, 169, 172
    see also marriage
  parent and child 39, 98–104, 118
  sibling 57, 72, 73, 99–100, 104, 106–7,
    108, 124–5, 126, 127, 129, 131, 137,
    141–2, 153–4, 160–1, 168–9, 170
  sisters 100, 124–5, 126, 127, 129,
    131, 137, 153–4, 168–9, 170
religion 4, 5, 37, 39–40, 73, 77, 110–11,
  129–31, 138–9, 161–2

Anglican 130
Episcopalian 130
and piety 39, 129–31, 138–9
Protestant 56–7, 73, 161–2
Quaker 110–11
Roman Catholic 54, 73
  converts to 175n.19, 176n.53
Republic of Letters 6, 14
Robinson, Elizabeth *see* Montagu,
  Elizabeth
Robinson, Frances 108, 124, 126, 135,
  137, 169
Robinson, Thomas 106, 108
Rollin, Charles 38, 45, 61n.49
Rousham House, Oxfordshire
  127, 128
Rousseau, Jean-Jacques 38
Royal Society 5, 42, 66, 67–8, 123, 130

Sayes Court, Deptford 66, 159, 183
Secker, Reverend/Bishop Thomas
  17–18, 41, 43, 82, 119, 133,
  148n.52
servants 15, 70, 85, 142, 166
Sévigné, Madame de 12
Shirley, Henry 102
Smith, Charlotte 124
sociability 14, 45–6, 57, 80, 82, 85, 99,
  114, 124, 125–7
  dancing 82
  singing 126–7
  visiting 14, 45–6, 80, 85, 114, 124,
    125–7, 157, 164
social status *see* class
solitude 22, 128, 136, 137, 140, 171–2
Soresby family 39

Talbot, Catherine 17–18, 40–50, 51–2,
  80–3, 92n.54, 107–8, 119, 127,
  132–4, 136–7, 171
Taylor, Bishop Jeremy 130–1,
  147n.33, 160
Taylor, Frances 101, 102
  daughters of 101

tea-drinking 41, 46, 127, 133
Temple, William 12, 65, 141
theatre and concerts 80, 81, 135
    criticism of 83
    reading plays 4, 12, 53, 69, 83
Tillotson, John 129–31, 147n.37
translation 37, 72, 73, 82
Trumbull, Elizabeth 127, 170
Trumbull, William 127
Tuke, Samuel 117, 156–9

Voiture, Vincent 12

William III (of Orange) and Mary II
    54, 56, 57, 143
Wimpole Hall, Cambridgeshire 43, 51

Wollstonecraft, Mary 7, 183
    feminism 5
women writers 7–8, 28n.48, 58, 72–4,
    82, 87–9, 124, 160
    marginalisation of 7–8, 87–8, 124
Worsley, Ann 17, 18, 21, 106–7, 108, 115,
    137, 160–1
Worsley, Eliza 17, 18, 115, 124–5, 126,
    137, 169, 171
Wotton, near Guilford 133, 163, 175n.37
Wrest Park, Bedfordshire 18, 43,
    44, 131–2

Yorke, Jemima *see* Grey, Jemima,
    Marchioness
Yorke, Philip 42, 43, 46, 51–2, 60n.36, 127